Robert's Rules
FOR
DUMMIES®

by C. Alan Jennings, PRP

D0179205

WILEY

Wiley Publishing, Inc.

Robert's Rules For Dummies®

Published by
Wiley Publishing, Inc.
111 River St.
Hoboken, NJ 07030-5774
www.wiley.com

WILEY

Dedication

To all the people who attend meetings and come home thinking, "Surely, there has to be a better way."

About the Author

C. Alan Jennings holds a Professional Registered Parliamentarian (PRP) credential from the National Association of Parliamentarians. He holds office in the Louisiana Association of Parliamentarians and is a member of the American Institute of Parliamentarians.

His experience as a parliamentarian began when it became his duty to establish a new congregation of a church. His education as a parliamentarian, as is true for most parliamentarians, is experiential. As he learned about Robert's Rules by using the book as the guide for forming new organizations, he applied the rules in another venue — creating an educational organization for Louisiana's Notaries at Civil Law. Alan encouraged the leadership teams of these organizations to develop a working knowledge of Robert's Rules and use it in their work with these organizations; he credits the success of the organizations (both have achieved international recognition) to the leadership's consistent application of the principles of procedure and leadership found in the pages of Robert's Rules.

In 2000, Alan retired as the executive director of the Louisiana Notary Association. He currently writes for several publications in his professional fields and publishes a regular newsletter for notaries at civil law in Louisiana. He is a consultant to the director of the Louisiana State University Center for Assessment and Evaluation on Civil Law Notary qualifying examinations, and he has recently concluded a year of service on the advisory committee to the Louisiana State 19th Judicial District Court on civil law notary examination procedures.

Alan is most active as a professional parliamentarian and serves as meeting parliamentarian for organizations on the local, state, and national level. He provides consulting services year-round for clients in a wide variety of situations and specializes in bylaws and corporate documentation.

Alan and his wife Hartwell Harris have been married for 24 years this year. Retired from 30 years of public service, Hartwell is an accomplished photographer/artist. Both Alan and Hartwell enjoy not only the day-to-day adventures at home in Baton Rouge (with their new dapple rat terrier puppy, Jaz, and Manx cat, Molly), but also their working (and vacation) travel time together.

Author's Acknowledgments

This book wouldn't be in your hands right now if it weren't for the generosity of so many. I've worried a bit that I have nowhere near the page count available to acknowledge them all if I were to start the list where it belongs, with my first-grade teacher who started me off with that big fat pencil and Big Chief writing pad. So, I'll just thank Miss Hill for that and move on to the more immediate friends, family, and colleagues who helped me with this particular work.

First, I thank my original parliamentarian–mentors, Eleanor Earle, PRP, and Myra Myers, PRP, who gave me their time and encouragement.

I am inspired by the example of these leadership role models who exemplify such special character attributes that no one can go wrong by seeking to emulate them: Eileen Armstrong, Loretta Simonson, Kathryn Scheld (this book's general reviewer), Judy Young, and Tommy French. I am inspired by the skill and dedication of these parliamentarian teachers: Nancy Sylvester and Eugene Bierbaum. I am inspired by the wisdom and loyalty of friends like Tom Austin, and I am at once inspired and humbled by the personal strength and dedication to learning of a protégé, Rapunzel Fontenot. And finally, I am inspired by the professionalism of Ann Rempel and Jim Lochrie.

Gratitude for personal and direct help on this manuscript is extended to my colleagues known as the Klatched Parliamentarians, especially Rod Davidson, Kim Goldsworthy, Jonathan M. Jacobs, and John Stackpole. And for the collection of notes and tips stacked in my reading files from Jim Lochrie, Teresa Dean, Michael Malamut, Dan Honneman, and Jim McCabe, I am grateful.

And what self-respecting author wouldn't let the whole world know how much he appreciated the help and hard work of the editors who not only helped him find his muse, but took his manuscript and made it into the book you hold in your hands today? I don't know of anybody who'd fail to be prolific in his words of appreciation for the gang at Wiley, namely Natasha Graf, Natalie Harris, and Elizabeth Rea.

And that brings me to the last-but-not-least list. There's no inspiration as great as that which I get from my wife Hartwell Harris. There's no gratitude like that I have for the life lessons taught me by my mother, Charleen. There's nothing that makes me want to do a good job like the expectations of my sister Carleen, and there's nothing like the confidence I have when my friend Richard Bullock gives me that approving nod. Of course, having a dog (Jaz) and a cat (Molly) that help me read *Robert's Rules* just tops it all off.

Thanks one and all. I appreciate you very much.

Publisher's Acknowledgments

We're proud of this book; please send us your comments through our Dummies online registration form located at www.dummies.com/register/.

Some of the people who helped bring this book to market include the following:

Acquisitions, Editorial, and Media Development

Project Editor: Natalie Faye Harris

Acquisitions Editors: Mikal E. Belicove, Natasha Graf

Copy Editor: Elizabeth Rea

General Reviewer: Kathryn C. Scheld, PRP

Senior Permissions Editor: Carmen Krikorian

Media Development Specialist: Pending Website info

Editorial Manager: Christine Beck

Media Development Manager: Laura VanWinkle

Editorial Assistants: Courtney Allen, Melissa Bennett

Cartoons: Rich Tennant, www.the5thwave.com

Composition

Project Coordinator: Maridee Ennis

Layout and Graphics: Kelly Emkow, Joyce Haughey, Jacque Roth, Heather Ryan

Proofreaders: Joe Niesen, Carl William Pierce, Charles Spencer, Aptara

Indexer: Aptara

Publishing and Editorial for Consumer Dummies

> **Diane Graves Steele,** Vice President and Publisher, Consumer Dummies
>
> **Joyce Pepple,** Acquisitions Director, Consumer Dummies
>
> **Kristin A. Cocks,** Product Development Director, Consumer Dummies
>
> **Michael Spring,** Vice President and Publisher, Travel
>
> **Brice Gosnell,** Associate Publisher, Travel
>
> **Kelly Regan,** Editorial Director, Travel

Publishing for Technology Dummies

> **Andy Cummings,** Vice President and Publisher, Dummies Technology/General User

Composition Services

> **Gerry Fahey,** Vice President of Production Services
>
> **Debbie Stailey,** Director of Composition Services

Contents at a Glance

Table of Contents

Introduction

Welcome to *Robert's Rules For Dummies* — a book with "Robert's Rules" in the title that doesn't pretend to be a substitute for Robert's Rules! It's written to serve as your personal guide to the principles of parliamentary procedure found in *Robert's Rules of Order Newly Revised.*

Just so you know, in this book, whenever I use the term "Robert's Rules," I'm referring to the current edition of *Robert's Rules of Order Newly Revised,* not to one of the many other books with "Robert's Rules" in the title.

I doubt that you *really* want to know anything about parliamentary procedure. But I'm pretty sure you're looking to get some quick information to help you participate more effectively in meetings, to serve in an office to which you've recently been elected, or both. Whatever your situation, if using parliamentary procedure is a must, then this book will go a long way toward helping you master the rules of Robert's Rules.

In 1989, I joined a local unit of the National Association of Parliamentarians in Baton Rouge, Louisiana. I didn't join because I wanted to be a parliamentarian or because I wanted to be a member of another organization; I joined because I wanted to learn enough to get a new organization off the ground. I needed some specific information, and I didn't even realize that all I needed to know could be found in a book entitled *Robert's Rules of Order Newly Revised.*

At first glance, the real Robert's Rules appeared to be naught but a tome of arcane spells to intimidate the masses and empower the erudite. But thanks to several very knowledgeable and experienced parliamentarians, I found that quite the opposite was true. Robert's Rules is actually just a great reference book.

So, when I was offered the opportunity to write this book, I thought it would be nice to finally pay forward all the personal help I received from the parliamentarians in the Baton Rouge unit. If I've accomplished my goals for this book, then you can keep *Robert's Rules For Dummies* handy and use it as if it were your own personal consulting parliamentarian.

When you need to make a point in a meeting, be prepared to cite the real Robert's Rules. Whatever you do, please don't go waving *this* book around to your presiding officer unless your bylaws say that your parliamentary authority is Jennings's *Robert's Rules For Dummies.* (Of course, I'm delighted that you've bought this book, but it's not a parliamentary authority. It's a book about one.)

About This Book

To get the most out of *Robert's Rules For Dummies,* use it to introduce yourself to the fundamental concepts that are covered in comprehensive detail in *Robert's Rules of Order Newly Revised.*

Don't try to read this book cover to cover. Instead, dive right into the chapter containing the information you need. Read it and you'll have a good and thorough overview of that particular topic. If I've done my job, you'll be well oriented to the subject matter. When you turn to the corresponding pages in the current edition of *Robert's Rules of Order Newly Revised,* the in-depth treatment of a particular subject will make much more sense to you, and you'll be able to apply it to your particular situation.

(Not So) Foolish Assumptions

Because you picked up this book, I assume a few things about you:

- ✔ You've heard of Robert's Rules, but you have little (or no) formal training or study in parliamentary procedure.
- ✔ You're a member of an organization that uses Robert's Rules.
- ✔ You want to participate effectively in meetings.
- ✔ Much of what you know about parliamentary procedure is what you've picked up here and there in meetings.
- ✔ You have to deal with others who attempt to minimize the importance of using proper procedures in meetings.
- ✔ You want to have a better understanding of Robert's Rules so that others can't take advantage of you in meetings.
- ✔ If you're an officer or director, you want to understand the proper way to handle your duties in the organization.

I also assume that you won't try to use this book as a substitute for Robert's Rules. It's *not* written to be a parliamentary authority. It's written to give you the perspective you need to make the best use of the real Robert's Rules when you need it.

That being the case, my final assumption is that you will obtain a copy of the real Robert's Rules. The right book is the current edition of *Robert's Rules of Order Newly Revised.* Get a copy if you don't already have one.

How This Book Is Organized

The real Robert's Rules is a reference book, and this is a reference book about a reference book. Ergo, arranging the material was easy. *Robert's Rules of Order Newly Revised* wasn't designed to be read from cover-to-cover. Neither is this book. I've divided the content into four major parts and include handy tips in the Part of Tens section that *For Dummies* books are famous for. Then, as *lagniappe* (Louisiana lingo for "something a little extra"), I include some appendixes with forms, sample reports, and other good stuff to help you understand some of the things discussed throughout the rest of the book.

Part I: It's Parliamentary, My Dear: Participating Effectively in Meetings

If you want to get the real lowdown on what parliamentary procedure is all about, turn to Part I. In these chapters, I cover some of the basics about parliamentary procedure and how to use it to have better meetings.

Part II: Motions: Putting Ideas into Action

This part is a long one, full of details about all the different parliamentary motions that help you turn an idea into an action plan for your group. True, nobody wants to know this much about so much at one time, but the way this part is set up, you can decide what you want to accomplish and find the procedure to help you do it.

Part III: Getting Involved in Leadership

Knowing the basics of parliamentary procedure and having the experience to get things done in meetings makes you a great candidate for leadership in your group. The more you know, the more you can help your fellow members make your organization all it can be. This part covers the process of selecting your leaders and the fundamentals for serving in an elective or appointive office. It also tells you how to remove a problem officer, whether he or she is a complete deadhead or a self-important dictator.

Part IV: The Part of Tens

David Letterman presents his Top Ten list every night, but he's got nothing on parliamentarians. We can come up with lists of lists. In fact, I had a lot of help with this part of the book. I give you lists of very useful information — essentially, the answers to the most frequently asked questions we parliamentarians field day-in and day-out from people who want to know what time it is but don't want to have to build a clock to find out.

Part V: Appendixes

As a parliamentarian who makes his home only a few short miles from the infamous Spanish Town Mardi Gras Parade, I'm used to getting — and giving — *lagniappe* (a little something extra). When planning this book, I decided I'd like to go beyond the usual chapter narratives, tables, lists, and discussions and add a glossary of parliamentary terms and some real-life examples of minutes, bylaws, forms, and reports. This way, you can see for yourself how these things look. I thought of this as lagniappe, but the editors call this part the Appendixes (and yes, they even spell it with the "x" instead of the "c"). Well, as we say down here, "I ax you dis," . . . which would you rather have: another appendix or a little lagniappe?

Icons Used in This Book

Icons are these peculiar little pictures that surface in the margin from time to time in each chapter to let you know that the following topic is special in some way. *Robert's Rules For Dummies* utilizes the following five icons:

When you see the Tip icon, you know you're about to read a helpful hint or tip that can save you some time or trouble. The tip may make things easier for you when you're in the thick of some difficult parliamentary situation.

When you see this icon, pay close attention. It lets you know that trouble or problems may be lurking, but you can avoid the trouble by taking the right precautions or paying heed to some advice born of experience in the school of hard knocks.

This one doesn't get a lot of use here, because just about everything in this book qualifies as technical stuff. So if you see this icon, it's sure to be the most technical of the technical stuff.

 I use this icon a good bit, but that's only because there's a lot to remember in this book. But the good news is that you don't have to memorize it because you can flip to the page and go straight for the icon. But generally, this icon highlights key points of whatever discussion you're reading.

 An important aspect of knowing the rules is knowing the exceptions. Whenever there's an important exception to an otherwise pretty hard-and-fast rule, I call it to your attention with this icon.

Where to Go from Here

Get with it! You bought this book for a reason, so look up whatever it is you need to understand about Robert's Rules. After you've read the discussion, turn to your copy of *Robert's Rules of Order Newly Revised* if you want or need to know more. Immerse yourself in an in-depth treatment of a topic as written by the somewhat droll but definitely learned authors.

Don't stop there! It's the very nature of parliamentary law that knowledge about one topic leads to interest in another. Learning a little more will make you that much more effective in your meetings and service as a leader. It feels good to gain a stronger grasp of the Robert's Rules principles.

If I can help at any time, let me know. I can be reached by e-mail through the contact page on my Web site. Point your browser to www.alanjennings.com/contact, and type in a message. I make every effort to respond to all my e-mail, so please drop me a line if there's something you need clarified or expanded.

Parliamentary procedure education in your area

If you really want to learn as much as you can, check with one or both of the following organizations to find the nearest local unit or chapter of parliamentarians. These local units have regular program meetings and offer educational programs in the community. They also usually have registered or professional members that can tailor-make a workshop for your group to help you have better meetings or develop leadership skills.

The National Association of Parliamentarians
213 South Main St.
Independence, MO 64050-3850
Phone: 888-627-2929
Web site: www.parliamentarians.org

American Institute of Parliamentarians
P.O. Box 2173
Wilmington, DE 19899-2173
Phone: 888-664-0428 or 302-762-1811
Web site: www.parliamentaryprocedure.org

Hiring a professional parliamentarian

More and more groups are looking to professional parliamentarians for training, consulting, or on-site meeting services.

If you have a large group and would like to have more orderly and productive meetings, or if your staff is overwhelmed when putting together your meetings and could use some help, it may be to your advantage to retain a professional parliamentarian for specific services.

And even if your group is small and local and is just interested in fixing some bylaws, you save a lot of time and angst if you enlist the help of a local certified, registered, or professional parliamentarian. Similarly, if your group gets into a rough situation and you just can't get past a particular issue, you may be able to break the impasse by asking a professional parliamentarian to give you a consultation and advise you on how to proceed.

Part I

It's Parliamentary, My Dear: Participating Effectively in Meetings

The 5th Wave   By Rich Tennant

"Okay, that's not a bad idea. Who would like to second the motion that we blast our guns wildly in the air when we leave town as well as when we first ride in?"

In this part . . .

You may think that everything about parliamentary procedure relates to meetings. And when it comes down to it, you're probably right. You sure don't get anything done as a group unless you have meetings, and you don't get anything done in meetings unless you know how to make the best use of your time.

To help you better manage your meetings, the chapters in this part provide short lessons in the fundamental principles of parliamentary law. The basics in Chapter 1, for example, make it an important chapter even if it's not the first one you turn to. And Chapter 2 is intended to help you understand the bylaws of any organization you belong to, and to help you know what may need to be changed if your bylaws are loaded with ambiguity or so much verbiage that you can't figure out what they mean.

Most of the rest of the book ties back to this first part, because ultimately, your meetings are where you make your decisions. So take it from me: The rest of the book makes a lot more sense if you have a good grasp of the information in these first few chapters.

Chapter 1

Following the Rules (Robert's, That Is)

In This Chapter

▶ Uncovering the source of Robert's Rules

▶ Defining parliamentary law

▶ Understanding the rules of parliamentary procedure

▶ Recognizing the personal benefits of learning Robert's Rules

A re you one of those people who see meetings as a wonderful and personally fulfilling activity that you look forward to with great anticipation?

I didn't think so. If you were, you probably wouldn't be reading this book. Truth is, I haven't met many folks who love meetings and can't wait for the next one. But I *have* met plenty of people who dread meetings and only attend because they're afraid of what may happen if they're absent. Attitudes like this develop most frequently when nobody in the group (especially the presiding officer) really knows how a good meeting should be run.

Lucky for you, I've found a remedy for antimeeting attitudes. Try out a well-run meeting conducted by a presiding officer who takes the time to learn and use the principles of parliamentary procedure in Robert's Rules. It really does work wonders!

Making Meetings Meaningful

One of the most marvelous things about Robert's Rules is that it makes meetings meaningful. I first experienced a true understanding of how Robert's Rules can really work to a group's advantage in a meeting of my state association of parliamentarians many years ago.

At that meeting, then president of the National Association of Parliamentarians (and now still-busy parliamentarian and technical reviewer for this book), Kathryn Scheld, presented a program entitled "Making Meetings Meaningful." I was really taken with that presentation, and I have since made it my goal in service as a parliamentarian to help my clients see their meetings as events that can and should be meaningful experiences for the members who invest their time and money in attending and participating.

Those three words — *making meetings meaningful* — so clearly describe the most immediate benefit to learning and applying the principles of parliamentary procedure contained in Robert's Rules.

Using *Robert's Rules For Dummies* as a handbook for making your meetings meaningful can give you a real edge on the knowledge that can help you put your organization on the fast track to greater success.

A Brief History of Robert's Rules

Robert's Rules is practically synonymous with *parliamentary procedure.* My colleagues conservatively estimate that well over 80 percent of all organizations use Robert's Rules as their parliamentary manual. But *Robert's Rules of Order Newly Revised* is just one of a number of parliamentary manuals. And because copyrights expire and the name *Robert's Rules* has assumed a generic usage, many books are published with *Robert's Rules* in their titles, but they're not the real thing.

The editions of Robert's Rules

RONR (the acronym for *Robert's Rules of Order Newly Revised*) refers to the most current edition of the parliamentary authority described by any of the following titles:

- *Robert's Rules of Order* (RO) (1st, 2nd, and 3rd editions)
- *Robert's Rules of Order Revised* (ROR) (4th, 5th, and 6th editions)
- *Robert's Rules of Order Newly Revised* (RONR) (7th, 8th, 9th, and 10th editions)

All the revised editions are revisions by the original copyright holder or his successor trustees of the copyrights. The original *Robert's Rules of Order* is out of copyright and consequently has been republished or rewritten by numerous authors and sold with the name *Robert's Rules* or *Robert's Rules of Order* in the title.

Robert's Rules For Dummies is intended as your guide to the current edition of *Robert's Rules of Order Newly Revised* and is based on the most current rules, not on the old and outdated rules of earlier editions.

Robert's Rules of Order was the cover title of a book first written in 1876 by Henry Martyn Robert. The actual title was *Pocket Manual of Rules of Order for Deliberative Assemblies.* The author was a civil engineer in the U.S. Army, and in 1863, when he was 26 years old, Robert was called on to preside at a meeting. He was reluctant to decline, but he didn't know how to properly preside at a meeting; despite his reservations, he accepted the duty hoping that his lack of knowledge wouldn't be an embarrassment to himself or a disservice to those at the meeting.

We don't know exactly what happened at that meeting, but we do know that Robert came away determined to learn something about parliamentary procedure before he even *attended* another meeting.

Some years later, Robert was transferred to San Francisco and found himself working with different organizations composed of persons from all over. Due to the differences of local customs, wide disagreement took place over what the "correct" meeting procedure was. Major Robert saw the need for uniformity and immersed himself in a study of the parliamentary law of the day. He developed a pocket manual of parliamentary procedure that was published in 1876 and was known as *Robert's Rules of Order.* Since then, the manual has seen two revisions in a total of ten editions.

General Robert's heirs continue to be actively involved as authors of each current edition. The Robert's Rules Association, the National Association of Parliamentarians, and the American Institute of Parliamentarians recognize *Robert's Rules of Order Newly Revised* (RONR) as the authoritative work on parliamentary procedure whenever Robert's Rules is designated as the parliamentary authority.

Empowering Yourself at Meetings

In groups where a presiding officer becomes truly knowledgeable about correct parliamentary procedure, things change for the better. When I hear someone complain about how parliamentary procedure just causes problems, I'm hearing from a member of a group that uses parliamentary procedure incorrectly. The things that members dislike about the so-called process aren't even accurate parliamentary procedures. The procedures they're using are usually just somebody's self-serving double-talk that snookers members who don't know better into accepting them at face value.

When it comes to having meaningful meetings, you're only successful if you empower yourself by gathering the right information. But just as important as having this information is knowing when to use it.

The rules in Robert's Rules aren't set up to give one side an edge over the other. They exist to help you arrive at the true will of the assembly with due consideration for all points of view.

Arming yourself with even a few basic rules of procedure puts you more in control. Preparation helps you know how to insist on technicalities when you need to and when not to worry about them.

Getting Comfortable with Parliamentary Procedure

You'll enhance your understanding of the principles in this book if you take a few minutes now and go over some of the basics.

Parliamentary procedure refers to the practices used in meetings to keep things orderly and give everybody a fair chance to be heard for at least as long as it takes for everybody to realize that nothing new is being said and a large majority is ready to make a decision and get on with other business. Parliamentary procedure really goes a lot further than that, but you've probably guessed as much. It takes a book or two to really cover the subject. You're on your way, though, and you'll have a much better understanding of the process after you've worked through some concrete examples like the ones in this book.

General parliamentary law

Parliamentary procedure is based on *parliamentary law.* Specifically, parliamentary procedure is the parliamentary law you follow in your organization along with any special rules of order you make just for your group.

The broad concept of *parliamentary law,* although not actually law in the sense of statutes and jurisprudence, is the body of accepted rules and practices of *deliberative assemblies* of all types and sizes. (Flip to Chapter 3 for more details on deliberative assemblies.)

If you've come together as a loosely knit group of friends (or enemies), then the chances are good that you follow some rules even if you haven't written them down and given them a name. You know what I mean, rules like "Only one person speaks at a time," "Don't interrupt somebody when they're talking," or "Let's decide what to do about this before we go on to something else."

The most basic rules about interacting with others are the basis of what you may hear referred to as the *common parliamentary law.*

That's a collection of rules and customs, many of which you know, understand, and use every day, even though you never really think about them much.

Parliamentary law isn't statutory law. It's just the body of rules that, written or unwritten, we use when we're assembled and discussing our business.

Principles of parliamentary law

Robert's Rules is generally regarded as the codification (or systematic arrangement) of general parliamentary law. Robert's Rules is written to be a concise but thorough treatment of the vast amount of interrelated information on parliamentary law.

The rules in Robert's Rules are soundly based in principles of parliamentary law that take into account the rights of the majority, the minority, the individual, any absent members, and the collective rights of all these groups.

Fundamental principles

One fundamental principle of parliamentary law is that a deliberative assembly (see Chapter 3) is an autonomous body that enjoys the freedom to conduct its business in accordance with its own provisions for the rights of its members and itself as an assembly. It is free to enact its own rules, choose its leadership, delegate to its leadership all or part of its authority, and retain whatever control over its business that it wishes.

Two other principles are so close to the heart of things that Robert's Rules also terms them *fundamental principles of parliamentary law.* The rules that embody these principles can never be suspended. The only way to avoid having these rules apply to your group is to provide differently in your bylaws (see Chapter 2). Those fundamental principles are as follows:

- ✔ The right to vote is limited to the members who are present in a meeting during the time a vote is actually taken. Therefore, even if the vote is unanimous,

    • Rules can't be suspended to give a right to vote to a nonmember.

    • Cumulative voting is prohibited (see Chapter 8).

    • Absentee voting is prohibited (see Chapter 8).

- ✔ Only one motion can be considered at a time. (You can, however, have several questions pending at one time.)

Other principles of parliamentary law

In addition to the etched-in-stone *fundamental* principles, parliamentary law includes the following general principles:

- The majority rules, but only after providing for the minority to be heard. The only way to keep a member from being heard is by a two-thirds vote of the entire group to stop debate. (Take a look at Chapter 7 for the details on bringing debate to a close.)

- Even though it's not always wise for them to do so, every person or minority faction has the right to take all legal measures to have their position adopted by the group. These measures, however, can't be taken in such a manner as to be disruptive to the peace of the entire group.

- A higher voting threshold is required to change something than to adopt it in the first place. (See Chapter 12 for more details on readdressing issues.) This requirement protects against the instability of changing rules that can develop easily with minor shifts in attendance from meeting to meeting.

Keeping Things Informal

For anyone reading this book who thinks that Robert's Rules is all about being stiff and formal in meetings, I hope you disregard that notion right away. Robert's Rules is about having good meetings without any more formality than is absolutely necessary to protect the rights of everyone and to keep things orderly. The rules are there to help, not hinder, business. General Robert (though not a general at the time) said in his original edition:

> *Know all about parliamentary law, but do not try to show off your knowledge. Never be technical or more strict than is absolutely necessary for the good of the meeting. Use your judgment; the assembly may be of such a nature, through its ignorance of parliamentary usage and peaceable disposition, that a strict enforcement of the rules, instead of assisting, would greatly hinder business; But in large assemblies where there is much work to be done, and especially where there is liability to trouble, the only safe course is to require a strict observance of the rules.*

The general's point should be taken to heart. Sprinkled throughout Robert's Rules are details of procedures that are available when you need them. The key theme of *Robert's Rules For Dummies,* as with Robert's Rules in general, is that you don't need to be any more formal than necessary. But you never want to be so informal that you compromise any rights — whether those of the individual, the minority, or the group as a whole.

Achieving Personal Goals

The benefits of understanding the principles of parliamentary law in Robert's Rules go beyond just running (or participating in) a meeting. By taking the time to better understand the ins-and-outs of Robert's Rules, you're able to save a lot of time at meetings and use motions to get your ideas on the fast track.

Understanding motion-making techniques develops your ability to concisely state exactly what needs to be done. The better you are at making motions in meetings, the better you are at processing your own particular action plans, both in and out of meetings.

Experiencing Personal Success

As you absorb tips for effective meeting participation, you're no doubt developing leadership skills you didn't even know you have. By focusing your knowledge of rules and your educated judgment of when and how to apply them, you'll find yourself successful in all your meetings.

The education you get from a hands-on application of Robert's Rules in your meetings helps you more naturally listen to others before making a decision. Ask any successful person if they would be where they are if they hadn't learned how to listen and respect other points of view!

Chapter 2

Defining the Organization: Bylaws and Other Rules

In This Chapter

▶ Knowing how to adopt, amend, and suspend your rules

▶ Changing your bylaws and applying them properly

▶ Keeping members informed of changes to bylaws and rules

"We the People. . . ." These famous words begin the definition of one of the greatest organizations in the world, The United States of America.

We the people adopted a rule early on that secures the right "peaceably to assemble." Your right to belong to an organization is based on the agreement of everybody that assembling is a natural and sacred right, and it's one of the first membership rules the founding fathers established. It was so important that they put it in the Constitution, making it pretty sure to stay in force unless a large majority of Americans agree to change it. And that's not likely to happen anytime soon.

A country *is* its citizens, and your organization *is* its membership. And the success of both depends on the members' agreement to the fundamental rules. If you think of your organization's rules as the framework for your mutual cooperation and benefit, then you can understand bylaws and other organizational rules much more clearly.

In this chapter, I focus primarily on bylaws because they establish the real framework of your organization. But my focus isn't intended to minimize the importance of other types of rules. It's just to say that your bylaws are to your organization pretty much what the Constitution is to the good ol' USA.

Covering the Rules about Rules

C'mon now, admit it: You saw it in the Table of Contents, but you really didn't believe that a whole chapter could be dedicated to covering rules about the rules. Well, after all, this is a book about a book full of rules, so this chapter shouldn't be a big surprise. But don't worry, it's not really all that complicated.

When it comes to the rules about rules, one rule stands out: A deliberative assembly is free to adopt whatever rules it may want or need as long as the procedure for adopting them conforms to any rules already in place, or to the general parliamentary law (which I define in Chapter 1).

The reason for having rules in the first place is so that you and your fellow group members can mutually agree on *governance* (that is, who your leaders are, how you choose them, when you have your meetings, and so forth), *procedures* for arriving at group decisions, and *policy* covering the details of administration for your organization.

Without rules, you don't last long as a group; you're unable to avoid conflicts, and you experience disagreements on things as basic as whether a particular assembly of individuals can really decide something in the name of the group. You don't know for sure whether some procedure used is inappropriate for arriving at an important decision. And without a way of classifying the different rules, you find yourself not knowing which rule takes precedence and when. Robert's Rules sets up some basic classifications to help you avoid these complications.

Classifying your rules

Different situations call for different types of rules. Robert's Rules classifies the different rules of organized groups based generally on their application and use and on how difficult they are to change or suspend.

Robert's Rules classifies rules for deliberative bodies as follows:

✔ **Charter:** The charter may be either your *articles of incorporation* or a *charter issued by a superior organization* if your group is a unit of a larger organization. A corporate charter is amendable as provided by law or according to provisions in the document for amendment. A charter issued by a superior organization is amendable only by the issuing organization.

✔ **Bylaws:** The *bylaws* are fundamental rules that define your organization. Bylaws are established in a single document of interrelated rules. (I discuss bylaws in detail in the sections following this one.)

✔ **Rules of order:** *Rules of order* are written rules of procedure for conducting meeting business in an orderly manner and the meeting-related duties of the officers. Because these rules are of a general nature about procedure rather than about the organization itself, it's customary for organizations to adopt a standard set of rules by adopting a parliamentary authority such as Robert's Rules. Rules of order can be customized then by adopting *special rules of order* to modify or supersede specific rules in an adopted parliamentary manual. For example, the rule of order in Robert's Rules limiting speeches in debate to ten minutes can be superseded permanently by adopting a special rule of order providing that speeches are limited to three minutes. Most of the rules in Robert's Rules and the other chapters of this book are rules of order.

✔ **Standing rules:** These rules are related to the details of administration rather than parliamentary procedure. For example, suppose your group adopts a motion that directs the treasurer to reimburse the secretary for postage up to $150 per month, provided the secretary provides a written request accompanied by receipts for postage purchased and a log of items mailed in the name of the organization. That policy becomes a standing rule. Motions that you adopt over the course of time that are related to policy and administration are collectively your *standing rules.*

Robert's Rules also mentions *custom,* referring to unwritten rules followed in actual practice. But because they're not written, they're not considered a "class" of rules.

Ranking the rules

When you're dealing with different types of rules, you need to know when to follow which rule. Among the more fundamental rules, then, are those about which rule takes precedence over other rules.

Finishing first: Charter

The charter, if you have one, reigns supreme. Nothing except a judge or the law of the land supersedes it. Fortunately, a charter is usually pretty succinct and operates like a franchise. It's a grant of authority by the state (if your group is incorporated) or a superior organization (if your group is a constituent unit of a larger body).

A charter usually lists the few conditions under which you must operate, but it usually provides for your organization to be subject to bylaws specifically tailored to your organization but which may not conflict with provisions of the charter.

Coming in second: Bylaws

Even though the bylaws contain the most important single set of rules for defining your organization and its governance, the content of the bylaws remains binding and enforceable only to the extent it doesn't conflict with your charter. If your group is not incorporated or not subject to a charter, then the bylaws are the highest-ranking rules of your organization. No matter what, no rules of order or standing rules can ever be enforced if they conflict in any way with your bylaws.

Because bylaws define specific characteristics of the organization itself — including (in most cases) which parliamentary authority will be used by the organization — bylaws are of such importance that they can't be changed without previous notice and the consent of a large majority of your members.

Tying for third: Special rules of order and standing rules

Special rules of order and standing rules have completely different applications and uses, but they rank together as immediately subordinate to bylaws because they have one particular thing in common: They contain individual rules (each of which is usually adopted separately from the other rules in the class) based on the specific need of the organization to accomplish a specific purpose for which the rule is adopted.

Coming in fourth: Robert's Rules (parliamentary authority)

Robert's Rules is a parliamentary manual, and if your organization has adopted it as your parliamentary authority, then Robert's Rules is binding on your group. But it's binding only to the extent that it isn't in conflict with the charter, bylaws, special rules of order, or standing rules.

Last place: Custom

By *custom,* I mean procedures that aren't written anywhere but are followed in actual practice just as if they were written rules. Custom has its place, and any practice that's taken on the standing of an unwritten rule is just as binding as if it were written, with one exception: If a written rule exists to the contrary, even in the parliamentary authority, then the custom must yield as soon as the conflict is pointed out to the membership through a point of order; the only way around this exception is if a *special rule of order* is adopted to place the custom formally in the body of written rules.

Laying down rule requirements

Fundamental differences exist in the procedures you use to adopt or amend each class of rules. Table 2-1 lists the rules by class and the requirements for their adoption, amendment, and suspension. (See Chapter 11 for rules on suspending rules.)

Table 2-1	Rule Classifications and Requirements		
Class of Rule	*Requirements to Adopt*	*Requirements to Amend*	*Requirements to Suspend*
Charter	Instrument initially adopted by majority vote or as provided by law or chartering authority	As provided in charter	Can't be suspended
Bylaws	Instrument initially adopted by majority vote	As provided in bylaws, or by two-thirds vote with previous notice if bylaws silent	Can't be suspended unless provisions for suspension are included for a particular rule or are clearly in the nature of a *rule of order*
Special rules of order	Previous notice and two-thirds vote, or a majority of the entire membership	Previous notice and two-thirds vote, or a majority of the entire membership	Two-thirds vote, subject to limitations (see Chapter 11)
Standing rules	Majority vote	Majority vote with notice, two-thirds vote without notice, or a majority of the entire membership	Can't be suspended if application is outside a meeting; can be suspended for the particular session by majority vote if application is in a meeting
Rules of Order (parliamentary manual)	Initially adopted by specifying in bylaws, but may be adopted by special rule of order	Not amendable, but special rule of order or standing rule takes precedence	Two-thirds vote, subject to limitations (see Chapter 11)

After you know the basics about the different classes of rules, it's time to drill down to bylaws, because your bylaws are the heart of your organization's structure.

Uncovering Bylaw Basics

Your *bylaws* comprise the fundamental rules that define your organization. They should include all the rules that your group determines are of such importance that

- ✔ They can't be changed unless the members get previous notice of any proposed change and a large majority (commonly two-thirds) is required to enact any proposed change.

- ✔ They can't be suspended (see Chapter 11) even by a unanimous vote.

A particular bylaw may be suspended if the bylaw provides for its own suspension or if it's a rule that otherwise would be considered a *rule of order* as defined in the section "Covering the Rules about Rules," earlier in this chapter. An example of such a bylaw that can be suspended is a provision that "the president shall preside at all meetings of the assembly." Because this bylaw is specifically a rule related to the duty of an officer in a meeting, it would otherwise be classed as a rule of order, and it could, therefore, be suspended. I discuss procedures for motions to suspend the rules in Chapter 11.

The exception permitting bylaws to be suspended in these cases must be narrowly construed. If there's any doubt as to whether a rule in the bylaws can be suspended, it probably cannot be suspended.

Because bylaws are such a closely interrelated and customized set of rules, they're gathered in a single document. With the exception of any laws governing your organization or your charter (if your organization is incorporated or is a unit of a larger organization), the bylaws take precedence over any and all other rules you may adopt.

The nature of bylaws is sufficient to establish a contract between members and define their rights, duties, and mutual obligations. Bylaws contain substantive rules relating to the rights of members whether they're present in meetings or not. The bylaws detail the extent to which the management of the organization's business is handled by the membership, a subordinate board, or an executive committee.

Whenever the United States Congress enacts a law that treads on the fundamental rights of a citizen, that citizen can take 'em to task and show Congress just how the law is unconstitutional. Well, bylaws are like that in a way. Adopting a motion or taking any action that's in conflict with your bylaws is wrong, and under Robert's Rules, any such action is null and void.

Origins of the constitution and bylaws

As stable as Robert's Rules are, styles change over time. It used to be much more common for an organization to have two separate governance documents — one being the *constitution,* and the other being the *bylaws.* Now, it's considered preferable to combine all the articles from both into one document called *bylaws.*

Then . . .

Up until about 1970, Robert's Rules took into account that organizations usually would establish two sets of rules to define themselves. The higher-ranking rules were called the *constitution,* and the rules ranked just below the constitution in importance were called the *bylaws.*

The constitution usually contained the articles establishing the name and object of the organization; and articles defining the qualifications of members, officers, and the essential details of meetings. (If the society was to be incorporated, the corporate charter contained these articles and no constitution was adopted.)

The bylaws, then, contained any other rules that the organization may have required that couldn't be changed without previous notice. These rules included any details related to meetings that weren't included in the constitution; the quorum requirement; and any provisions for executive boards, committees, and parliamentary authority.

Both the constitution and bylaws contained specific provisions for amendment, with the constitution a little more difficult to amend.

And now . . .

The only substantive difference between then and now is the recognition that unless some real purpose is served by having two documents with one more difficult to amend than the other, having a separate constitution and bylaws is unnecessary.

In fact, the only time a separate constitution is a good idea is when some law requires it.

Robert's Rules now includes in the bylaws all the articles once placed in the two separate documents. Furthermore, whenever the term *bylaws* is used in Robert's Rules (or in *Robert's Rules For Dummies,* for that matter), it refers not only to bylaws but also to the constitution (when one exists).

You don't have to go to all the trouble of taking your violation to the Supreme Court, however. You just have to take it to the membership by raising a point of order (see Chapter 11). And even though the membership is pretty supreme, it can't even use a unanimous vote to make legal something that conflicts with the bylaws without amending the bylaws, because to do so would violate the rights of the absentees.

Because of the nature and importance of bylaws, and because members' rights are spelled out there, a copy of your bylaws should be given to every member upon joining your organization. And anybody who's considering joining your organization should also be given a copy of your bylaws upon request. By joining, your prospective member agrees to be bound by these rules, and it's reasonable for him or her to want to look over your bylaws in advance. For just that reason, I usually request a copy of an organization's bylaws in advance of making a commitment to become a member. I figure there's nothing wrong with looking at what I may be getting myself into!

Breaking Down the Content of Bylaws

Your bylaws may have more articles than the basic list provided by Robert's Rules. (And that's okay unless you're adding a lot of stuff that you shouldn't.) In any case, the following list outlines the articles you should have in your bylaws (and the order in which they should appear) in order to cover the basic subjects common to most organizations.

1. **Name:** Specify the official name of your organization in this article.

2. **Object:** This article includes a succinct statement of the object for which your society is organized. This statement should be broad enough to cover anything your group may want to do as a group, but it should avoid enumerating details because when you list things, anything you leave out is deemed excluded.

3. **Membership:** Begin this article with details of the classes and types of membership as well as the voting rights of each class. If you have eligibility requirements or any special procedures for admission, then include them under this article. Also include any requirements for dues, including due dates, rights or restrictions of delinquent members, explanations of when members are dropped from the rolls for nonpayment, and reinstatement rights. Any rules related to resignations or any intricate requirements related to memberships in subordinate or superior societies are included here, too.

4. **Officers:** This article is the place to explain specifications about the officers your organization requires and any duties beyond those established by rule in your parliamentary authority (see Chapter 15). Sections including qualifications of officers; details of nomination, election, and terms of office

(including restrictions on the number of consecutive terms, if any); and rules for succession and filling vacancies are appropriately placed in this article. You may include a separate article to describe the duties of each officer.

5. **Meetings:** This article contains the dates for all regular meetings. Authority for special meetings, if they're to be allowed, must appear in the bylaws. Details related to how and by whom special meetings can be called and the notice required are included here. Also, the quorum for meetings should be included in a section of this article.

6. **Executive Board:** If your organization plans to have a board of directors to take care of business between your regular meetings (or all the time, if that's the way you set it up), then your bylaws *must* include an article establishing the board and providing all the details regarding the board's authority and responsibility. Be clear and specific about who is on the board, how board members are elected or appointed, when the board is to meet, any special rules it must abide by, whether it can make rules for itself, and, of course, specific details of the board's powers.

The powers and duties of boards vary widely from one group to the next, and problems arise for many organizations whenever the members and the board have different ideas about the role and duties of the board. This article, therefore, should be developed or amended only with the greatest care.

It's common not only to have an *executive board* to handle the business of the organization between membership meetings, but also to have an *executive committee* (that reports to the board) comprised of selected officers who are authorized to act for the board in the time between board meetings. The same amount of care must be taken when establishing the composition and power of an executive committee as when establishing a board. Furthermore, as with the executive board, no executive committee can exist except as is expressly provided for in the bylaws.

7. **Committees:** All regular standing committees that your group anticipates needing to carry out its business are defined, each in its own section, under this article. The description of each standing committee should include the name of the committee, how its members are selected, and its role and function in the organization. If it's desired or expected that other standing committees may be needed, then this article must contain an authorization for the formation of additional standing committees. Otherwise, the bylaws have to be amended to create a standing committee.

8. **Parliamentary Authority:** Adopting a parliamentary authority in your bylaws is the simplest and most efficient way to provide your group with binding *rules of order* under which to operate. The statement adopting the parliamentary authority should define clearly any rules to which the rules in your parliamentary authority must yield.

9. **Amendment:** The precise requirements for previous notice and size of the majority required to change the bylaws are specified in the bylaws. If your bylaws say nothing about amendment, and if Robert's Rules is your parliamentary authority, then amending your bylaws requires previous notice and a two-thirds vote.

Making Sure the Bylaws Are Complete

If your bylaws include at least the basic articles I outline in the section "Breaking Down the Content of Bylaws," then you're at least able to say that you have a set of bylaws. But a basic set of bylaws often isn't enough. There are plenty of things that you just can't do unless you make provisions for them in your bylaws.

The actions in the following list are collected from throughout Robert's Rules, but this list is by no means a complete one. It's accurate, though, and it may help you if you're wondering whether you can (or can't) do something in your own organization.

If your bylaws don't specifically authorize it, you can't

- Elect by plurality, cumulative, or preferential voting
- Submit absentee votes (including votes by mail, fax, e-mail, or proxy)
- Hold a runoff between the top two candidates
- Suspend a requirement for a ballot vote
- Suspend a bylaw
- Limit officers to those who are members of your organization
- Restrict the right of a member to cast a write-in vote
- Keep a vice-president from assuming the office of the president if a vacancy opens in the office of president
- Allow honorary officers or members to vote
- Create an executive board

> ✔ Appoint an executive committee
>
> ✔ Impose financial assessments on members
>
> ✔ Suspend a member's voting rights or drop a member from the rolls for nonpayment of dues or assessments
>
> ✔ Hold meetings by telephone conference, videoconference, or (heaven forbid) e-mail
>
> ✔ Hold special meetings

Amending Your Bylaws

No matter how good a job you've done in creating your bylaws, it's inevitable that sooner or later, you'll need to change something. If you followed all the guidelines and instructions for creating proper bylaws, then they can't be too easily amended, but amending them isn't so difficult that you can't consider and make changes within a reasonable time when necessary.

Setting the conditions for amending your bylaws

Normally, amending something previously adopted (see Chapter 12) takes a majority vote if previous notice is given, a two-thirds vote without any previous notice, or a majority of the entire membership (see Chapter 8).

But amending a previously adopted bylaw is a different story. You want to ensure that the rights of all members continue to be protected. The surest way to provide this protection is to prevent bylaws from being changed without first giving every member an opportunity to weigh in on a change. And bylaws should never be changed as long as a minority greater than one-third disagrees with the proposal.

Just think: If you can amend your bylaws by a majority vote at any meeting without notice, then Pete Sneak, Mabel Malevolent, and Connie Slink can assemble a small group on a slow night and, by excluding everyone not present from the right to vote, push through changes that allow the evil threesome to effectively take over all the group's bank accounts.

This worst-case scenario illustrates why you make it just a little more difficult to amend bylaws than to amend anything else. And you should always specify in your bylaws the exact requirements for their amendment.

According to Robert's Rules, you should, at the very least, require a two-thirds vote *and* previous notice to make any change at all in your bylaws. The previous notice ensures that anybody who cares about a bylaw amendment knows it's going to be voted on at a particular meeting, so they can attend the meeting if they want to help the vote reach (or fail to reach) the threshold. The rule also makes sure that if more than one-third of the members voting are opposed to the change, then they win and nothing changes. When deciding what amendment requirements to put in your bylaws, consider two things: the *details of the previous notice* and the *vote threshold required to adopt*. For detailed information concerning previous notice, turn to Chapter 4; you can find a discussion of voting thresholds in Chapter 8.

Giving notice of bylaw amendments

Bylaws are important to orderly, productive organizations, so even if you don't know many specifics about them, you can probably guess that bylaw amendments are pretty serious undertakings. Amending bylaws essentially changes the contract you've made with your fellow members about how your organization operates, so you need to be really technical and precise. The proper notice for a bylaw amendment contains three fundamental components:

- ✔ The proposed amendment, precisely worded
- ✔ The current bylaw
- ✔ The bylaw as it will read if the amendment is adopted

Additionally, the notice should include the proposers' names and their rationale for offering the amendment. It may also include other information such as whether a committee or board endorses or opposes the amendment.

I furnish a Web link to an example form for a bylaw notice in Appendix B.

Handling a motion to amend bylaws

When the time comes to deal with the amendment on the floor, you're handling a special application of the motion to *Amend Something Previously Adopted* (see Chapter 12). The bylaw amendment is subject to all the rules for that motion except for the following:

- ✔ The provisions for amendment contained in your bylaws determine the requirements for previous notice and the vote required to adopt a bylaws amendment. But if your bylaws have no provisions for their amendment, the requirement is a two-thirds vote with previous notice, or without notice, a majority of the entire membership. Otherwise, unless you say so in your bylaws (and you shouldn't), amending bylaws by a majority vote or a majority of the entire membership is never in order.

✔ Primary and secondary amendments to your proposed bylaw amendment can't exceed the *scope* of the notice. For example, if the proposed amendment was noticed as one to raise the dues by $10, then you can't amend the proposal to up the dues by more than $10. (Nor can you amend the proposal to lower the dues by any amount!) But you can amend the proposal to increase the dues only $8, because an $8 increase is within the scope of notice.

✔ After you've adopted an amendment, that's it. You can't reconsider the vote. (But if the amendment fails, you can reconsider *that* vote.) See Chapter 12 for more information on the motion to *Reconsider.*

✔ The rule against considering essentially the same question twice in a meeting doesn't apply when you're amending bylaws. Members may offer different ideas on how to handle things, and all bylaw amendments included in the notice are eligible for consideration.

Even though other amendments addressing the same issue have to be considered if proper notice has been given, you can't get around the possibility that after you adopt a particular bylaw amendment, other proposals may become moot because any change in the bylaws may make a yet-to-be-considered amendment impossible to enact.

Amending specific articles, sections, or subsections of your bylaws

Proposed amendments to bylaws are main motions, which means that the amendments are themselves open to primary and secondary amendments.

When you're amending parts of your bylaws, you propose the amendment as a main motion and specify one of the same processes you would for any amendment. The processes of the motion to amend, which are described in detail in Chapter 9, are

✔ Strike out words, sentences, or paragraphs

✔ Insert (or add) words, sentences, or paragraphs

✔ Strike out and insert (or *substitute*) words, sentences, or paragraphs

Any primary or secondary amendments to the proposed bylaws amendment must be within the scope of notice as I describe it in the previous section. However, when your amendment is noticed as a substitution of an article or section, and some part of the substitution is no different from the original bylaw, then you're prohibited from amending that particular part when considering the substitution. When no change is proposed, any change is considered outside the scope of the notice.

Tackling a full revision of your bylaws

A *revision* to bylaws is an extensive rewrite that often makes fundamental changes in the structure of the organization.

By considering a revision of your bylaws, you're proposing to substitute a new set of bylaws for the existing ones. Therefore, the rules regarding scope of notice that limit primary and secondary amendments don't apply. Your group is free to amend anything in the proposed revision before it's adopted, as if the bylaws were being considered and adopted for the first time.

Recording the results of the vote

Bylaw amendments (requiring a two-thirds vote) are handled as a rising vote (see Chapter 8) unless the amendments are adopted by unanimous consent. However, because of the importance of bylaws and the impact of their amendment, unless the vote is practically unanimous, the best and fairest procedure is to count the vote and record the result in the minutes.

Interpreting Bylaws

Your bylaws belong to your group, and only your group can decide what they mean. Sure, a parliamentarian can help you understand the technical meaning of a phrase or a section here and there. But when you come across something ambiguous (meaning that there's more than one way to *reasonably* interpret something), then the question remains to be answered by your organization by a majority vote at a meeting.

If you find your group has to adopt a specific interpretation to resolve an ambiguity, then make the interpretation. But as soon as you can, follow up by amending the bylaws to remove the ambiguity. Making the adjustment to the bylaws keeps you from having to go round-and-round with the same issue depending on who attends the meeting!

Robert's Rules lists some *principles of interpretation* to help you narrow down what's truly ambiguous and what's just a matter of following a rule for interpretation. I list and discuss these principles here in the context of bylaws, but the principles apply to other rules, too.

- ✔ Bylaws are subject to interpretation only when ambiguity arises. If the meaning is clear, not even a unanimous vote can impute to them a different meaning. In other words, if you want a bylaw to have a different meaning, then you have to amend it.

- ✔ When bylaws are subject to interpretation, no interpretation can be made that creates a conflict with another bylaw. You're also obligated to take into account the original intent of the bylaw if it can be ascertained.

- ✔ If a provision of the bylaws has two reasonable interpretations, but one interpretation makes another bylaw absurd or impossible to reconcile and the other interpretation doesn't, then you have to go with the one that doesn't have a negative effect on existing bylaws.

- ✔ A more specific rule takes control when you have a conflict between the specific rule and a more general rule. For example, if your bylaws say that no relatives are permitted at meetings and another individual bylaw says that you can bring your spouse to the annual meeting and barn dance, then be prepared to buy your spouse a new dress or a new tie before the festivities begin.

- ✔ When bylaws authorize specific things in the same class, other things of the same class are not permitted. For example, if your bylaws allow members to enter cats, dogs, hamsters, and ferrets in the annual pet parade, then elephants are off-limits.

- ✔ When a bylaw authorizes a specific privilege, no privilege greater than the one that's authorized is permitted. For example, if your bylaws say that your board can provide refreshments for the members at meetings, that doesn't mean the board can host a banquet at the Ritz.

- ✔ If a bylaw prohibits something, then everything beyond that which is prohibited (or limited) is also prohibited. However, other things not expressly prohibited or not as far-reaching as the prohibition are still permitted. For example, if your bylaws say that you can't throw rotten fruit at your president during a meeting, then you probably *can* get away with catapulting a spoonful of fresh stewed tomatoes in his direction.

✔ If a bylaw prescribes a specific penalty, the penalty can't be increased or decreased except by amending the bylaws. For example, if you say a member shall be expelled for speaking ill of the Grand Mazonka, then a member who calls the GM a louse must be expelled but you can't kick him on the backside as he heads for the exit.

✔ If a bylaw uses a general term and then establishes specific terms that are completely included in the general term, then rule that's applicable to the general term applies to all the specific terms. For example, if your bylaws define a class of membership as *Royal Pains* and that class includes *Hot Shots* and *Know-It-Alls,* then a rule applying to Royal Pains applies to both the Hot Shots and the Know-It-Alls, as well.

Publishing Your Bylaws and Other Rules

As I explain in Chapter 15, one of the duties of the secretary is to maintain a record book containing the current bylaws and rules of your group. This book should be available at meetings for easy reference.

Furnishing every member with a copy of the bylaws when they join the organization is good practice. Because special rules of order are indispensable to a member's effective participation in meetings, it's customary for special rules of order to be printed with, but under a separate heading from, the bylaws.

Standing rules, which are for the most part policies related to the details of administration, are maintained as a current list. Update the list as rules are added, amended, or rescinded. Unlike the bylaws and special rules of order, the list of standing rules is normally only furnished to your officers and staff in order that they can perform their duties in accordance with the policies adopted by the membership.

Some organizations periodically publish an updated booklet containing all their rules except those that appear in the parliamentary authority. By publishing this type of booklet, you communicate that you intend for your rules to mean something. Your members are encouraged to know and understand the rules, which helps everybody become more effective participants in your meetings. Everybody wins when you foster a high level of respect for, and awareness of, the rules of your organization.

Chapter 3

Meetings: Making Group Decisions

. . . .

. . . .

Meetings are the official gatherings of your group and where you make the decisions that bind your organization. Not everybody will agree on every issue, but that's just part of the process.

With Robert's Rules, everybody wins in one way or another because you have an agreed-up-front deal: You may not win, but you do get your say. This premise is the key to what makes your group a *deliberative assembly,* and meetings are the time and place for your assembly (group) to conduct its deliberations (discussions and decisions).

Defining the Deliberative Assembly

You're probably familiar with all the types of groups in which Robert's Rules generally comes into play. These time-tested rules of parliamentary procedure are applicable to meetings of several types of organizations. Examples include the organizational meeting for a new society, a local meeting of a service club, a monthly meeting of the board of directors of your neighborhood association, or maybe even the national convention of your professional association.

Boning up on terms of art

Terms with precise parliamentary definitions, like *meeting* and *session,* often are used in everyday speech without giving much thought to their precise parliamentary meaning. The same is true for terms like *recess* and *adjournment.*

For example, many groups call their two- or three-day annual session an *Annual Meeting* and refer to the meetings in the session as *sessions* (the *Friday morning session*). Or they may call the time between those separate meetings a *recess* when they really *adjourned* the morning meeting.

The following list defines meeting-related terms as they're used in this book:

✔ A *meeting* is any official convening of the members for any length of time to trans- act official business, with no break in the proceedings for more than a few minutes. Such a break is called a *recess,* not to be confused with an *adjournment.*

✔ A *recess* is a short break in a meeting, but declaring a recess does not adjourn the meeting.

✔ An *adjournment* ends a meeting, but it doesn't necessarily end the *session.* For a session that carries over to more than one meeting, when any but the last meeting of the session adjourns, that meeting is said to "adjourn to meet again at [specify a time]." The act of adjourning is termed an *adjournment,* and also the next meet- ing is called an *adjourned meeting,* or an *adjournment of* the previous meeting.

✔ A *session* refers to a meeting or series of meetings working completely through an entire agenda or order of business (see Chapter 5). If the session is more than one meeting, each meeting picks up where the previous one left off.

Most of these groups are what are known as *deliberative assemblies,* and it's the meetings of these groups and the bodies subordinate to them that Robert's Rules was designed to assist.

Your group is a deliberative assembly if:

✔ You meet to act together in the name of the group, and you make your decisions after thorough *deliberation* (that is, an airing of the pros and cons), where the majority gives the minority full opportunity to present its case and increase its number to a majority.

✔ Your meetings are attended in one physical location where all the participants can hear each other. This includes teleconfer- ences or videoconferences, but the use of these technologies to hold meetings must be authorized in your group's bylaws. (For more on bylaws, flip back to Chapter 2.) The point is that members *must be able to participate simultaneously* in the discussion.

✔ Your meeting attendance is large enough that you need some formal structure to keep things on track and business moving along.

✔ Your members are free to use their own judgments in connection with making the group decisions, and each member's vote counts the same.

✔ You don't have to quit, or resign from, the group if you don't concur in the final decision.

✔ You have rules protecting the rights of absentees, and you require some absolute minimum number of participants to be present before taking action in the name of the group.

In general, the groups I discuss in this book are divided into two types of deliberative assemblies (and the committees subordinate to them). They are

✔ **The local assembly of an organized society:** This is the deliberative assembly with which you're probably most familiar. For the most part, the material in this book is geared to this type of assembly; examples include your civic or service club, your neighborhood association, or a professional or trade association meeting at the local (or maybe state) level.

✔ **The board:** The board is an administrative or management group, the members of which are appointed or elected. It may be an executive board that is subordinate to a larger assembly; or it may be an autonomous body elected in public elections, appointed by public officials or government agencies, or appointed by the membership of a private organization.

There are three other general types of deliberative assemblies: *mass meetings, conventions of delegates,* and *legislative bodies.* The *legislative body* includes lawmaking bodies like state and national legislatures. Except for small legislative bodies such as city or town councils that are run like the boards described above, legislative bodies operate under very specialized parliamentary rules and authority. Robert's Rules wasn't written for them, so I don't discuss them beyond this mention.

Understanding Types of Business Meetings

In most deliberative assemblies, meetings are classified as one of the following types.

Regular meetings

Regular meetings are just that: regular! You can count on having one every week, month, quarter, or whatever your schedule calls for. The days on which you hold regular meetings are probably spelled out in your bylaws, and if you've done the smart thing, you've even established the time of the meeting by adopting a standing rule. Regular meeting times can be established in other ways, but if the times aren't fixed in the rules in some way, you must provide for a definite notice procedure in your bylaws.

Regular meetings are generally conducted to complete a standard order of business (see Chapter 5), so your *meeting* and the *session* are the same thing.

Any business that needs to be handled by the assembly can be dealt with at a regular meeting. However, any motions that require previous notice (such as bylaw amendments) must be noticed in strict accordance with your bylaws or rules of order, as the case may be.

Special meetings

Special meetings, sometimes referred to as *called meetings,* are held for the purpose of taking up business that requires the urgent attention of your group and that can't wait until the next regular meeting.

Special meetings cannot be held unless your bylaws specifically authorize them. Bylaws should be very clear on just how a special meeting may be called. Commonly, bylaws will provide that "special meetings may be called by the president, and shall be called on the request of any five members." The number is not as important as the example that it's a good idea to have some number of members that can demand a special meeting, especially if there's a need, say, to jack up the president for extreme misfeasance (or just plain obtuse recalcitrance!). After all, he's not likely to call that meeting on his own initiative.

Special meetings always require notice to the members a reasonable time in advance, and the notice must include not only the time and place of the meeting, but also the specifics of the business to be transacted. I go into detail about meeting notices in Chapter 4, so be sure to read that chapter before you call any special meetings!

Absolutely *nothing* can be done in a special meeting if it was not specifically included in the notice, or *call,* of the meeting. This rule protects the rights of absentees and can't be suspended.

Sometimes a special meeting notice lists a couple of items of business to be dealt with, and then says, ". . . and any other business that may come before the assembly." But this language in a notice for a special meeting is meaningless. Anything done in a special meeting that was not *specifically* declared in the notice as business to be considered is null and void.

Adjourned meetings

An *adjourned meeting* is a continuation of a meeting (regular or special) that has adjourned without completing its agenda or order of business, and which was scheduled either as part of a session of several meetings, or just provided for in the previous meeting by adjourning to a particular time, thus extending the session to include another meeting. In the adjourned meeting, the order of business continues at the point where it left off in the previous meeting (except that the minutes of the previous meeting are read before the meeting continues).

Adjourned meetings are appropriate when it's important to continue the business of a particular meeting before the beginning of the next regular meeting (session).

Suppose you're in your annual meeting in the middle of elections and balloting is taking an unusually long time. Your group wants to complete the election without having to wait until your next regular meeting, but everyone is tired, and if you don't stop soon, you'll lose your quorum and have to quit anyway.

So you move to *Fix the Time to Which to Adjourn* (see Chapter 10) before actually adjourning your meeting. With that motion, you have established an *adjourned meeting* to be held next week. Next week, you hold your adjourned meeting and continue your election process; you conclude the session when you finally adjourn that meeting.

The term *adjourned meeting* also applies to the prescheduled meetings that comprise a *session* of several meetings; each successive meeting in a session is an *adjournment of* the previous meeting.

Annual meetings

Some groups have only one meeting of the membership each year. At this meeting, they elect officers, or an executive board, or both; hear a lot of reports and approve the auditors' report; have some refreshments; and go home. After this *annual meeting,* the new officers and the board run the show for the next 12 months until it's time for another annual meeting. Minutes of annual meetings of this sort should be approved as soon as possible, and it's customary for the members to appoint a special committee for that purpose.

Other groups don't have an executive board but instead make all the decisions themselves at regular meetings scheduled throughout the year. But these groups have annual meetings just the same, because the bylaws designate one particular meeting as the annual meeting. At the annual meetings of these groups, the officers and standing committees present their annual reports, and the members elect new officers. With the exception of *special orders of business* (see Chapter 5) designated in the bylaws to be handled at the annual meeting, the organization handles its usual order of business, including approval of the minutes of the previous regular meeting.

Executive session

An *executive session* is any meeting or part of a meeting in which the proceedings are considered secret and nonmembers are excluded (unless they're invited for specific purposes of providing information to the assembly). Commonly, fraternal lodges conduct all their meetings in executive session.

Board and committee meetings are customarily held in executive session. Nonmembers may be invited, as is often the case when a nonmember of a board is a reporting member of a committee that reports to the board. Even in those cases, the nonmember only attends at the pleasure of the board.

With the exception of public bodies required by law to hold meetings open to the public, no assembly (whether that of the organization's full membership, its executive board, or just a committee) is obligated to admit any nonmember to its proceedings unless ordered to do so by a superior body.

Conducting Your Business

Everything you do in meetings revolves around using Robert's Rules to get your business taken care of so that, ultimately, you can go home. And the whole purpose of parliamentary procedure is to facilitate the conduct of business in your meeting so that the deliberate will of the majority is achieved, while still protecting members' rights.

Giving notice and getting people to the meeting

The first requirement for any meeting is members — enough members so that the decided-upon action is in all likelihood representative of the wishes of the entire group. Robert's Rules calls that minimum number a *quorum*. Part and parcel to achieving a quorum is making sure that all the members know about the meeting. Kind of hard to show up if you don't know about the meeting, right? That means you need to send a meeting notice to your members. I discuss notice and quorum in detail in Chapter 4.

Getting some help up front

In addition to having a room full of members, your meeting needs a minimum of two people to officiate. A presiding officer and a recording secretary are essential to holding a meeting and creating a record of what was done. If you don't already have officers, or if your regular officers can't make it to the meeting, you need to know how to select temporary replacements. I cover officers and their duties in Chapter 15.

How formal does it have to be?

One of the things I hear from members and presiding officers alike is that "we don't like to get too formal with all this parliamentary procedure stuff." I understand. But it's usually one of these groups that has a Puggy Knuckleknocker in attendance at its meeting.

Puggy is somewhat of a bully who likes to show off his knowledge of parliamentary procedure (that he remembers from the fifth grade). As elementary and convenient as his knowledge may be, he has a way of intimidating the members and the presiding officer. He's able to control the meeting because the other members don't even know enough to show him just how little he really knows. So the only way they can disarm him is to just avoid using parliamentary procedure or anything that sounds too formal; the goal is just to keep him from being able to insist on having his way because he knows how to holler, "Point of Order!" or "I move to table that motion!"

But the best way to handle Puggy is not to avoid making good use of Robert's Rules, but to learn them so that you can't be buffaloed.

I can almost guarantee that if you learn a few of the basics, including the secondary motions and their rank (discussed in Part II), and if you start handling business (especially recognizing members and assigning the floor) with a little formality, ol' Puggy won't know what hit him. And as a bonus, you'll have more meaningful meetings.

Planning the work

To conduct a productive and efficient meeting, you need a plan, or *agenda* — a schedule of what's going to be discussed and when. Find out all you need to know about using an agenda to get through your order of business in Chapter 5.

Getting down to business

If a meeting were a meal, this would be where the waiter shows up with your order! After an appetizer of opening ceremonies and the soup and salad of reports, you get to the main course of making your decisions by making motions and voting, followed by adjournment (always a great dessert!).

Making motions

Nothing can get done until somebody has an idea and shares it with the group. You do this by making motions. I discuss the process of making main motions in Chapter 6.

Discussing and debating

Nobody's idea is perfect. Some members may want to improve it, and some may want to just forget about it. Debating motions, making amendments, and voting are covered in Chapters 7 through 10.

Adjourning

Probably the best part of any meeting is when the chair declares the meeting adjourned. If you've had a good meeting, then you're glad you were a part of it, and you feel a great sense of accomplishment. If you've had a bad meeting, then you're probably even happier it's over!

Participating in Meetings As a Member

Fundamental to effective meeting participation is knowing how to get the attention of your presiding officer so you can be recognized and permitted to speak. Just as important is understanding the way to avoid getting personal in debate by asking questions of the other members through the chair. (Jump to Chapter 7 for more information on debate decorum.)

Addressing the presiding officer

In meetings, your presiding officer should be addressed by title, such as "Madam Chairman" or "Mr. President." Robert's Rules provides that an officer's title should be used as defined in the *bylaws,* or the rules of order. In Robert's Rules, "Chairman" is considered as gender neutral as "Director" or "Governor." (Not many female members of a board of directors or a board of governors want to be called a "Directrix" or a "Governess," the traditional feminine forms of "Director" and "Governor.") But courtesy demands that a person's preference as to the usage of their title be honored. Accordingly, "Madam Chair" or "Madam Chairperson" is not incorrect if it's the pleasure of a woman holding the position of presiding officer.

A vice-president is addressed as Mr./Madam President when actually presiding. If the president is only temporarily out of the chair and is still present at the meeting, Mr./Madam Vice President is appropriate. Any other person temporarily occupying the chair is properly addressed as Mr./Madam Chairman.

When addressing the presiding officer, avoid the second person, as in "Madam Chairman, are you sure that . . .?" Instead, use "Madam Chairman, is the chair certain of . . .?"

Speaking through the chair

When addressing another member, you never go wrong by speaking through the chair. Refrain from using the member's name if you can avoid it. Respect is conveyed by depersonalizing comments made in debate. For example, "Mr. Chairman, does the member who just spoke have information on the cost of his proposal?" works much better than, "Dang it Fred, have you thought about how much your stupid idea is gonna cost us?" Formality has its benefits.

Waiting for recognition before speaking

Before you launch into your speech, get recognition. When you and your fellow members properly seek recognition and refrain from speaking until the chair has recognized you, you allow the presiding officer to do his job. A presiding officer who understands the rules for preference in obtaining recognition (see Chapter 7) and applies them impartially has the control necessary to conduct balanced debate, and this control gives him the respect due to the station.

Presiding Over Meetings with Style

When you're *in the chair* at a meeting, your job is to always maintain the appearance of impartiality. The quickest way to lose control is to allow your personal agenda to control the decisions you make while presiding. You can run things, and you can have an agenda, but your floor leaders have to stand on their own when you're in the chair. Otherwise, you're sunk. To ensure that you're seen as the leader of your group:

✔ **Speak of yourself in the person of your position:** "The chair rules the point not well taken," not, "Oh, come on, George, get real!" Or "Your president is proud to announce that . . .", not "I just found out that. . . ."

✔ **Avoid directing instructions to members by name:** "The member will please take his seat," not "Puggy, sit down and shut up!" It is appropriate, however, to use a member's name when assigning the floor, as in, "The chair recognizes Mr. Phister." In cases where delegates represent specific constituencies, it's appropriate to recognize them by delegation, as in, "The chair recognizes the member from Tribble County."

✔ **Know your bylaws and rules of order:** Probably the single most dutiful thing you can do as a presiding officer is to become intimately familiar with your organization's charter, bylaws, special rules of order, and sections in your parliamentary authority related to serving in the leadership position you have accepted.

Relaxing the Rules at Meetings

It's essential to order and expediency to maintain a degree of formality of proceedings. Nobody wants to get bogged down in minutia or listen to a lot of mindless chatter in a business meeting. But sometimes things are just better suited to a little less formality. This need for less formality occurs in meetings of ordinary assemblies when some issues just need to be discussed with a little flexibility on the rules of debate. And in committees and small boards, when the group is comprised of as few as a dozen or so members, some aspects of formality can actually slow things down.

Considering things informally

A regular assembly, no matter how large or small, has some options to relax its rules and deliberate on any particular subject under the rules for committees and boards. It may:

✔ **Resolve itself into a committee of the whole,** in which the entire assembly makes itself one big committee and uses committee rules as the rules of debate on a particular subject.

Committee of the whole is the procedure commonly chosen by very large bodies of more than about 100 members. This procedure officially turns the organization into a committee, and the presiding officer steps down and a committee chairman steps up to run the show. A committee of the whole is formed by motion and vote as a variation of the subsidiary motion to *Commit* (see Chapter 9). When a committee concludes its work, it reports back to the group that appointed it. When a committee of the whole finishes, it *rises and reports,* reconvening back into the regular meeting and voting as that group on the recommendation of the committee.

✔ **Resolve itself into a quasi-committee of the whole,** which is much like a committee of the whole, except it doesn't change presiding officers.

In both the quasi- and full committee of the whole, members aren't voting as the original assembly. Rather, they're voting on things as recommendations to the full assembly, which they become when they rise and report to the assembly. Quasi-committee of the whole is used by groups of 50 to 100 members.

✔ **Simply relax the rules and consider a particular subject informally.** This move essentially relaxes the limits on debate. Votes during informal consideration are votes of the assembly.

✔ **Establish breakout groups.** This method requires some planning in advance so that facilitators can be appointed to bring back the results of these short committee meetings.

Taking it easy in committees and small boards

For larger groups, the need for formality is more important, so you start off formal and use special procedures to relax formality in some circumstances. But with smaller assemblies and committees, things work just the opposite. You start off with more relaxed rules and only get formal if such a change becomes necessary.

Boards are usually smaller than most deliberative assemblies. Depending on size, the board may operate as any deliberative assembly, but if its meetings aren't generally attended by many more than a dozen members, then the board is subject to the relaxed rules of procedure generally available to committees.

Your board and committee meetings are generally subject to the same rules as the organization they serve, and you can't adopt special rules of procedure unless the bylaws authorize it. However, many of the procedural rules important in large groups are relaxed in boards and committees — unless the committee is so large that the formality of a regular membership assembly is a practical necessity.

Under the relaxed rules of procedure for committees and small boards:

- You can make motions or speak without the necessity of formal recognition.

- Your motions don't have to be seconded.

- You can speak as often as you can politely obtain the attention of the other members. In fact, motions to *Limit Debate* aren't in order, and the motion to *Reconsider* practically knows no limit in a committee.

- You can discuss things without a motion being on the floor.

- You don't have to take minutes in committees. However, having some record is useful, and it may be customary for your chairman to keep notes of committee proceedings for reference.

- Your chairman can make motions, participate in discussion, and vote.

One more thing about procedure in committees and small boards that's exemplary of the relaxed rules available to these groups: A vote can be taken by assuming a motion even where none has been formally made, and, if it's abundantly clear that a particular decision is pending, that decision can be made by *unanimous consent* (see Chapter 8).

An example may help here. Suppose you've been talking about whether the fire truck you're recommending to the company commander should be a red fire truck or a white fire truck. Your committee is sitting around the table, and you say, "The red one is cheaper. Besides, the white one will show more dirt." Bill says, "Yeah, I like red fire trucks better anyway." The chairman then says, "Then I guess we go with the red fire truck. Any objections?"

You've just decided to buy a red fire truck, or at least to recommend the purchase to your membership. Wasn't that easy?

Chapter 4

Starting with Notice and a Quorum

In This Chapter

▶ Understanding the basic requirements for a legal meeting

▶ Protecting the rights of all members

▶ Knowing what you can do if you don't have a quorum

*I*t doesn't matter whether your organization is a three-member refreshment committee for the Myrtle B. Glutz chapter of the Georgia Crumpet Tasters Society, or a 250,000-member General Assembly of the Congress of Delegates of *For Dummies* Readers International, or some group of some size somewhere in between. No matter how large or small your voting membership, you can't have a meeting where you do anything in the name of the group unless there has been some sort of previous notice for the meeting. And even then, if too few voting members show up, you can't do much at the meeting anyway.

In this chapter, I explain how to set requirements for notifying your members about meetings, and I help you figure out the minimum number of members who have to show up to do anything in the name of your group.

Giving Notice of Meetings

Robert's Rules says that if you expect to do business in the name of a group, then every voting member has a right to *previous notice* of the meeting. It's easy to understand why: If you have a right to vote, then you have a fundamental right to attend. And you can't attend a meeting if you don't know about it, right?

Regular meetings

Regular meetings are just that — regularly scheduled and open for any regular business that needs to be discussed. The bylaws of your organization should include the information about how often your organization's membership (and its executive board, if you have one) is supposed to hold regular business meetings.

The content and the delivery requirements of the notice for regular meetings depend mostly on the details of scheduling that are already contained in your bylaws. For example, if your bylaws provide for your board to meet at the public library on the second Tuesday of every month, then your board may just fix the hour by adopting a standing rule (see Chapter 2), and no additional notice would be required unless a change is necessary or some business is scheduled that requires special notice.

But most bylaws are more general, narrowing meeting times down only to a particular day if regular meetings are held monthly, or to a particular month (or season) if meetings are held quarterly or annually.

E-notice? Think twice!

I get asked at least once a week if it's okay to give notice of meetings using e-mail or fax communication. My answer is always, "It depends. . . ."

Despite the widespread use and convenience of e-mail and other electronic means of communication, technologically challenged voting members still populate membership rolls in great numbers. And even the technologically gifted can find themselves at the mercy of a system that's nowhere near dependable enough for important time-sensitive, mission-critical communication.

Because notice is a fundamental right of members, my advice is always to make sure that the group's bylaws establish a policy for meeting notice lead time and method(s) of distribution, and add policy details either in bylaws or in standing rules.

Without clear policy and even some written waivers of liability covering the possibility of e-mail notice failure, you may find your whole meeting (and some important decisions made there) legally challenged on a claim of improper notice.

E-notice sounds like a great idea, and it can be very convenient, especially if you have a small group and all the members consent (and are able) to receive notices this way. But if your secretary has a long membership list to contend with and has to keep three lists to manage notices in different media, you'll be turning to my chapter about filling vacancies in office (that's Chapter 14) a lot more than you want to.

Spelling out notice requirements

Unless the bylaws include details of the hour and location of regular meetings (a fairly uncommon scenario), they should provide specifics about when and how meeting notices are given. The lead time always should take into account the frequency and importance of a particular meeting and the distance members have to travel to attend. Notice should be given far enough in advance for voting members to receive the notice and arrange their schedules so they can attend.

Including special items of business

In addition to the hour and location, the content of the meeting's notice, or *call,* must specify all items of business that require previous notice under your rules. Common examples of such special items of business include proposals to amend bylaws, to adopt or amend special rules of order (see Chapter 2), or to amend or rescind — by majority instead of two-thirds vote — something previously adopted (see Chapter 12).

Notice for regular meetings, which must at the very least specify the hour and location of the regular meeting and could possibly include additional information about what business is on tap for the meeting, is referred to as the *call of the meeting,* and it must be furnished to all the voting members.

Special meetings

Special meetings (see Chapter 3) are, well, *special.* They're only called if something important comes up that *must* be dealt with before the next regular meeting. After all, you already have enough to do. It's not like you're not busy, so special meetings had better be important, right?

Now, because these meetings are special, the notice announcing them is special as well. You have to take a little more care with notices for special meetings than you do for regular meetings.

To be on the safe side and to eliminate doubt, I always suggest that my clients provide for written notice of special meetings to be *mailed* within a specified time frame before the meeting. For example, "Notice of special meetings shall be mailed to the members at least 14 days but no more than 30 days before the meeting." The actual range for notice will vary depending on the size of your group and the distance members must travel. The important thing is that the range for notice is reasonable and that everyone is assured of receiving the notice.

All the notice principles for regular meetings still ring true for special meetings, so I just touch on the additional material in this section. You can flip back to the section "Regular meetings" for the more general details.

Special meetings can't be held if your bylaws don't provide for them, so the information in this section may not even apply to your group. Check your bylaws before you worry about special meetings. If your bylaws don't say you can have special meetings to handle things that come up between regular meetings, then skip down to the next section of this chapter, "Selecting forms of giving notice." Otherwise, read on.

Calling a special meeting

If you need to have a meeting before the next regular meeting, go ahead. But be sure it's important and can't wait. And don't try to cover anything more than what is absolutely necessary. Write your notice, include the pertinent details, and get the notice out as far in advance as you can. (Hopefully, your bylaws dictate the lead time requirements for special meeting notice. If not, you need to amend the bylaws to include this info.)

Drawing up the special meeting notice

Make your notice simple and to the point. The subject of the meeting must be something urgent that can't wait. So don't try to do anything else at this meeting. Just write down exactly what you need to address and get the notice in the mail.

Suppose Peter Piper just applied for membership on your Parched Peanut Purveyors panel. Piper promised to pick a peck of pickled peppers for each of your panelists if he's permitted to petition for a position on the panel prior to the time his pickled pepper patch pays out.

Pickled peppers dry on the vine long before your next regular meeting. You really want Mr. Piper to belong to the club because, not only is he a person of patience and prestige, but you and the other panelists have postulated that the prospects for pickled peppers packed with parched peanuts is a profitable possibility.

The opportunity to present Peter to the panel and permit Peter's promise to perhaps profit the panel is something that would require a special meeting. So, in accordance with provisions of your bylaws, a special meeting is called, and you send a notice to all the voting members of the panel that reads as follows:

Parched Peanut Purveyors Panel

Notice of Special Meeting

There will be a special meeting of the Parched Peanut Purveyors Panel held at the Peanut Patch on Wednesday, March 22, at 3:00 p.m. to peruse the petition of Peter Piper and prognosticate on the possibility of permitting Piper to hold a permanent post on our panel.

Please plan to participate.

Sincerely,

Lilbo Peep
Secretary

Now, as long as a *quorum* is present (the minimum number of voting members required to be present to legally conduct business in the name of the assembly), and provided the proposal is adopted by a majority of the panelists, Peter Piper's petition will pass and that fact will be placed in the proceedings of the panel. (For more info on quorum, fast forward to that section in this chapter.)

Special meetings *always* require previous notice. Special meeting notices must include not only the date, time, place, and location, but they also must *specify all the business to be included in the meeting*. Nothing, repeat *nothing*, can be considered in a special meeting if it's not included in the notice.

Special meetings should only be called in circumstances in which something must be addressed before the next regular meeting. Your time is important, so use this tool judiciously. Save everything that can wait for the next regular meeting.

Selecting forms of giving notice

Depending on the rules of the organization, previous notice can take any of several forms. Meeting notices can be given

> ✔ **By a simple announcement at a regular meeting.** Small informal committees that meet frequently to work on a project often adopt this method. A simple, "We'll meet same time same place next week" is a proper notice.

> ✔ **By a fixed rule in the bylaws establishing a regular meeting time and place.** For example, "Regular meetings of the Second Thursday Club will be held on the third Wednesday of every month, at noon in Tuesday's restaurant."

> ✔ **By mailing (or otherwise distributing) written notice of the time and place of the meeting a reasonable time in advance.** This is the most common method.

Defining the time and method for giving notice in your bylaws makes things much easier down the road. A good bylaw provision for this might read something like, "Notice of the time and place of the annual meeting shall be mailed to each member at their address of record at least three weeks prior to the meeting." In this example, the bylaw defines the method of distribution and the time in advance of the meeting it is to be sent.

The important thing about giving notice is that everybody who has a right to be at the meeting must have a reasonable opportunity to be informed that a meeting will be held. And if your group is a public body, like a school board or a town council, then you probably face some legal requirement for *public* notice, too.

Protecting the rights of absentees

According to Robert's Rules, members have the absolute right to expect that nothing except business specified in the call will take place in a special meeting. If I receive notice of a meeting, I still have rights even if I decide not to attend.

For a good example of absentee rights, I'm going back to the Peter Piper petition scenario from the section, "Drawing up the special meeting notice," earlier in this chapter. Suppose I'm on the Parched Peanut Purveyors panel. Even though I want to be a good member who attends all meetings, it's very difficult for me to get to this special meeting for some reason. I have no particular objection to Peter Piper's petition, so I decide that it isn't a problem for me or the other members if I miss the meeting. And I'm okay with the action proposed, and I know that enough people will attend so that my presence is not vital, so I can miss the meeting and continue to pull up peanuts in my peanut patch.

So what happens if the rest of the panel members attending the special meeting decide, all of a sudden, to invest the panel's money in a pickled pepper-packing machine? Why shouldn't they? Everybody's there but me, and they all want to do it! Why, indeed! If I'd had any reason to think that an investment discussion might take place, then I would have done anything to be at that meeting and stop such a stupid idea. I would have tried my darnedest to convince them not to do it. I may not have succeeded, but I have a right to decide whether I want to go to the meeting and make my point.

Robert's Rules says that I don't have to worry about being absent from a special meeting. The rule requiring previous notice of the specifics of the business to be conducted at a special meeting protects me as an absentee; this rule is so important that even if the panel did decide to make the investment, the decision would be a null-and-void action (because it violates the absentee protection rule). If I'm too late to keep the money from being spent, then I can probably force the other members to pay the money back to the treasury from their own personal funds. Oh, I may have to wave my Robert's Rules around and hire a professional parliamentarian (or even threaten to sue) to get things straightened out, but I'm right, and that's the point.

After you know how to notify everybody of the when, where, and what of your meetings, the last hitch to having your meeting hooked up and ready to roll is the how many, as in "How many members have to be there?"

Quorum Defined: Acting in the Name of the Organization

Some number of members — more than one, but less than the total number of voting members of any deliberative assembly — is a magic number. That magic number, called a *quorum*, is the minimum number of voting members who must be present at a properly called meeting in order to conduct business in the name of the group. If the quorum isn't defined in your bylaws, then Robert's Rules fixes the number at a *majority*, or more than half, of all the members.

How many is enough for a meeting?

Robert's Rules is full of practical guidance when it comes to how many members you need to have present to hold a meeting, and General Robert continues to guide readers with the same rule that he came up with over 100 years ago.

According to General Robert, the bylaws should provide for a quorum "as large as can be depended upon for being present at all meetings when the weather is not exceptionally bad." In other words, at best a quorum is just an educated guess.

Establishing a quorum

Some groups set a quorum as a percentage of membership, and others use a fixed number. What's best for your organization is anybody's guess.

In fact, you really need a track record for your group before you can come up with a number that doesn't allow too few people to spend all the money in the treasury, or doesn't call for some number that's way too high. Unfortunately, most of the time you don't have a track record to go off of when you're just getting started. So, proceed with caution, and think about your quorum carefully. Use common sense and be willing to change the quorum frequently as your organization grows.

Until you make a different decision for your group and include it in your bylaws, Robert's Rules sets your quorum at a *majority of the members.*

Dealing with the absence of a quorum

No matter what the reason, sometimes too few members show up for a meeting. When this happens, you've got options, but they're pretty limited. That's a good thing, though. You don't want three of your members voting to divide the treasury between them and dissolve the association!

Here's an example of a quorum at work. The quorum for the Mountainview County Potbellied Pig Society is defined as 20 members. It wasn't always like that, though.

When the society began, nobody thought much about fixing a quorum in the bylaws. A majority was fine, especially when the membership was low. As the membership grew, however, so did the quorum! By the time the members numbered more than 50, they started having problems (boring meetings and too many silly pig stories). Achieving attendance of more than 25 members became impossible.

The Mountainview County Potbellied Pig Society had a problem. After all, at a meeting without a quorum, you can't do much more than say you held the meeting. You can have the program, but you can't approve last month's meeting minutes, you can't adopt any committee recommendations, you can't deal with unfinished business, and you can't entertain new business.

All is not lost if you're quorumless, however. Robert's Rules lays out four things you can do during a meeting in which a quorum is not present. You can

 ✔ **Fix the time to which to adjourn.** Doing so makes it possible for the meeting to continue on a later day, after you've chased down enough people to achieve a quorum.

 ✔ **Adjourn.** You can call it quits for the time being and wait for the next regular meeting.

 ✔ **Recess.** Sometimes achieving a quorum is as simple as taking a short break to go out into the hall and round up more members;

then you can proceed with the business of the assembly. Recess is often used when attendees wander out of the meeting room in the middle of a meeting and suddenly somebody notices that there aren't enough members in the room anymore.

✔ **Take other measures to assemble a quorum.** You could, for example, appoint a committee to go make calls and round up enough members for your business meeting; while you're waiting for additional members to arrive, you can continue with the program or scheduled speaker. A motion to do something to obtain a quorum is treated as a privileged motion and takes precedence over a motion to recess.

In cases like that of the Mountainview County Potbellied Pig Society, when you don't expect to achieve quorum given your membership situation, the only real solution is to entice enough members to a meeting (or drag them, kicking and screaming if need be) so that you have a quorum, and then amend the bylaws! You should do this as soon as you realize you have a problem so the default quorum doesn't continue to grow.

True, you could go on just having program meetings, but until you change your bylaws to specify a quorum you know you can achieve, your group is helpless to conduct any business. You can't even make a decision to disband until you get a quorum!

Here's how the Mountainview County Potbellied Pig Society handled their problem: After three regular meetings were adjourned because they didn't have a quorum, the president and the founder decided to ask the members to amend the bylaws, fixing the quorum at 20 before the club grew any larger. With plenty of notice (and the promise of refreshments, including the president's famous lemon rum pound cake), a majority of the club's members showed up to a meeting and passed an amendment to the bylaws. Now, their quorum is 20, and that seems to be the magic number!

See Chapter 2 for the rules for amending bylaws — you need to know how to do this in case you ever have a problem getting a quorum for your meetings.

Taking a risk while quorumless in an emergency

You can't get around the requirement that a quorum must be present to take official action in the name of your group. The quorum rule holds fast even if everybody in attendance votes unanimously to do something. In fact, Robert's Rules says that *any* action (other than the four things discussed in the section "Dealing with the absence of a quorum") done by those in attendance at an inquorate meeting is *null and void,* at least as an action of the organization.

But what if you *have* to do something? I mean you *really* have to do something? What if the circumstances are such that you call a special meeting to discuss making repairs to the heating system in your neighborhood clubhouse, and a snowstorm blows in and keeps everybody away except you and the other members who live no more than one or two doors away from the clubhouse. And while you're shivering in your boots in the clubhouse with your neighbors wondering what to do, a huge limb on the old tree next to the building breaks under the weight of its icy branches it crashes through the roof leaving a huge gaping hole, and the snow, tree debris, roofing materials, and broken rafters are all over the place, and the storm is getting worse, and. . . .

The answer is really simple: You still can do nothing *in the name of the organization.* Even if you all agree that the clubhouse's heating system will have to wait on the quorum, but decide that the roof must be fixed immediately at the expense of the group, you can't bind the group to pay the bill unless a quorum is present at a properly called meeting.

You and the others can certainly make a decision to call in a roofer to make emergency repairs, but you do it *at your own risk.* If the membership doesn't agree that you did the right thing, or even if they agree but vote against a motion to ratify your action, you're "out in the cold," so to speak! In that case, the club doesn't have to pay the bill. You and your buddies do.

The motion to ratify allows the group to approve, by majority vote at a regular meeting (or properly called special meeting) with a quorum, your action and adopt it as the action of the group. After that happens, you and the others are off the hook, and your action is no longer null and void.

Things happen, and sometimes decisions must be made in the absence of proper authority. But the rule is that without a quorum, or without proper notice, nothing done is binding on the organization unless and until the organization ratifies the action in a properly called meeting with a quorum present. And this rule can't be changed, even by a unanimous vote. It's a fundamental principle that there must be a quorum and proper notice to do business in the name of your group.

Chapter 5

Taking Care of Business without Wasting Time: Order of Business and Agenda

. . . .

In This Chapter

▶ Following the standard order of business

▶ Understanding why things are taken up in a particular order

▶ Using an agenda to plan your meeting and keep things on track

. . . .

*T*he meetings you attend are probably a lot like business trips. You want to get the business over with and get back home or back to work or play. You probably don't even *consider* going on a business trip without some sort of itinerary. Not unless you have all the time in the world and you don't care about the people you have to meet or the deals you have to make. My guess is that you *don't* have that kind of time and that you *do* care about others and about successfully handling your business.

In this chapter, I walk you through *order of business* — that is, the sequence you establish by rule to handle all the different types of things that need to come before your members in the meetings. Then I show you how to develop an *agenda,* or itinerary, for your meeting and how to use it to work through your order of business.

If you want to know how to get in and out of your meeting quickly and still get everything done you need to do, you're reading the right chapter.

Making Order of Order of Business

At the foundation of every good meeting is a good meeting plan. And Robert is the man with the plan. His rule book provides your group with this standard *order of business,* which is simply a sequence for taking up each different class of business in order as follows:

1. **Reading and approval of minutes:** Important things happened in your previous meeting. Before you do anything else, make sure that everyone agrees with the record of that meeting.

2. **Reports of officers, boards, and standing committees:** Your leadership team should be working in the time between membership meetings, and you need to hear what they've been up to before you venture into making too many decisions.

3. **Reports of special committees:** If your group has appointed any special committees for specific purposes, you need their info, too. But these committees wait their turn and report after the standing committees make their reports.

4. **Special orders:** Sometimes you need to schedule particular items of business before going over the things postponed from a previous meeting. And sometimes the bylaws require something to be done at a particular meeting, like a "nominations in November" rule in your bylaws. Such items of business and bylaw requirements qualify as special orders.

5. **Unfinished business and general orders:** Before you do anything else, you need to finish up what you already started. This is the time to get back to the postponed motions and any business that was pending when your previous meeting adjourned.

6. **New business:** If time permits, you can broach the subject of new business. You've done the wise thing by waiting until you've taken a shot at all the other stuff. It's sort of like how you have to clean your plate before you get dessert.

If you've adopted Robert's Rules, much of your meeting planning has been done for you. This order of business framework is really all you need to develop your meeting agenda. All you have to do to make the best use of your meeting time is plug your specifics into the program and *go!*

The term *order of business* refers not only to the complete sequence of the classes of business within the order of business, but also to any individual class of business. In other words, when referring to a single *class* of business within the order of business, the single class can also be referred to as an *order* of business.

Approving the minutes

In the years before word processors and copy machines, the secretary would handwrite the minutes of meetings in a book kept for that purpose. When the next meeting rolled around, the secretary would read the minutes, and the chairman would ask for any corrections, which would be noted in the margins of the minutes being corrected.

Today, technology has made things a little different. Minutes can be drafted by the secretary and easily copied and sent to the members ahead of time for them to read; then members can come to the meeting prepared with any corrections. You can still read the minutes aloud to the members in the meeting if you want to, but if time is precious, distributing the draft of the minutes ahead of time is the thing to do.

You need to be mindful that minutes drafted ahead of time are not the official minutes *until the members approve them*. Because changes may be made in the minutes before they're approved, it's good practice for the secretary to note somewhere on the distribution copy that it's a "draft for approval" at the next regular meeting. Flip to Chapter 17 for the complete breakdown of how to write good minutes.

Members who make notes of any corrections to meeting minutes are able to keep accurate records if they keep their copy of the draft minutes on file or if a final version is not automatically distributed to them at a later date.

Handling the motion for approval

The most efficient way of approving minutes is for the chair to assume the motion and obtain general consent (see Chapter 8) that the minutes be approved as distributed (or as corrected).

The presiding officer handles things by saying, "The minutes have been [read/distributed] to you. Are there any corrections?" If corrections are offered, the chair handles each by offering the correction to the membership just to be sure all agree that the correction is accurate. The secretary then enters the corrections on the master copy. When no further corrections are offered, the presiding officer says, "If there are no further corrections (pause) the minutes are approved as read/distributed/corrected."

If members of your group like to make motions and vote, however, it's just as permissible for a member to make a motion to approve the minutes, for another to second it, and then for a vote to be taken on the motion. Voting just takes more time than approving the minutes by general consent.

Approving minutes by committee

In situations where the assembly is not meeting again for a long time (if at all), such as is the case in annual membership meetings or conventions of delegates, the process of approval of the minutes is delegated to a special committee or an executive board. This practice produces an approved and legal record of the meeting shortly after the meeting closes but before memories of what occurred in the meeting fade.

If yours is a group that customarily deals with minutes by a motion to "dispense with the reading of the minutes," you need to make a change. Your intent is probably to approve them with that motion, but you don't actually approve anything. You just agree not to read them. If you want to use the term *dispense* in your meeting, let it be to "dispense with the reading of the minutes and approve them as distributed/printed."

Hearing reports of officers, boards, and standing committees

After you've approved your minutes, your leadership team gets to bend your ears telling you what they think you need to know and what they think you should do about it. Except for the big-deal annual meetings, when everybody likes to get into the act of telling you about all the hard work they've done during the year, this order of business is usually short, sweet, and to-the-point. For details on how to compose good reports, take a look in Chapter 17.

For the most part, the officers (except for the treasurer) don't usually have a report at regular membership meetings. Neither does the board, unless it's handling something that needs the membership's attention. Standing committee reports are the reports heard most frequently in this portion of the order of business. But despite their infrequency, reports from the leadership team tend to include things of high importance, so Robert's Rules places them second from the top in the standard order of business.

The prepared presiding officer knows in advance which officers and committees have reports, and she doesn't waste any time calling for reports unless she knows someone has a report to give.

Under this order of business, reports (if there are any in this portion of the agenda) are taken up in this order:

1. **Officers:** Reports are taken up in the order that the officers are listed in the bylaws. If an officer's report includes recommendations, another member moves for the adoption of the

recommendation or otherwise makes any appropriate motions that arise from the report. (It's not good form for the officer to move his own recommendations.)

2. **Boards:** After the officers' reports, the boards make their reports. If a board has recommendations, the reporting member makes the necessary motion. The motion doesn't require a second because the board is a body of more than one person. If the report gives rise to a motion by any member, it's in order to entertain that motion at this time.

3. **Standing Committees:** Reports and recommendations of standing committees are made one by one, in the order that the standing committees are listed in the bylaws. Just as with boards, the reporting member makes any motions, which require no second unless a committee is a committee of one, and if the report gives rise to a motion by any member, it's proper to entertain the motion at this time.

Two types of standing committees have *completely* different procedures for properly handling their reports. They are *resolutions* committees and *nominating* committees. Not only are reports from these committees never adopted, but also the committees' recommendations are never directly voted on.

If an officer or committee report doesn't contain any recommendations, it really doesn't require any action at all. In these situations, I advise my clients generally to avoid *adopting* reports. Even a motion to *receive* a report is not proper, because the report has already been received. Only motions dealing with report recommendations are in order.

If a report contains no recommendations, the proper handling of the report is for the chair to thank the reporting member and move on to the next item of business. However, because so many people (not you, thank goodness) still don't have a clue about good form and procedure in meetings, I usually recommend that presiding officers spell it out and say, at the conclusion of information-only reports, "Thank you. The report requires no action and will be placed on file. The next item of business is. . . ."

Accepting reports from special committees

If your organization has learned how to save meeting time and operate efficiently by making good use of committees, you'll see special committee reports often in your meetings. Check out Chapter 16 for details about working on committees. Also, take a look at Chapter 17 for the info you need to produce great committee reports.

You consider reports from special committees in the order the committees were appointed. These reports are only called for if the committee has asked to report or is due to report based on its instructions. The rules for handling special committee reports are the same as for handling the standing committee reports.

Addressing special orders

After you've worked through the routine things, what's left to handle is an assortment of items of business that can cover a wide range of topics. But each item has a priority for consideration based on what was done in earlier meetings.

The class of business for items of this type with the highest priority is called *special orders*. This class refers to special items of business that have been given top priority by being made an order of the day through the express wishes of your members.

An *order of the day* is any item of business that your group is scheduled to consider at a particular session, meeting, day, or hour.

Special orders (of the day) are considered in the following order:

1. **Unfinished special orders:** These are orders not yet disposed of, held over from an earlier meeting. Consideration starts with any special order that was pending when an earlier meeting adjourned, and other orders are then taken up in the order that the item was made a special order.

2. **Items made special orders for the current meeting:** Because order is important, the group finishes old things before getting started with new items, even if the new items are on tonight's agenda.

3. **Items provided for in bylaws to be done at a particular meeting:** Examples include items such as nominations and elections, or bylaw amendments where previous notice was given for them to be considered in your current meeting.

Turning to unfinished business and general orders

Under this class of business, motions that were before the assembly but not disposed of (for whatever reason) in earlier meetings, but that weren't made special orders, are the next things in order. At this point in the order of business, items fall into two categories: unfinished business and general orders.

Unfinished business

Suppose you're considering a motion to lease a pink limousine for the Elvis impersonator scheduled to headline your annual talent show, and before you can finish your debate, a motion to adjourn is adopted. You have unfinished business, and it will be the first thing you take up (after special orders) under this order of business in your next meeting. After you decide what to do about the limousine, you'll take up any business that was left under unfinished business in your previous meeting's order of business.

Unfinished business includes the following items, which are considered in the order listed:

1. **Any item (not a special order) that was pending when the previous meeting adjourned.**

2. **Business items that were on the "unfinished business" list in your previous meeting but were still not taken up before adjournment.**

3. **Items that were** *general orders* **(see the next section) in your previous meeting but were not reached in that meeting.** (They're considered now in the order in which they were made.)

General orders

General orders are those items that were made orders of the day by being postponed to a certain time (see Chapter 9) in the previous meeting to come up in this meeting. For example, you're considering a motion to install a second phone line at the neighborhood clubhouse, and somebody moves to postpone the motion until next month's meeting. The postponed motion becomes a *general order* for next month.

You can also make something a general order by adopting an agenda containing the item of business, or by adopting a motion by majority vote to consider a question that's not currently pending, such as, "I move that next month we consider a motion to host a picnic for all the soccer teams in our league."

Accepting new business

It's no accident that new business is the last order of business. After all, by the time you get through dealing with all the other business you have going on, you just may not want to open up any more cans of worms.

But unless you just want to wind down your organization and disband, you need to provide the opportunity for members to introduce new items of business to the assembly. The chair is obligated to make the opportunity available; he does this by announcing that new business is in order and asking if any member has such business to present. At this time, it's in order for any member to make any main motion or to take from the table any item previously laid on the table.

If it's been a long meeting, you may be getting the idea that tonight's new business may be showing up under unfinished business and general orders at your next meeting. But if you team the order of business with an agenda and good planning strategies, and if you spend quality time working in committees (as I discuss in Chapter 16), then you're on your way to making meetings meaningful (see Chapter 3).

Using an Agenda to Produce Better Meetings

It's 7 p.m. on Tuesday night. You're attending the regular monthly meeting of your neighborhood association. Your president, Prissy Gardner (who was elected because nobody else wanted the job), is ready to start the meeting. Prissy's really a stickler when it comes to keeping the petunias watered at the front entrance to your neighborhood, but she thinks the board is just one big beautification committee. So, she starts the meeting off by going over last month's minutes — well, just the part about the new flowerbed she wants. When she gets through with that, she starts talking about the possibility of spending some money on a sprinkler system.

In spite of the great organizational tools and techniques available in Robert's Rules, for some reason meetings happen all the time in which presiding officers like Prissy fly by the seat of their pants — going over last month's minutes, rehashing old decisions, interspersing real discussions with commentary, and suppressing anybody who tries to move things along.

If you're unlucky enough to be a member of one such organization, then you already know the importance of knowing how to make a meeting run with a reasonable amount of dispatch. If not, believe me when I say that the future is now for anyone who can be efficient and effective when it comes to running meetings.

Understanding the agenda

If you're like me, you know the only way to get the most out of your time is to spend it wisely, and you want to make every second you have count. When it comes to meetings, the way to be efficient and effective simultaneously is to prepare and make good use of an *agenda*.

An *agenda* is essentially a program or listing of the events and items of business that will come before the meeting. It may be a detailed program covering several meetings in a session (see Chapter 3 for info on sessions), or it may be a short list of the items of business to be handled in a routine board meeting. The agenda may (but doesn't have to) indicate the hour for each event, or it may just show the total time allotted to each item.

The agenda may be *adopted* (that is, be made binding on the meeting), or it may simply be a guide to keep the meeting on track. Adopting your agenda is sometimes a good idea because it gets everybody in agreement with the meeting plan at the beginning of the meeting.

Robert's Rules' basic agenda

Robert gives us an order of business but doesn't mandate any particular agenda. However, he does give us an agenda protocol that has been so widely used that it's almost universally accepted as a fundamental meeting plan. Not everything in the agenda shown here is necessary in every situation, and your agenda may even need to be more extensive and detailed. But in its own right, this basic agenda is a great arrangement of events, consistent with the standard order of business discussed throughout this chapter; you can find it at the heart of just about every good business meeting you ever attend. In the following section, I list the basics and add some commentary to help you put it to use in your organization as the need arises.

Call to order

When the time comes, start the meeting on time. A single rap of the gavel at the appointed hour and the declaration, "The meeting will come to order" is sufficient. You can't finish on time if you don't start on time, and everybody knows when the meeting starts. A good chairman is known for starting meetings on time and will always be respected for doing so.

Opening ceremonies

Your group may customarily open meetings with an invocation and a recitation of the Pledge of Allegiance. Maybe you sing a hymn or the national anthem. The protocol is "God before country" (meaning you invoke the deity before you salute the flag), so plan to make your invocation before you say the Pledge. This part of the agenda is also the place to include any special opening fraternal rituals, a greeting given by one of your officers, or anything else that might reasonably fall under the category of ceremony. You don't have to use it, of course, and in many types of meetings, you'll skip this item.

Roll call

If your group is a public body, or if you have a rule that certain officers must be in attendance before the meeting can proceed, this is the time to call the roll. But if you don't have a rule requiring it, you shouldn't waste your time on this item.

Consent calendar

This item isn't used often, except in specialized organizations such as public legislative bodies or a large professional society's house of delegates. A consent calendar quickly processes a lot of noncontroversial items that can be disposed of quickly by placing them on a list (the consent calendar) of items to be adopted all at once. The list can also contain special preference items to be considered in order at the appropriate time. This consent calendar is usually placed in an order of business by a special rule of order (see Chapter 2), and its placement is generally of relatively high rank.

Standard order of business

Everything on the agenda outside of the standard order of business is really just ancillary to the meeting. All the business really begins with the approval of the minutes, and ends when you're finished with any new business. Refer to the section "Making Order of Order of Business," earlier in this chapter, for a detailed treatment of this agenda section, including a complete discussion of the six classes of business and the items included under each.

Good of the order

This is a time set aside for members to offer comments or observations (without formal motions) about the society and its work. The good of the order is also the time to offer a resolution to bring a disciplinary charge against a member for offenses committed outside of a meeting. (Flip to Chapter 18 for the lowdown on discipline and member removal.)

Announcements

This portion of the basic agenda sets aside time for officers (and members, when appropriate) to make announcements. However, the fact that this is an agenda item does not prevent the chair from making an emergency announcement at any time.

Program

If you're offering some other general presentation of interest to your members, whether it's a film, a guest speaker, a lecturer, or any other program, it should be presented before the meeting is adjourned. If you would rather conduct the program at some other place in the agenda, it may be scheduled to take place before the minutes are read or, by suspending the rules, inserted within the standard order of business.

Guest speakers are often on tight schedules, so it's quite proper for the chair to ask for unanimous consent to place the program at any convenient place on the agenda, even if the only convenient place is within the order of business.

Adjourn

This part of the agenda marks the end of the meeting — time to go home. But don't leave until the chair declares the meeting adjourned, or you may just miss something important. Chapter 10 contains everything you need to know about properly adjourning a meeting.

Part II
Motions: Putting Ideas into Action

The 5th Wave   By Rich Tennant

"I think the electing of officers to the garden club has gotten a little out of hand. According to last Month's minutes, we've elected a Sergeant at Arms, a doorkeeper, a maitre'd, a bartender and a bullfighter to serve on the board..."

In this part . . .

"Well done is better than well said." — Benjamin Franklin

Poor Richard is right, but meetings are all about getting things said so you can agree on what's to be done. The chapters in this part guide you through the journey from idea to action. I explain the mechanics of bringing an idea formally before your group and how to make sure everybody has a chance to have their say. One chapter covers all the standard motions that can help you make a final decision . . . or help you decide *not* to make a final decision. In addition to chapters on the different parliamentary motions, you can read about how to have a good discussion and finally how to vote and move on to the next idea. Or maybe even go home.

The more you know about these motions, the better you're able to get things done. Isn't that why you're having a meeting in the first place — to decide how to get things done? If it's not, it should be!

Chapter 6

Main Motions: Proposing Ideas for Group Action

- -

- -

Y ou're sitting in a meeting, and that little idea light bulb that floats above your head starts flashing. You have a brilliant idea, and you're convinced that it will further the goals of your group. It may be a brand-new idea that your group has never considered, or it may be an idea to do something in a new or different way. No matter what the idea is, in order for your group to consider it, you have to offer your idea to the group as a proposal for action. In parliamentary lingo, your proposal is called a *main motion.* In this chapter, I explain how to use a main motion to take action in the name of your group. I explain the different types of main motions and their characteristics and give you some examples of how to use them in a meeting. I offer some basic information about other classes of motions as they relate to the main motion, and I walk you through the eight steps of handling a motion so that you feel comfortable and empowered to bring any idea to the floor in any meeting.

Understanding Motion Basics

A favorite saying among parliamentarians, is, "When all is said and done, there's a lot more said than done!" This little quip has a lot of meaning, though. The real reason your organization holds business meetings is to bring interested members together to talk about ideas for action and to make decisions and take action in the name of the group.

Even though it's the nature of meetings to have [LB1]more said than done, Robert's Rules helps keep things on track by requiring that no discussion be undertaken until somebody proposes an idea for action.

It's through *motions* that everything your group ever accomplishes gets its start. So, while it's more than just a truism that in meetings a lot more gets said than done, nothing can get done without the motion. The length of time you discuss something and the ultimate decision your group makes are both based on your members' use and understanding of the nature of the different types of motions, their relationship to each other, and how the different motions are best used as your tools for effective decision-making.

Classifying motions

Motions come in all types and sizes, but they fall into five basic classes (and the first class breaks down into two types):

- Main motions
    - Original main motions
    - Incidental main motions
- Subsidiary motions
- Privileged motions
- Incidental motions
- Motions that bring a question again before the assembly (I use the term "restorative motions" for this classification.)

Defining relationships between the classes

I was once at a meeting when a member came up to me and said, "Why don't you parliamentarians stop confusing us with all this stuff about motions and just teach people to say, 'Let's do this . . .' and then we can just talk about it?"

I replied that she made a really great point and that understanding "all this stuff about motions" can be viewed in precisely the terms she preferred. Using her suggestion, I explain the relationships between the classes and types of motions briefly here, and I refer you to other chapters for more detail.

Starting things off with main motions

The first class, main motions, is the most basic motion of all: The main motion introduces before your group a new subject for discussion and action.

A *main motion* says: Let's do this about that.

Digging in deeper with secondary motions

The next three classes, subsidiary, privileged, and incidental motions, are all used to help you process a pending main motion. Collectively, these three are termed *secondary motions*.

A *subsidiary motion* says: Let's do this . . . with the main motion.

A *privileged motion* says: Let's do this . . . even though there is a pending main motion.

An *incidental motion* says: Let's do this . . . to better handle the pending motion.

Rewinding with restorative motions

The fifth class, restorative motions, is a special class of motion by which your group can undo or make changes to decisions already made. This type of motion is a special tool used when changes to a decision become necessary "after the fact." You can find everything you need to know about these motions in Chapter 12.

A *restorative motion* says: Let's undo this and maybe do that instead.

Knowing when to use secondary motions

The main motion proposes action, but it's a rare meeting where every motion is decided without some discussion. After an idea is put before your group, the fun starts. Some folks will be all for the idea. Some will be dead-set against it. Others will think it's fine but want to consider a different approach.

You would never get anything done if you didn't have a system for dealing with all the different things members offer in response to your idea. So Robert's Rules provides you with *secondary motions* — the tools you need to handle the different approaches members may want to take to arrive at a final decision.

Secondary motions fall into one of the following three classes:

- **Subsidiary motions** are motions that are applied directly to a pending main motion (or pending secondary motion) and help the group arrive at a final decision on the main motion. (For example, the motion to *Amend* is a subsidiary motion. You use it to propose a change to the main motion. Another example is the motion to *Refer* the main motion to a committee. You use it when you don't want to spend all night talking about something that could be done at another time by people who are interested in working out the details.) I cover subsidiary motions in detail in Chapter 9.

- **Privileged motions** are motions that deal with things relating to the comfort of the assembly or other situations that are so important they may interrupt pending business and must be decided immediately by the chair or by the members without debate. (For example, the motion to *Adjourn* is privileged when made if another motion is under consideration. You make this motion when you're ready to go home.) I cover privileged motions in detail in Chapter 10.

- **Incidental motions** are motions that generally deal with procedures and help process other motions. (For example, making a *Point of Order* during debate on a main motion is an incidental motion.) You use incidental motions to help the group go about conducting its business in meetings. I cover incidental motions in detail in Chapter 11.

Many individual motions make up these three classes of secondary motions, and collectively, secondary motions — and the restorative motions discussed in Chapter 12 — are often referred to as the *parliamentary motions*. I mention parliamentary motions here to illustrate their relationship to main motions, but I cover them more completely and provide examples of their applications in the individual chapters in Part II.

Taking the Plunge with a Main Motion

The main motion is a proposal for specific action and marks the beginning of consideration of a subject by your group.

That's simple enough! You're a member, you're at a meeting, and you have an idea for action. All you have to do now is make a motion for the group to decide if it accepts your idea and authorizes the action you propose.

The motion opens discussion

Examples of main motions

Suppose you're attending a monthly meeting of your community service club. Your speaker from the county library tells everyone about the new bookmobile program to make books available to members of the community who find it difficult to get to the library. Your club's president thanks the speaker and addresses the club members, asking if anyone has any new business. You think the club should make a donation to the county library to support the bookmobile, so you address the chair, are recognized, and suggest your idea by making a motion. You say, "Mr. President, I move that we donate $1,000 to the county library to purchase books for the bookmobile." You've just made a main motion.

Resolutions: A matter of form

Some main motions need to be expressed very formally in writing in order to attach a special level of importance to them. Because of the form — beginning with the word "Resolved" and followed by either a statement of opinion or a statement authorizing or directing that some action to be taken — such a motion is called a *resolution*.

Here's an example of a common resolution: "*Resolved,* That it is the sense of this assembly that the organization commend our city council for repairing our streets without raising our taxes."

You make this kind of motion by saying, "I move the adoption of the following resolution," and then you read the resolution.

Of course, the same opinion can be considered by your group if you make a motion by stating, "I move we commend the city council. . . ." But resolutions afford the group a way of adding emphasis to the expression.

Another thing about resolutions is that because they're very formal, you get to add a *preamble* if you want to. A preamble is parliamentary lingo for all those "Whereas" paragraphs that precede the "Resolved"s. Using a preamble gives you a chance to list the reasons for the resolution and keeps you from having to use all your debate time justifying your motion.

When I was a student, I wondered a lot about the difference between a main motion and a resolution. After all, if they do the same thing, how do you know when to make your motion in the form of a resolution? My mentor told me, "Well, it's like this: You use a resolution when you want to make it like a law!"

The difference has a lot to do with how you want the record to look when all is said and done. (I explain what the record is when I discuss minutes and reports in Chapter 17 and the duties of the secretary in Chapter 15.) No matter the differences, a resolution is a main motion just the same. It's just a matter of form.

That's just one example. Main motions are also used to

- ✔ **Express an opinion:** "I move that we commend the president for a job well done!"

- ✔ **Authorize a purchase:** "I move that we buy a new computer for the club secretary."

- ✔ **Create a policy or rule:** "I move that we limit the use of the swimming pool only to residents of the neighborhood and their preregistered guests."

- ✔ **Adopt a recommendation made in a report:** "I move that we adopt the recommendations of the Membership Committee to take out advertising in the Sunday newspaper."

Understanding the main motion's purpose

The main motion is the starting point on the way to making a group decision. Essential for orderly decision-making, the main motion's purpose is to introduce business for discussion, and, ultimately, it results in your group making a decision.

Until a motion is made, seconded, and stated by the chair, no discussion is in order. (I cover this and other rules about discussion in Chapter 7.) This rule of "motion before discussion" saves valuable meeting time. When you start off with a definite proposal — "I move that . . ." — your group discusses the motion's merits and all the details necessary to make a decision. And during the discussion, you and the other members are free to alter your motion as much as necessary before reaching the final decision. This process is much more productive than just starting off jabbering about some vague idea hoping to work it out as you go, and then getting around to making a motion summarizing what you think you may have just proposed, wasting meeting time and leaving your group confused.

Brainstorming is great, but you need to do it outside of your business meeting. Time is limited, and often many decisions need to be made at the meeting in a very short time. The rule requiring you to have a motion on the floor before discussing it means that you have to be responsible and have your idea fairly well thought out before turning it over to the group for its consideration.

Putting your motion in writing

Experience has taught me to write out my main motion before I stand up and make it in a meeting. Writing out the motion helps me organize my thoughts and compose a motion that's clear and covers the necessary details but is as concise as possible. A well-prepared motion helps other members understand my idea and how I think the group should proceed.

If a member has something to bring before the group, writing it ahead of time is the thing to do. As often as not, however, ideas come during the meeting. An effective member will work out a motion's wording before rising to make the motion. It's not always easy to follow along in a meeting *and* compose a motion, but that's what happens in meetings. As soon as a member gets to thinking about making a motion on the fly, writing it is the most effective way to compose one's thoughts.

If you reduce your ideas to writing so that you express your proposals as concisely as possible before any discussion occurs, you not only save time, but you help the group reach the right decision (whether that's the decision you hoped for or the decision that's best for the group). A side benefit of being prepared and having your motion in writing is that you won't find yourself grasping for words and cause a meeting delay, especially if you have a long motion.

In fact, Robert's Rules gives the presiding officer the right to ask that you submit your motion in writing. The secretary has the duty of recording all main motions in the meeting's minutes. But that duty doesn't involve transcribing your motion on the fly. For all but the simplest motions, handing the secretary your motion in writing (after you make it) is the thing to do. An important benefit is that offering your written motion eliminates the chance of error when the chair states your motion or when the secretary writes it in the minutes.

In any event, you achieve your goal more effectively if you state your proposal clearly without fumbling around for words. You *sound* prepared because you *are* prepared, having thought about exactly what you want the group to do and how best to propose that they do it.

Making your motion in proper form

In addition to writing your motions down before you make them, you also want to use proper form when stating your motion.

- ✔ **Do** use words like, "I move that . . ." or "I propose that. . . ."

- ✔ **Don't** use words like, "I motion that . . ." or "I want to make a motion that. . . ."

  One of my mentors always responded to members who said, "I want to make a motion that . . ." by answering, "Okay then, make it!"

Using proper form makes you sound natural, relaxed, and confident. Without it, you may sound like you don't know what you're doing, thus lessening your effectiveness in the meeting.

Breaking Down the Types of Main Motions

Main motions are divided into two different classifications: original main motions and incidental main motions.

Original main motions

An *original main motion* is one that deals not so much with the internal business of the assembly as with the goals and objects of the organization itself. Its most distinguishing characteristic is that, when made, the original main motion marks the beginning of a group's involvement in a substantially new question. Check out a few examples of original main motions:

- ✓ "I move that we buy a copy of *Robert's Rules For Dummies* for our president."

- ✓ "I move that we appoint a committee of three to plan a Christmas social for the residents of the Senior Citizen's Center and to report their recommendations at the November meeting."

- ✓ "I move that we adopt the following resolution: *Resolved,* That the Lakeside Acres Homeowners Association opposes the construction of a new causeway entrance across from the main entrance to Lakeside Acres subdivision."

Incidental main motions

An *incidental main motion* is a main motion that deals with things directly related (or *incidental*) to the business of the group, including previously made decisions.

Distinguishing incidental main from original main motions

An incidental main motion is distinguished from an original main motion in that

✔ **The incidental main motion deals with business that started out as an original main motion and on which the group reached a decision. Now the subject matter is being revisited in some way and is the subject of further discussion or decision-making.**

Suppose that the committee responsible for planning a Christmas social for a senior citizens center has found a caterer, but the caterer wants a $400 deposit before he will book the event. At the next meeting, the committee reports back to the group with a recommendation that the members authorize and direct the treasurer to issue a check for $400 to Party Hearty Catering Service. The chairman of the committee then makes an incidental main motion to adopt the recommendation of the committee.

✔ **The incidental motion to *Object to the Consideration of the Question* may only be applied to an original main motion, and it's never proper to use it to keep an incidental main motion from being discussed.**

By definition, this kind of objection can only be applied to an *original* main motion. To understand this, just think of the incidental main motion example above. It would make no sense to have the group vote on *whether to consider* the recommendations of a committee your group has appointed. If a member is opposed to adopting their recommendation because he thinks $400 is too much to spend, his duty is to speak against the motion to adopt — not to stifle discussion about the recommendation. The motion to object to consideration of the question is fully discussed in Chapter 11.

Some examples of incidental main motions include

✔ **Motion to *Adopt:*** "I move that we adopt the recommendations of the Christmas Social Planning Committee to authorize and direct the treasurer to issue a check for $400 to Party Hearty Catering Service for our annual event for the Senior Citizens Center."

✔ **Motion to *Ratify:*** "I move that we ratify the decision made by the president to contract for emergency repairs to the clubhouse after the storm."

✔ **Motion to *Recess* (made when no other motion is pending):** "I move that we take a ten-minute recess before we move on to the election of officers."

If made when another main motion is pending, the motion to recess isn't an incidental main motion but is a *privileged motion* — a special type of secondary motion.

✔ **Motion to *Limit Debate* (made when no other motion is pending):** "I move that we spend no more than 20 minutes tonight discussing the budget."

If made when the budget is already under discussion, the motion to limit debate isn't an incidental main motion, but is a *subsidiary motion* — a type of secondary motion.

✔ **Point of Order (made when no other motion is pending):** "Mr. President, the bylaw amendment reported in the minutes as adopted last month was not included in the notice of that meeting. Bylaw amendments require previous notice and publication in the call of the meeting at which they are to be considered, therefore my point is the action taken to adopt the bylaw amendment is null and void and the bylaws were not amended."

If a point of order is raised during consideration of a motion, it is not an incidental main motion, but is an *incidental motion* — a type of secondary motion.

Distinguishing incidental main motions from incidental motions

An incidental main motion is not the same as an *incidental motion,* which is one of the secondary motion types you can read about in Chapter 11. The differences between these motions are briefly highlighted in this section.

The incidental main motion is first and foremost a main motion, and it's never made when another main motion is being made or discussed. By contrast, the incidental motion is always a secondary motion being applied to and used to help with processing some other pending motion.

To understand the difference, consider these examples:

✔ **Incidental main motion:** No motion is pending, and the election of officers is coming up. You rise, address the chair, are recognized, and say, "Mr. Chairman, I move that when we vote on our officers we vote by ballot." This is a *main motion* because it brings a new question before the group, and it's *incidental* to the business of the assembly.

✔ **Incidental motion:** The election of the treasurer is pending, and there are two nominees. The chairman proceeds to take the vote on the first nominee by voice, and it cannot be determined whether the first candidate received a majority. You rise, address the chair, are recognized, and say, "Mr. Chairman, I move that we vote on the treasurer by ballot." This is a *motion* that is *incidental* to the currently pending election of an officer.

Working within Limits: Basic Rules for Main Motions

In order to participate effectively in a meeting, you need to know some basic things about the various motions: Is the motion applicable in this situation? Can it interrupt a speaker? Does it need to be seconded? Is it amendable? Is it debatable? What vote is required to adopt it? Can it be reconsidered?

The answers to these questions make up what Robert's Rules terms the *standard descriptive characteristics* of motions. For a particular motion, these characteristics are made up of a concise set of rules that fairly describe when a motion is in order and what it takes to adopt such a motion.

The standard descriptive characteristics for main motions are the following:

✔ A main motion takes precedence over nothing. It is only in order to make a main motion when no other business is pending. Further, a main motion must yield to almost all secondary motions.

✔ A main motion is never "applied to" another motion, but all subsidiary motions can be applied to it.

✔ A main motion that is made when someone else has the floor is out of order.

✔ A main motion requires a second.

✔ A main motion is debatable.

✔ A main motion is amendable.

✔ A main motion requires a majority vote to adopt except

- When bylaws provide for a higher vote requirement, as they usually will for some special situations.

- When its adoption requires overriding any procedural rules in place. In such a case, the main motion requires a two-thirds vote.

- When it has the effect of changing a decision already made. The vote in such a case is the same as for restorative motions (covered in Chapter 12).

✔ A main motion can be reconsidered, subject to some special rules about the motion to *Reconsider* (see Chapter 12).

all in favor
all opposed
any abstentions

Handling a Main Motion in Eight Easy Steps

When it comes to handling a main motion, Robert's Rules streamlines the process and saves your group a lot of time.

Using the following eight steps to consider ideas brought to the group in a systematic and orderly manner doesn't guarantee that everybody gets their way, but it does guarantee that everybody has their say.

Step 1: The member rises and addresses the chair

Members have the right to make motions during a meeting almost any time no other business is pending. The chair's responsibility is to know whether it is in order to entertain a particular main motion.

When you're ready to make your motion, be sure no one else has the floor, and then stand up and say, "Mr./Madam Chairman (or Mr./Madam President)."

Step 2: The chair recognizes the member

If the member is entitled to recognition by the chair, the chair responds by saying something along the lines of, "The chair recognizes the member from Elm Acres." (The chair needs to maintain the appearance of impartiality here. If the member from Elm Acres is a constant pain, the chair may have to work hard to avoid say anything like, "What is it *now*, George?" But that's the job!) In some situations when the chair needs to determine the purpose for which the member seeks recognition before recognizing the member, the chair says something like, "For what purpose does the member from Elm Acres rise?" In this case, the member responds, "I rise to offer a motion to. . . ." If the motion is in order, the chair proceeds by recognizing the member.

Sometimes several people rise at once to address the chair, and when this happens, the chair follows the rules for preference in recognition. These rules are discussed in detail in Chapter 7.

Step 3: The member states the motion

After the chair recognizes the member, the member makes the motion concisely (and with only minimal advance comment, if any at all) by saying, "Mr. Chairman, I move that. . . ."

For all but the simplest original main motions, the judicious member has written out the motion ahead of time and is prepared to immediately submit the written motion to the chair or the secretary after making the motion.

Step 4: Another member seconds the motion

Main motions must be *seconded,* meaning that a second member expresses a desire to have the motion considered by the group.

Contrary to popular belief, a second is not necessarily an endorsement of the idea. The procedure requires a second mainly to ensure that at least one other person thinks the motion should be discussed. A member who opposes the motion may want it to come before the meeting so it can be voted down.

To second a motion, a member simply calls from his place, "Second!"

If no second is forthcoming, the chair asks, "Is there a second to the motion?" If a second still doesn't come, the motion is said to *fall to the ground* and simply does not come before the group. If this happens, the chair states that as the case and moves on to the next item of business.

However, if someone rises and starts making comments in support or opposition (even without being recognized by the chair or without saying "Second!"), then the motion is considered seconded because another member has expressed interest in discussing the motion. Then the chair (after asking the member whose speech is out of order to please be seated) proceeds to the next step.

Up to this point, the member who offered the motion still has complete control of the motion. If for some reason he wishes to withdraw it, he may do so. If he needs to make a minor change, he may do so — the permission of the assembly is not required.

The motion has been made by —
seconded by —

Step 5: The chair states the motion

This step is simple. The chair says, "It is moved and seconded that . . ." and then reads the motion to the members. By then asking, "Is there any discussion?" the motion is put in the control of the group, and the member who made the motion needs the approval of the assembly to withdraw the motion or to make or approve changes on his own.

In some cases minor adjustments to language or clarifications of content are needed before the motion is stated to the members. It's the chair's responsibility to assist the member with his motion in making any such adjustments when necessary. The time spent at this point is well worth the investment because it expedites business and helps the group arrive at its decision without being bogged down amending intricate details.

After the chair states the motion and asks for discussion, the motion belongs to the group. However, Robert's Rules provides that the member who made the motion is entitled to be recognized to speak to the merits of his motion before any other member.

Step 6: The members debate the motion

The chair recognizes the member who made the motion by saying, "The chair recognizes the member from Elm Acres." The member now has the floor to explain his motion and the reasons behind its creation.

Other members may then take the opportunity to seek recognition of the chair to speak for or against the motion. The member wishing to speak rises and addresses the chair by simply saying, "Mr./Madam Chairman/President" and waiting to be recognized.

During the discussion, any of the secondary motions may be considered, subject, of course, to the specific rules for their uses and applications.

Discussion and debate of the motion can be a complicated process, and because of that, it has its own chapter in this book. In Chapter 7, I cover the rules and procedures for this part of the process.

Step 7: The chair puts the question and the members vote

When all have spoken who wish to do so, it's decision time.

Putting the question

The presiding officer now asks the members whether they want to adopt the motion. The motion is voted on by answering a yes-or-no question; hence, the term "question" is often used interchangeably with "motion" in parliamentary usage.

For this step, assume the motion is "To purchase a new copying machine for the staff at a cost not to exceed six-hundred dollars." The chair puts the question by saying, "The question is on purchasing a new copying machine for the staff at a cost not to exceed six-hundred dollars. [pause] All those in favor say, 'Aye.'"

After the ayes have been heard, the chair then takes the negative vote by saying, "All opposed say 'No.'"

Presenting, in a clear manner, exactly what the members are being asked to decide is very important in this step. The chair should be very deliberate about incorporating the actual language of the motion in the question.

The members vote

Motions are commonly decided by voice vote (or *viva voce* in Robert's Rules). That's the method assumed in the example for this step. But the presiding officer may, on her own initiative, call for a rising vote or a counted vote. Additionally, before the voting actually begins, any member may offer an incidental motion to conduct the vote using a different method.

Voting procedures are discussed at length in Chapter 8.

Step 8: The chair announces the result

It's all over now, and one side or the other has prevailed. The chair's duty is to make the declaration of fact and to announce the result. She either says, "The ayes have it and the motion carries (or 'is adopted')" or "The noes have it and the motion is lost (or 'fails')."

The motion carries
fails

But that's not all. The chair also needs to tell the assembly what will happen as a result of the vote.

In the example used in this section, if the motion passes, the chair adds, ". . . and we will purchase a new copying machine for the staff at a cost not to exceed six-hundred dollars."

If the motion fails, the chair adds, ". . . and a new copying machine will not be purchased."

If the vote is viva voce and any member doubts the result, then that single member may demand that the vote be redone by a rising vote. To make such a demand, the member simply rises in his place and calls out "Division." This incidental motion and its use are covered in Chapter 11.

✳ Chapter 7

Debate: Discussing the Pros and Cons of Ideas

. . . .

In This Chapter

▶ Getting recognized by the chair

▶ Assigning the floor to the right person

▶ Focusing discussion on the merits of the question

▶ Interrupting a member who has the floor

▶ Knowing which motions are debatable

. . . .

*W*hen it comes to meetings, the fun doesn't really start until you're standing in front of everybody, and, except for Mr. Boor rudely whispering to Miss Priss, they're all tuned in to hear what you've got to say. Some members are eagerly waiting to cheer you on, while others are probably thinking about how to get everyone to listen to them instead. Either way, it's your turn to talk, and you need to make the most of it.

Whether you're the presiding officer or simply a member at the meeting, you won't last long without a working knowledge of the rules of debate. If you're the presiding officer, you need to know how to decide who gets to speak so that the meeting runs fairly. If you're part of the assembly, you need to know how to claim an opportunity to speak when you want to make a point.

This chapter guides you through the nuances of debating. For the presiding officer, it's about managing the floor. For the member, it's about listening and being heard. And for both, it's about being nice and professional when you're in the thick of it.

Understanding the Debate Process

Debate is Robert's Rules lingo for the time you spend discussing, amending, or otherwise dealing with a motion in order to arrive at its final disposition. Members take turns having their say, and in many cases, debate involves nothing more than spending a little time on a couple of amendments. However, it can also be a time when a lot of people have a lot to say about whether or not the group should agree on a motion and take the action it proposes.

When it comes to debating a motion in a meeting, you really have no such thing as pure and unencumbered freedom of speech. Because you're a deliberative assembly, you're concerned not only with the rights of individual members to have their say, but also with the rights of the group. That's why debate is subject to rules and limitations on who's allowed to speak on an issue, and how often and how long speakers can hold the floor. Protecting the rights of both the members and the group is also why rules for debate can be limited or extended, but only by a two-thirds vote.

Rules for debate are designed to balance members' rights to speak with the assembly's right to make its decision and move on to something else.

To Debate or Not to Debate, That Is the Question!

A quick look at the tables of subsidiary and privileged motions in Chapters 9 and 10 shows you that all the motions that rank above *Postpone to a Certain Time (or Definitely)* are undebatable. If you think about it, it makes perfect sense because everything of any higher rank is pretty much a yes-or-no question. Motions to *Limit Debate, Lay (a motion) on the Table,* or *Adjourn* just don't leave much room for question. Except for tweaks to the amendable motions, you don't really have anything to discuss.

The same is true for most incidental motions. As you can see in Chapter 11, incidental motions deal with questions of procedure. Except for appeals and resignations, procedure is procedure — what's there to discuss?

When it comes to procedural motions, in most cases you're either for the motion or against it, depending on the immediate parliamentary situation. So, by defining a motion as undebatable, Robert's Rules is really just saying, "Take the vote and move on!"

Questioning limits on debate

I have to confess: One of my pet peeves is the obvious misuse of the rules of debate. Like when Mr. Smartypants wants to wax eloquent about how adopting a motion to limit debate violates the first amendment or wants to argue about taking a recess. Some questions (in fact, *most* questions) are undebatable. I usually don't raise points of order about every little thing, even when I'm right. But when people start to debate an undebatable motion, I can't help myself. I almost always rise to a point of order, and if I'm presiding, I'm quick to rule improper debate out of order.

It doesn't take long for most of my fellow members to catch on to the list of debatable motions and to appreciate the time we save by cutting to the chase and voting them up or down without a lot of fuss. It's like starting a meeting exactly on time — sooner or later, people start actually showing up on time. When you start learning and following the rules of debate, you save time and have better meetings.

Table 7-1 lays out the debatable motions and provides you with some key information about each one. You may find it ironic that meetings are all about discussing ideas and taking action, yet the list of debatable motions is really quite short. The good thing about the short list is that you don't really have to remember too much to know what's debatable and what's not. (Browse through Chapters 6, 9, 11, and 12 for more information on these motions.)

Table 7-1	Debatable Motions
Motion	*Key Points*
Main motions	Debate is limited only by rules for length and number of speeches, and, of course, rules of decorum.
Postpone Indefinitely	Discussion can encompass the merits of the main motion.
Amend	Debate is limited to merits of the proposed amendment. (Motion to amend is undebatable if the underlying motion is undebatable.)
Commit	Discussion is limited to merits and details of referring.
Postpone to a Certain Time (or Definitely)	Discussion is limited to merits and details of postponing.

(continued)

Table 7-1 *(continued)*

Motion	Key Points
Appeal	Discussion is limited to the subject matter of the appeal. (But if debate serves no purpose and gets in the way of business, as is sometimes the case when the underlying motion is undebatable, then the motion to appeal isn't debatable.)
Request to be Excused from a Duty	Discussion is not limited because each situation in which this motion is used is unique, and it's vital to have the information necessary to make a proper decision.
Rescind or Amend Something Previously Adopted (and Discharge a Committee)	Discussion can go fully into the merits of the subject matter.
Reconsider	Discussion can go fully into the merits of the motion to be reconsidered, unless that motion is undebatable.

Presiding over the Debate

If you're a presiding officer, there's one time when your leadership skills are clearly on display: You're chairing a meeting during the consideration of a motion on which a lot of people have a lot to say.

When it comes to presiding, your number-one duty is to know the rules. The rules for discussion and debate get quite a workout in meetings, so if you know the rules, you'll do just fine. And if you don't know them, sooner or later you'll wish you did.

Starting the debate

In meetings, discussion (also known as *debate*) is in order only when a motion is on the floor. A motion is on the floor after the presiding officer (also known as the *chair*) states the motion (see Chapter 6). For example, the chair may say something like, "It is moved and seconded to buy a fire truck for County Volunteer Company No. 2."

The discussion of ideas is the key component of any meeting. After the motion is on the floor, it's up to the members and you as the presiding officer to work as a team to figure out what, if anything, the assembly wants to do with the motion.

Your job while presiding is to keep up with who has spoken and who wants to speak. You control the assignment of the floor and handle discussion and secondary motions until no further discussion is forthcoming, or until members close debate or otherwise dispose of the motion.

The way you move things along is a matter of style. You call for debate by asking, "Is there discussion?" or "Are you ready for the question?" Or perhaps even by saying, "Ms. Gliggenschlapp, do you wish to speak to your motion?

You also need to know rules relating to discussion and debate and how to apply them, especially with regard to

✔ Assigning the floor

✔ Maintaining the appearance of impartiality

✔ Handling an appeal

✔ Taking the vote

Assigning the floor

Knowing that members control decisions but the chair controls the floor is at the heart of successful presiding.

Early in a discussion, the situation is pretty clear. Members rise and address the chair, and you basically want to take them in the order they seek recognition — first come, first served.

But deciding who gets the floor isn't always that easy. When the masses clamor for your attention, how do you decide whom to recognize? The needs and rights of the assembly are a big consideration in this decision. Knowing who's up first isn't enough; you often need to know why a member seeks recognition. And entitlement to preference in recognition is dependent not only on who wants to speak and why, but also on the parliamentary situation, which can only be one of the following:

✔ No question is pending.

✔ A debatable question is immediately pending.

✔ An undebatable question is immediately pending.

When no question is pending

This is your situation after you've finished up with a particular item of business but before you've moved on to the next order of business (see Chapter 5) or stated a new motion.

✔ In a special meeting, a member planning to offer a motion for which the meeting was called has preference in recognition over others who may offer competing motions. (See Chapter 3 for more information on special meetings.)

✔ When getting a motion before the group requires a series of motions, such as needing to lay a motion on the table to take up a more urgent motion, the member who made the intervening motion (in this case, the motion to lay on the table) is entitled to recognition in order to make the motion he's trying to get on the floor.

✔ If a motion is voted down because a member offers to make a certain motion if the assembly defeats a pending motion, that member is entitled to preference in recognition for the purpose of making the new motion.

✔ Motions that are necessary to determine composition of a committee that's established in another motion preempt any other motions until the necessary details of the committee have been decided. Members seeking the floor to make motions to decide committee details have preference in recognition.

✔ Even when a member is entitled to recognition to make a main motion, if another member seeks recognition to do one of the following things, then that member must be recognized first:

- To make a motion to reconsider and enter onto the minutes (see Chapter 12)

- To make a motion to reconsider a vote (see Chapter 12)

- To call up a motion to reconsider (see Chapter 12)

- To give previous notice (see Chapter 4)

- To make the motion to take from the table (see Chapter 12)

When a debatable motion is immediately pending

This is your situation most of the time during the discussion and debate. As the presiding officer, you may quite often find yourself asking, "For what purpose does the member rise?" If it's not one of the following, your job is to inform the member, "That's not in order at this time," and move on to the next member seeking recognition.

✔ A member rising to give notice is entitled to recognition (see Chapter 4).

✔ The member who made the immediately pending motion is entitled to preference in recognition if he hasn't already spoken.

✔ A member is entitled to speak a second time only after everybody else who wishes to speak has done so.

✔ The chair alternates recognition between proponents and opponents of the pending motion.

✔ If the pending motion is one that was adopted earlier and is now being reconsidered for the purpose of being amended, then the member who made the motion to *Reconsider* (see Chapter 12) — for the specific purpose of amending the motion now being reconsidered — is entitled to preference in recognition to move his amendment.

When an undebatable question is immediately pending

If a motion is undebatable, well, it's not in order to say much of anything. Only the following two situations give anybody any reason to claim the floor:

✔ A member rising to give notice (see Chapter 4) is entitled to recognition.

✔ A member rising to make a motion that takes precedence over the pending motion is entitled to recognition. For example, *Previous Question* (see Chapter 9) isn't debatable. But if Andy Doorhugger wants to move to *Adjourn* (see Chapter 10), he's entitled to the floor.

Deciding who to recognize

As the presiding officer, you decide which members get recognized and assigned the floor. And, as with any other decision of the chair, if you're in doubt as to who's entitled to recognition, you can ask the members and let them vote on who should be recognized.

If you're not sure if an interruption by a member is in order, before recognizing the member, simply say, "For what purpose does the member rise?" Based on his response, you make your decision on whether to recognize the member; if his purpose is in order, you recognize him. If not, you inform him that his purpose is not in order at this time.

In any case, if you err in assigning the floor, your assignment is subject to a point of order. And for the most part, except in mass meetings and large meetings such as conventions, the chair's ruling is subject to appeal (see Chapter 11).

Refraining from debate

Allowing yourself to be drawn into a debate is one of the surest ways to lose the confidence your members have in your ability to preside impartially. Your job is to facilitate the members making all the points, pro and con, on an issue. If you feel strongly about an issue, you'd best hope your political allies can handle advancing your goals from the floor. You must not give them any edge or advantage.

The *appearance* of impartiality is the key to presiding over debate. Nobody expects you to *be* impartial; chances are good that you were elected because you have a program you hope to advance. But when you're presiding, stick to the job at hand.

If you absolutely must engage in the debate, you're obligated to turn the chair over to a chairman *pro tem* and step down from the chair until the motion is disposed of.

Handling an appeal

The rules for assigning the floor during a debatable appeal (see Chapter 11) are generally the same as in any discussion, except that members may only speak once, and you, as the chair, may speak. Not only once, but twice! You get to speak first — after the appeal has been moved and seconded — to explain your ruling. Then, after everyone else has had their say, you get to speak again to respond to the points made by the members and explain further your ruling before you take the vote on the appeal.

Closing debate and taking the vote

Your duty as a presiding officer is to enable the group to conduct a full and free hearing of both sides of an issue. However, debate is not permitted to continue after voting begins. But because of the right of members to enjoy all the time the group is willing to spend in debate, it's not in order to move so quickly to the voting as to silence a member who legitimately seeks the floor to speak or make a secondary motion.

Robert's Rules calls this practice of silencing members *gaveling through,* and it's looked upon as particularly contemptible. If you ignore a member who seeks recognition before voting starts and proceed to take a vote, then the vote must be disregarded and debate reopened, even if the result has been announced. However, when you've made sure the members have a full opportunity to claim the floor before you move on to the voting, it's too late to reopen debate after voting has begun.

don't hurry to the vote, make sure that every one who wants to speak does

EXCEPTIONS

Discussion without a motion

The rule that no discussion is in order unless a motion is before your group has two exceptions that can make it easier for your group to arrive at some decisions.

One exception occurs when the subject of discussion isn't particularly complex and the group isn't large. In this case, the purpose of the discussion isn't to debate the pros and cons of a motion, but rather to frame a motion that the group wants to adopt. For example, a member in a board meeting may say, "You know, we've all been talking about setting up a scholarship for a member to attend our convention. Can we take a minute now to compose a formal motion and adopt it?" Situations in which this exception comes into play are limited, and usually it's better to just make a motion to establish a special committee to compose the motion outside the meeting.

The other exception occurs when a member wants to briefly discuss a subject and conclude his remarks with a motion. Technically, when he starts explaining the reasons for a motion he hasn't yet made, his discussion is out of order. However, if you have a clear idea of what's coming and can tell that it doesn't abuse the rule against speaking while no motion is on the floor, then unanimous consent is all you need to suspend the rule.

Watch out, though, because a fine line lies between making an exception to a rule and abusing the members' rights to have a proposal before them before spending any time on discussion.

But these two exceptions, in the right place and at the right time, can help your members arrive at good decisions with a minimum of fuss.

WARNING!

The debate remains closed even if the vote is not conclusive and if additional votes are necessary to determine the result.

Debating As a Member

It's not enough just to know the rules of debate as they apply to a presiding officer and his duties. You don't want to be without that knowledge, but there's more! Whether you're presiding or participating as a member, it's to your advantage (if not your duty) to know the rules for members' participation in debate.

Taking your turn

You've been patiently waiting for the chairman to recognize you. You've listened to everybody else so you won't waste time repeating points already made. Now you're ready to have your say.

If members try, as sometimes they will, to shut you out by making demands for adjournment or calls to table, they're out of order. As long as you've been assigned the floor, your presiding officer has a duty to help you have your say. Motions from those other members who have not been recognized and assigned the floor are just so much hot air.

Seeking recognition and obtaining the floor

Seeking recognition is at first as simple as rising and addressing the chair with the statement, "Madam president!" And unless someone else has preference in recognition, the chair should say, "The chair recognizes Ms. Goodsense."

You may be competing for recognition, and the chair may need to ask you about why you seek recognition. Be prepared to answer that question, and take care only to seek the floor for a purpose that's in order at the time. And if you think the chair has improperly recognized another person when you're entitled to preference in recognition, you can make a point of order, forcing the chair to stop whatever else may be happening and listen to your concern.

You have to follow a timeliness requirement to make a *point of order* (see Chapter 11). If you're entitled to preference in recognition, then you must make your point before the other person begins to speak!

Because the chair has the prerogative of assigning the floor, you need to be aware of the things that entitle you to preference in recognition. (Jump back to the section "Assigning the floor," earlier in this chapter, for an explanation.)

Limitations on debate

Unless your group has adopted special rules of order (see Chapter 2), you come to every meeting entitled to speak twice on every motion, with a limit of ten minutes per speech. That's 20 minutes per person, per motion, per meeting. It's a wonder meetings don't last for weeks!

Well, not really. Limits exist within the limits, and your group always has access to one of the most useful subsidiary motions: the motion to limit debate. I cover that motion in Chapter 9, and it's a great tool for keeping things short and sweet. In fact, it's not uncommon for a group to adopt a motion to limit discussion to a set period of time, to a set number of speeches for or against, to a shorter time per speech, or to some combination of these options.

In order for you to be sure you have your say, though, you need to be familiar with how the limitations on debate work.

- ✔ **Speaking a second time:** Under Robert's Rules, you can't speak a second time until everybody else who wishes to speak has done so. This means that if Mr. Smartypants has spoken once and the chair lets him speak again while you're attempting to be recognized, you have every right to claim the floor, even if you have to rise to a point of order (see Chapter 11) to do so.

- ✔ **Requesting an extension of time:** The chair is responsible for letting you (or any other member) know when your time is up, and it's your duty to honor the chair's polite notice that your time has expired and immediately conclude your remarks. If you need more time, you can ask for it, or the chair can, if he deems it appropriate, offer the members the opportunity to consent to an extension.

- ✔ **Yielding time:** You can't transfer time. When you yield the floor, you waive your remaining time, but that remaining time doesn't get added to another member's time. Yielding for a question counts against your time.

Like many elements of Robert's Rules, the limits on debate aren't completely without exceptions.

- ✔ **Committee reports:** Time limits don't apply when a committee report is being given. But if the reporting member speaks to a motion to enact one of the committee's recommendations, then his discussion is on the clock.

- ✔ **Making secondary motions:** Introducing a secondary motion isn't considered debate on the pending motion unless a member goes into the merits of the pending motion while making the secondary motion.

- ✔ **Debating secondary motions:** When secondary motions are debatable, limits on debate apply anew to debate on the merits of the secondary motions, but debate on the secondary motion may not go into the merits of the main motion except for the motion to *Postpone Indefinitely* (see Chapter 9).

- ✔ **Sessions of more than one day:** If a member exhausts his rights to speak on a motion and the motion is carried forward to a meeting on the next day, then his rights to debate the motion are completely restored.

Getting around the rules by changing the limits of debate

By using the motion to *Limit or Extend the Limits of Debate* (see Chapter 9), you have some options to change the default rules of ten minutes per speech and two speeches per person.

You can make changes as follows:

- ✔ **Adopt a special rule of order.** Taking this approach (see Chapter 2) can establish a different length for speeches or change the number of speeches permitted. A special rule of order makes the changes basically permanent, because special rules supersede Robert's Rules. However, they can still be changed temporarily, just like Robert's Rules.

- ✔ **Adopt a rule for a single session.** By a two-thirds vote without notice at any meeting, your group can adopt an incidental main motion to change the rules for time and length of speeches per person for one session only, or you can set a period for debate and a time for the vote.

- ✔ **Adopt a rule for a particular motion.** With this approach, you can change the limits of number and duration of speeches or the total time for debate of the motion; you can also set a time for debate to close, or set a limit of the number of pro and con speakers, or determine a workable combination of these. Adopting a rule for a particular motion takes a two-thirds vote.

When it's okay to interrupt

Most people were taught (or at least were told) that it's never polite to interrupt someone who's speaking. That etiquette rule works when it comes to interviews, dinner parties, and the like, but not when you're dealing with Robert's Rules. During debate in a business meeting, interrupting a speaker is often necessary to protect your rights or those of the other members.

Your presiding officer's duty is to know when interruptions are permissible and to recognize you for such things as points of order or giving notice. Recognized members who have begun to speak are entitled to their time, but they can be interrupted (using the motions in the following list) for specific purposes, if urgency requires it.

✔ **Motions that can interrupt a speaker who is speaking and that don't require a second:**

- Call for Orders of the Day

- Point of Order/Call a member to order

- Call for a separate vote on a series of independent resolutions or main motions dealing with different subjects that have been offered under one main motion

- Requests (or motions to grant another member's request)

- Parliamentary Inquiry

- Point of Information

- Call for Division of the Assembly

- Raise a Question of Privilege

✔ **Motions that can interrupt a speaker who is speaking but that must be seconded:**

- Appeal

- A motion to grant the maker's own request

✔ **Motions that are in order when another speaker has been recognized but has not yet begun to speak:**

- Notice of intent to make a motion requiring such notice (no second required)

- Objection to Consideration of the Question (no second required)

- A motion to reconsider (but not reconsideration itself; must be seconded)

- A motion to reconsider and enter on the minutes (must be seconded)

Playing Nice: Decorum in Debate

Nothing stands to ruin an organization's spirit and sense of group pride quicker than an acrimonious debate. When things get heated and personal, good members quit, and the antagonists generally don't have what it takes to keep the organization going.

Nobody likes acrimony, and nothing should keep you from having a spirited debate while still keeping discussion focused on the issues. The following list contains some things to keep in mind when the soup gets thick at those meetings where you talk about a dues increase or what to do with a budget surplus:

- **Listen to the other side.** You expect the presiding officer to protect your right to speak even if it turns out that you're a minority of one. You also expect the other members to hear you out and to allow you the same time as everybody else to get in your two cents' worth. Give your fellow members their rightful turn. Listen to them — you may hear something that affects the way you think.

- **Focus on issues, not personalities.** You don't want somebody across the aisle saying (about you), "I don't see how that idiot who just spoke can even hold a job, with as much sense as he has about spending money!" It's much better to just stick to the issues. You may disagree with the point, but you won't feel personally attacked if your opponent simply says, "If we make this purchase at this time, we'll have less money in the treasury than I think we need to maintain."

- **Avoid questioning motives.** It's not a good idea to say, "Mr. Chairman, the dweeb who just spoke is obviously trying to raise the salary of the executive director because he wants to get the director fired and hire his own brother-in-law." The dweeb may in fact be glad to see the director go, and he may indeed be working to set up a raise for the next employee, hoping it's his brother-in-law. But when you're in the meeting, express your opinion based on the proposal's merits. Try saying, "Raising the salary of the executive director is unwise at this time because we haven't yet completed the assessment of a performance review."

- **Address remarks through the chair.** One of the ways things can deteriorate quickly is by forgetting the rule that requires you to address the chair, not a member directly, during debate. Instead of turning to the member who made the motion to buy a fire truck and asking, "Just how much money do you think we need to spend on the fire truck?" try, "Madam Chairman, I'd like to ask how much money the member suggests we allocate to the purchase of the fire truck."

- **Use titles, not names.** Things are more likely to stay impersonal if you avoid using names during debate. Refer to "the secretary" instead of "George." Refer to "The member who offered the motion" rather than "Myrtle." It feels a bit formal, but the idea is to keep the focus on issues, not individuals.

- **Be polite.** Don't get the floor and start reading some paper, don't argue with the presiding officer except by legitimate appeal, and don't do anything that otherwise disturbs the assembly.

At some point, you've probably been in a meeting listening to something of interest, and Mr. Sluggo behind you isn't the least bit interested. He starts talking about how his pet parakeet is better looking than the lady at the microphone. He's disturbing the assembly with his distracting chatter, but Robert's Rules comes to your rescue with a way to remind Sluggo that his chatter isn't appropriate. If you have to handle such a disturbance and you can't deal with it quickly and quietly in your place, rise to a question of privilege that the buzz and chatter are affecting your ability to hear the speaker, and let the chair help you out. See Chapter 10 for more details on this privileged motion and how to use it.

Dealing with Disruption: Dilatory and Improper Motions

The purpose of Robert's Rules (and parliamentary procedure in general) is to facilitate the transaction of business and to achieve the deliberate will of the majority after giving the minority a full hearing of its position, with full consideration of the rights of all the members whether present or not.

However, some people learn about a few different types of motions and think they can use them to force their will on the group or to thwart the process that rules of order are designed to protect.

Everybody has run into Joe Noe, the malcontent who stirs up trouble and tries to interrupt discussion and debate with points of order, appeals, and motions to table. All these motions have their rightful place in the big picture, but if they're used to hinder business instead of help it, they're properly termed *dilatory* and can be ruled out of order by the chair.

Dilatory motions include motions that are

- ✔ Misused with the purpose of obstructing business (such as a series of points of order and appeals, motions to table, or motions to adjourn offered every time a little discussion has passed by a few members who don't like the way things are going)

- ✔ Absurd in substance

- ✔ Frivolous, especially amendments

- ✔ Unwarranted (such as calling "division" when the result is clear)

Just as disruptive are the motions Robert describes as improper. *Improper motions* are those that

- ✔ Are inconsistent with the organization's charter, bylaws, or procedural laws

- ✔ Conflict with an adopted motion that hasn't been rescinded

- ✔ Present essentially the same question that has been defeated earlier in the same meeting

- ✔ Present a question that the membership still has within its reach (as it has when something has been postponed or referred to a committee, or is the object of a motion to reconsider)

- ✔ Are outside the scope of the purpose of the organization (unless the motion is agreed to be considered by a two-thirds vote)

A meeting's success depends upon the good faith of the members and leaders to give everybody their say, but not at the expense of letting a troublemaker take over.

In his book *Parliamentary Law* (1923), General Robert says, "The greatest lesson for democracies to learn is for the majority to give to the minority a full, free opportunity to present their side of the case, and then for the minority, having failed to win a majority to their views, gracefully to submit and to recognize the action as that of the entire organization, and cheerfully to assist in carrying it out until they can secure its repeal." That about says it all!

Chapter 8

Making Group Decisions: Voting on the Motion

*V*oting is the heart of the deliberative process. What started as a proposal for action has been discussed, debated, changed, and tweaked to the point that everybody's ready to make a decision and get on with it.

In this chapter, I cover some general principles about voting and tell you about all the different methods of voting you can use and when you should (or shouldn't) use each one.

Of course, after you've voted, you have to figure out the result and what it means. Believe it or not, it's not always as simple as "the majority wins." So, I cover the different options for deciding the result of your vote.

Robert's Rules gives a good bit of coverage to the voting process and your rights in that regard. I summarize the voting process rules in this chapter, but you can also find references throughout the book that refine these concepts as they apply to specific situations.

Knowing Your Voting Rights and Responsibilities

Before I get into too much detail about the different methods of voting and the specific procedures for each method, I want to cover some fundamental points about voting in general. This section deals with your rights and responsibilities when it comes to voting. Knowing these points will help you keep the voting process fair and efficient.

Voting as a duty

Voting isn't just a right of membership; it's your duty to vote when you have an opinion about a matter being decided. I won't waste my breath telling you how important one vote can be; I'm sure you've heard countless anecdotes making that point. By failing to vote, you allow others to make the decision, which is the same as having voted for the prevailing side. Whether you vote or not, you're still in some way responsible for the decision that's made.

Abstaining from voting

Although it's your duty to vote when you have an opinion, you can't be forced to vote. You have the right to remain neutral! In fact, some situations demand that you refrain from voting even if you have a legal right to vote.

According to Robert's Rules, you should abstain from voting whenever you have an interest in the outcome that directly affects you personally (or monetarily) in a manner not shared by the other members of your group. The key here is that the other members don't share your interest. For example, it's certainly okay for you to vote in favor of, say, holding a banquet, even though you have a direct personal interest. You benefit from having the association buy your dinner. But so does everybody else. However, if the motion decides whether to give your company the catering contract, good form compels you to abstain from voting.

Just to be clear, the abstention rule is a *should* rule. Just as you can't be forced to vote, you can't actually be compelled not to vote. As a voting member, you can vote to swing the contract your way, but it's bad form if you do.

Abstentions do not count. Let me say that again: *Abstentions do not count.* If you abstain from voting, you have not voted. The fact that you were in the room doesn't make any difference unless the result is based on the number of members present.

Figuring abstentions into vote totals or noting them in the record is never correct unless the vote is a roll-call vote. Then, it's only important that the record shows you were present. Your abstention still doesn't count as a vote.

Voting for yourself

The rule that you should abstain from voting on matters of a direct personal interest to you doesn't apply if you're nominated for office. If your status as a member makes you eligible for the office, you're entitled to benefit from a vote as any other member would. So go ahead and vote for yourself if you want to.

Explaining your vote

When the group has moved on from the debate stage and voting is underway, you're not permitted to get a little debate in edgewise under the guise of explaining your vote. The right of free speech stops when the voting starts.

Changing your vote

When voting by any method except by ballot, if the result of a vote has been declared, you can change your vote, but only with the unanimous consent of the assembly without debate. Otherwise, it's too late. However, you have an absolute right to change your (nonballot) vote at any time up until the result is announced.

Deciding questions of procedure

All questions related to the manner and methods of voting are within the control of your group except as may be limited in your bylaws. Your group, through the use of incidental *motions related to voting and the polls* (see Chapter 11), remains in control of its own voting procedures.

Taking Your Pick of Voting Methods

Whether voting on motions or having elections, you've got quite a selection of voting methods to choose from. Although many voting methods exist, they can be easily grouped into two categories:

- ✔ **Usual voting methods for motions:** In most situations other than elections, you indicate your affirmative or negative vote by voice or by rising. The chair discerns the result and announces it, and then you move on to the next item of business. However, when using voice vote or rising vote, the judgment of the chair is subject to *verification.* A voice vote is verified by a rising vote either on the chair's own initiative or on the demand of a single member. A rising vote is verified by a counted vote either at the call of the chair or by a motion adopted by the membership.

- ✔ **Voting methods provided by rule or ordered by membership:** These methods of voting are usually established in your rules or bylaws depending on the type of organization or the nature of the decision. For example, elections often require ballot votes so that members can vote without disclosing their choice of candidate. Similarly, representative assemblies often require roll-call votes because the representatives are accountable to their constituents.

Unanimous consent

Quite possibly the most efficient way of conducting a vote, *unanimous consent* is the voting method of choice because it saves so much time. The process involves simply asking the members if there's any objection to adopting the motion. If no one objects, then the motion is adopted.

If even one member objects, then you proceed to take a vote using one of the other methods explained in this section.

Unanimous consent can't be used in all situations, but it's perfect for situations in which a motion isn't controversial and it appears that you have universal agreement, or at least that the minority is likely to agree to the decision without protest. For example, you can use unanimous consent to reach approval of the minutes: "If there is no objection, the minutes are approved as distributed." But unanimous consent can be used even on complex motions or when a two-thirds vote is required, because unless you encounter an objection, the minority has, in effect, said, "Okay with us! Do it!"

Voice vote (viva voce)

Viva voce (pronounced VEE-vah VOE-see, parliamentary lingo for voting "by voice") is the customary method for voting on motions requiring a majority vote for adoption.

To initiate a voice vote, the presiding officer simply says, "All those in favor say 'Aye,'" then, "All those opposed, say 'No.'" This method handles votes effectively because it's efficient and because determining whether a motion carries or not isn't difficult unless the vote is close. When the vote *is* close, your presiding officer can re-take the vote as a rising or counted vote on his own initiative.

If the chair doesn't think the vote is close enough to ask for a rising vote and declares a result that you doubt, you can require him to take a rising vote just by calling for a *Division* (see Chapter 11).

Rising vote

When a motion is to be decided by a two-thirds vote or some other proportion greater than a majority, or when a voice vote is too close to call, you have a more definitive method in your voting arsenal. A *rising vote* is just what the name implies. The chair says, "All those in favor will rise. [pause] Be seated." Then, "All those opposed rise. [pause] Be seated."

What the ears can't discern, the eyes generally can. Odds are that everybody will be able to agree whether the required threshold has been met. Only when the rising vote is too close to call do you need to move on to a counted vote. (Jump to the next section, "Counted vote," for details on this method.)

The rising vote has some variations that generally depend on the size of the group.

- **Voting by show of hands:** A vote by show of hands can be used instead of a rising vote when you're in a small group, such as a committee or a board meeting.

- **Voting by voting cards:** In some assemblies (usually very large ones), members are given colored voting cards to hold up appropriately signifying their vote. In very large assemblies, voting cards are probably the most efficient means for deciding most questions because large groups require large rooms, making it all the more difficult for a presiding officer to discern the result of a voice vote or to tell who's standing and who is not.

If the chair decides that the rising vote isn't conclusive enough, then he should retake the vote as a counted vote to ascertain the result. However, if the chair is comfortable with his call, he's not required to take a counted vote unless the membership adopts a motion to order a counted vote. Such a motion requires a second and is adopted by majority vote (see Chapter 11).

Counted vote

The procedure for taking a counted vote is the same as for a rising vote, except that you ask the members to remain standing (or keep their hands or voting cards raised) until they can be counted. And, you need to appoint someone, the *teller,* to do the counting. In a small meeting, the secretary usually handles the count. In a larger meeting, trusted members should be appointed as tellers by the chair with the consent of the members.

In very large meetings, you're probably better off conducting a ballot vote than a counted vote. But there's no hard and fast rule on when ballot votes become easier to tally than counting heads. It depends largely on your group and the time available.

With viva voce, rising, or counted votes, the presiding officer should always call for the negative vote (except, of course, for courtesy resolutions expressing appreciation, thanks, and so on). Even if it sounds like the ayes have it or it looks like enough members rise in favor, you still need the comparison to decide if you've really made the right call.

Roll-call vote

Roll-call voting is used in representative assemblies in which the members represent constituencies and it's important for con-stituents to know how their representatives vote on particular issues.

If your group is a representative assembly, your bylaws should provide details for how and when roll-call votes are ordered. Many such groups require all main motions to be decided by roll-call vote. Others provide that a specified minority may order such a vote. This is because without such provisions, a majority vote is required to order a roll-call vote. In cases where a majority prefers *not* to have to go on the record, the constituents (especially those of the minority) are prevented from knowing how their representatives vote.

Roll-call votes can be conducted by ballot or by voice. If by ballot, each member indicates his name and vote on the ballot. If by voice, the chair puts the question (see Chapter 6) and the secretary calls the members' names alphabetically (or according to some other adopted order), except that the chair's vote is taken last. Each member responds "Yea" for an affirmative vote, "Nay" for a negative vote, or "Present" if abstaining. The secretary repeats the name of each member and states his or her vote to ensure accuracy in recording.

The record of how each member votes is recorded in the minutes.

Voting by ballot

Voting by ballot is used whenever it's desirable that the members' individual views on the matter being decided not be disclosed.

Ballots, the slips of paper on which voters indicate their preferences, are understood to be *secret ballots* unless otherwise specified, such as with *signed ballots,* which may be used in voting by mail (covered in the section "Voting by mail" in this chapter) when secrecy is *not* required.

If your bylaws provide for ballot votes on any matter, it's to protect you, as an individual member, from having to disclose your vote. Because the rule protects the rights of an individual, it's a rule that can't be suspended (even by a unanimous vote), and no vote that would force you to disclose your views in order to protect that right is ever in order.

Ballots assume one of two general purposes: They either decide a motion or decide an election.

> ✔ **If the ballot vote decides a motion,** the question is clearly stated by the chair, and you're instructed to mark your ballot *Yes* or *No* (or *For* or *Against*).
>
> ✔ **If the ballot vote decides an election,** you're instructed to write the name of the nominee of your choice on your ballot.

It's never in order to vote *Yes* or *No* (or *For* or *Against*) a candidate when electing persons to office. The only way you can vote *against* a candidate is to vote *for* another person.

In cases when the motion to be decided is known ahead of time or when the nominees are known, ballots may be preprinted to save time and make things easier for members at voting time.

Conducting the ballot vote

Depending on your organization and the decisions being made, balloting may take place during a meeting, or polls may be open during polling periods including times when no meeting is in progress. In either case, you need to appoint tellers to hand out and collect ballots and to count the votes.

Tellers should be people known for their integrity. They don't have to be impartial, but whatever direct personal interest they have in the outcome shouldn't be uncommon to the other members. Some organizations appoint tellers representing each opposing side to ensure that all sides of the decision have complete confidence in the result.

Limiting ballot access to members

Only members entitled to vote are given ballots or are allowed to deposit ballots with a teller or place them in the ballot receptacle. If polling is conducted outside of a meeting, members should verify their credentials with election officials when casting their votes at the polls, and members' names should be checked on a list showing who has voted.

In meetings where persons who aren't entitled to vote are present, take whatever measures are necessary to limit balloting to voting members. In this situation, the tellers distribute the ballots to the members, and the members return their marked ballots to the tellers.

Closing the polls

If a member arrives late and wants to cast his vote, he may not be completely out of luck. If polls haven't been closed when he arrives, then he's entitled to vote. If the polls have been formally closed, then he can only vote with the members' consent by majority vote.

Voting by the presiding officer

During a ballot vote, your presiding officer votes along with all the other members. This rule holds even if he's been absorbed in doing his job overseeing the election; if he fails to vote before the polls are closed, then he needs the permission of the members to vote.

Your presiding officer is *never* allowed to cast a tie-breaker in a ballot vote. When the vote is by ballot, he votes with the other members. If the vote winds up being tied, the assembly votes again. Mr. Prez doesn't get to vote a second time by himself. Everybody votes again, and you keep your fingers crossed that you don't have another tie.

Counting the ballots

When counting ballots, tellers need to keep a few key points in mind:

- ✔ Blank ballots are treated as scrap paper and don't count at all.

- ✔ Illegal votes cast by legal voters count toward the total votes cast, but they don't count for any individual choice or candidate. Illegal votes are

  - Unintelligible ballots

  - Ballots cast for a fictional character

  - Ballots cast for an ineligible candidate

  - Two or more marked ballots folded together (together they count as only one illegal vote)

- ✔ If a marked ballot is folded together with a blank ballot, the marked ballot counts as one legal vote, and the blank ballot is considered scrap paper.

- ✔ Each question on a multipart ballot is counted as a separate ballot. If a member leaves one part blank, the votes entered on the other questions aren't negated.

- ✔ If a member votes for more choices than positions to be elected, the vote is considered illegal.

- ✔ If a member votes for fewer choices than positions to be elected, the vote is not illegal.

- ✔ Small technical errors, such as spelling mistakes or marking an X when a checkmark is called for, don't make a vote illegal as long as the voter's intent is discernable.

- ✔ Votes cast by illegal voters must not be counted at all, not even included in the number of total votes cast. If it's determined that enough illegal votes were cast by illegal voters to affect the result, and these votes can't be identified and removed from the count, then the vote is deemed null and must be retaken.

Reporting to the chair

After the votes are counted, the chairman of the tellers reads aloud to the membership the complete report of the vote counts, but she doesn't declare the result. That job belongs to the presiding officer. You can check out some links to sample tellers' reports in Appendix B.

Declaring the result

After the Tellers' Committee chairman concludes her reading, the presiding officer reads the report again to the members, concluding with a formal declaration of the result. For example, he may say, ". . . and Mr. Turkey is declared elected as the Birdbrain of the Year." The entire tellers' report should be included in the minutes of the meeting.

Destroying the ballots

To avoid running up a storage bill or having the secretary quit because his wife doesn't want so much junk in the house, destruction of the ballots should be ordered. When determining how long to hold the ballots before destroying them, your main consideration is the possibility of needing a recount. After the period during which a recount can be conducted has passed, you don't need to keep the ballots. A decision on how long to keep them can be made at the meeting when the vote takes place, or a short retention period for ballots can be adopted as a standing rule.

Absentee Voting

A fundamental principle of parliamentary law is that decisions are only made by the members present in a properly called meeting at which a quorum is present. This principle makes a lot of sense when you think about it: If you don't attend the meeting, you don't benefit from information that's presented during the discussion that precedes voting. If you haven't been exposed to any discussion or debate on the topic, you simply can't make a truly informed decision.

Voting by proxy

If anything's likely to cause trouble for a group, it's proxy voting. *Voting by proxy*, which is giving somebody a power of attorney to cast a vote for you, is inconsistent with the fundamental concepts that voting rights are not transferable and members must be present at the time a vote is taken.

Proxy voting is so contrary to the principles of parliamentary law for deliberative assemblies that Robert's Rules strictly prohibits this method unless your bylaws or charter specifically authorize it or your state's corporation law requires it. (See the section "Proxies in incorporated societies" for more details.)

Types of proxies

Proxies are powers of attorney, and they come in two types:

✔ **General:** A person is authorized to cast your vote as he chooses.

✔ **Limited:** A person is authorized to cast your vote on one or more particular matters or in a particular way. The actual authority depends on the document being used.

Proxies in incorporated societies

In several states, members of corporations have absolute rights to vote on some matters by proxy unless prohibited in the bylaws, while board members are absolutely prohibited from voting by proxy unless specifically authorized in the charter.

Proxies in shareholder meetings

Proxy voting finds its most common application in business corporation shareholder meetings where shareholders have different voting power based on the number of shares. Usually the voting in these kinds of meetings relates to electing directors and approving recommendations of the board.

Proxies in membership meetings

For most groups (whether incorporated or not), proxies are rarely necessary if each member has equal voting power. If your group is authorizing any sort of voting by proxy, it's a good idea to be very specific on how and when a proxy can be used.

If your group is incorporated, you need to find out exactly what the corporation laws of the chartering state say about the use of proxies. If you ever experience the surprise of having a large faction someday show up represented by a member holding a block of proxies, you'll know why it's important to know the laws.

Take the case of the Southside Sillysteppers. The group's bylaws were silent on proxy votes, and they depended on Robert's Rules' statement that proxies weren't allowed. That practice was fine until they were incorporated in a state where the law gives members of incorporated societies the right to vote by proxy unless their bylaws expressly prohibit it. Nobody thought about it much until the election when Sally Slink slunk into the room with proxies from over 100 absent members authorizing her to cast their votes for the stoop of the Supreme Sillystepper. She handed the proxies to the secretary and said she was casting 100 proxy votes plus her own for herself. The 70 other members present, all of whom thought Sally was a real stinker, rose up in protest. They were intent on electing Skipper Stoopstep. Skipper raised a point of order (see Chapter 11) about the proxies, and the point was ruled well-taken because according to bylaws, Robert's Rules was the adopted parliamentary authority. Skipper was declared elected, but Sally took the decision to court;

the judge said no matter what Robert said, the *bylaws* did not *expressly* prohibit proxy voting. So, Sally Slink secured the stoop of the Supreme Sillystepper, Skipper Stoopstep stepped down from the stoop, and the Southside Sillysteppers had to pay Sally's lawyer and the court costs.

To avoid surprise proxies and make sure that only members who have made it to the meeting make your group's decisions, you can adopt clear and direct language in your charter or bylaws to prohibit proxy voting to the extent allowed by law. Otherwise, your group may wind up like the Southside Sillysteppers and have to deal with interpretations of laws, bylaws, or the proxy documents themselves that sufficiently put an election or some other decision in limbo until a judge decides the outcome. Not only is this complication no fun, it's also expensive and can cripple or ruin an organization.

According to Robert's Rules, adopting a bylaw establishing Robert's Rules as your parliamentary authority is as good as adopting a bylaw to prohibit the use of proxies. In fact, it's the same thing — *unless your group is incorporated!* Then, the law reigns supreme. My advice is to have your lawyer and your parliamentarian work together to help you coordinate provisions in your bylaws with your laws and articles of incorporation so that you have things set up like you want them.

Voting by mail

Voting by mail is a trade-off: You give up the benefits of discussion and debate in favor of giving all your members an opportunity to vote. Voting by mail probably isn't worth the extra expense if most of your members can make it to meetings. But in large state, national, or international organizations that don't have some sort of delegate assembly, mail voting in elections (or to decide bylaw amendments) may make sense.

Mail voting is subject to the following considerations:

- ✔ **Mail voting must be authorized in bylaws.** If your group wants to permit voting by mail, fax, or e-mail, then whatever method you choose must be authorized in your bylaws, and provisions should always be in place to ensure that such votes are verifiable as being cast by members entitled to vote.

- ✔ **The question must not be changed at a meeting!** Any time your organization wants to allow members to vote by mail, you must be sure that you don't enable a decision on a question to combine mail votes with votes cast after discussion, amendments, or floor nominations at a meeting. A mail vote can decide something fairly only when *all* the votes cast are on the question as it was posed to members on the mail ballot.

For example, you poll your membership by mail on whether to hold a bake sale or a bingo game as your fundraiser. But then at your meeting, somebody moves to throw a raffle into the mix. How do you count the votes and be fair to the members who voted without the third option? It's just not possible.

✔ **Mailing lists must be complete and accurate.** Ballots must only go out to members who are entitled to vote, so maintaining mailing list integrity is important when it comes to mail voting. If you're going to authorize mail ballots, you need to keep your address records up-to-date. When the time comes to send ballots out to your members, your treasurer and secretary need to work together to make sure the mailing list is up-to-date and all the current members are on the list. They also need to ensure that purged members don't get ballots in error.

✔ **The secrecy and integrity of the vote must be preserved.** It's possible to preserve secrecy with mail voting (as opposed to voting by fax or e-mail), so that's the form to use if you're extending absentee voting to a large membership. If your group makes provisions for voting by fax or e-mail, you don't have any real means of assuring that the votes you receive are from people legally entitled to vote, unless the member's name is somehow disclosed on the vote itself. Therefore, avoid voting by fax or e-mail unless secrecy isn't important. If yours is a small group with considerable trust in each other, then the less-secretive options shouldn't present a real problem. But even then, you should have some very explicit rules about when and how these kinds of votes should be used.

With mail voting, you have to be able to confirm that each vote is from a member who's entitled to vote. But you also have to be able to ensure that each member's vote can remain secret. Both goals are accomplished by providing for a dual-envelope return system along with a special procedure for opening and counting ballots.

Sending the ballots to the members

For secret, mail-in ballots, each voter receives

✔ **A ballot and all the information necessary for the member to mark it properly and return it in a timely manner.** The ballot should be folded in such a manner that the member can mark it and refold it so that only the tellers can see the vote when they open the ballot at the meeting where it's being counted.

✔ **A small envelope on which the voter signs and prints his name and in which he places his folded, marked ballot.**

  ✔ **A separate, self-addressed return envelope into which the
  sealed envelope containing the ballot is placed for mailing
  back to the tellers.** This envelope should be distinctive and
  recognizable as containing a sealed ballot so that it's not inad-
  vertently opened before the election.

  ✔ **Any additional information, such as brief statements from
  the candidates for elective office, or summaries or ratio-
  nales related to items that are the subject of a vote.**

Preferential voting

Preferential voting is a method of ballot voting that has excellent application in mail balloting because it avoids the cost of re-balloting in the event of a tie. (Remember, deciding by plurality is not an automatic option!) It also has considerable advantages over electing by plurality (see the section "Plurality," later in this chapter) because it enables a group to make the best choice by taking into account the each voter's second (or third, or fourth) choice. For example, suppose you're voting by mail for your next president. You have a choice between Mr. I.M. Great, Ms. Raz M'tazz, Mr. Slug, and Ms. Gliggenschlapp. Mr. Great receives 91 votes, Ms. M'tazz receives 96 votes, Mr. Slug receives 35 votes, and Ms. Gliggenschlapp receives 75 votes. Who wins?

If you're electing by plurality, then Ms. Raz M'tazz wins. But out of 297 votes, 201 members want somebody else. So, Ms. M'tazz is hardly the right choice for the group. She wins because only first choices matter in a plurality vote.

Now, consider if you could redistribute based on their second choice the votes of those whose first choice was Mr. Slug. If all of them had Ms. Gliggenschlapp as their second choice, and you were using preferential voting, then she's the holder of 110 votes including secondary preference. That puts Mr. Great in last place. Now, if the members who voted him as their first choice had other ideas as their second choice, then his votes could be redistributed to Ms. M'tazz and Ms. Gliggenschlapp and one of the two of them would come out with the biggest stack of ballots. Preferential voting decides the election by taking into account everyone's prefer-ences, and thus avoids the cost of taking another mail ballot.

Preferential voting is a simple process, really. Members indicate their choices by order of preference, and the ballots are sorted based on the first choice listed, with each option having its own stack. The smallest stack is redistributed among the others based on the second choice indicated on the ballot. The next round takes the remaining smallest stack and redistributes it based on the second or third choice indicated. This process continues until one choice receives a majority of the bal-lots, and that choice becomes the winner.

Preferential voting is a good system because it comes closer than plurality to choos-ing the most desirable option and because it's less costly and time-consuming than continuing to re-ballot until a majority is achieved.

If the ballot doesn't require secrecy, then the small ballot envelope isn't necessary, and the ballot itself should have a place for the signature and printed name of the voter. (You still have to verify the voter is entitled to vote!)

Processing returned ballots

When the outer envelopes are returned, the designated recipient should keep them (unopened) until the election. At the meeting when the votes are to be counted, these envelopes are opened in the presence of the tellers. The signed inner envelopes are removed, and the name on each inner envelope is compared to the list of eligible voters. When your tellers confirm the voter is eligible, his name is checked on the list as having voted. Only then does the teller remove the ballot from the signed envelope and deposit it, without unfolding it, into the ballot box.

Determining Voting Results

You've no doubt heard the phrase, "The majority rules!" It's an age-old axiom, and in most cases, it's true. But according to the true definition and practice of democracy, *might* doesn't always make *right*. The primary democratic concept that everyone has an equal voice means that the minority, even a minority of one, has rights that must be respected. Robert's Rules are designed to protect the minority against the "tyranny of the majority."

Parliamentary law establishes two fundamental voting thresholds:

- ✔ **Majority vote:** Except when governed by a specific rule to the contrary, a *majority vote* is the fundamental requirement to pass a motion. A *majority,* simply stated, is *more than half.* Not 50 percent plus one. Not one more than half. Just more than half. And, a majority vote refers to more than half of the votes actually cast, not to more than half of the votes that could be cast if everybody voted. Unless a motion receives a majority vote, the motion is lost. If the vote is tied, it doesn't receive a majority vote, so it is lost.

- ✔ **Two-thirds vote:** As a means of balancing the rights of the entire group with the rights of individuals, some decisions require the affirmative consent of at least twice the number of members as are not in favor. This vote is called a *two-thirds vote* and refers to two-thirds of the votes cast. It protects any minority greater than one-third. As with a majority vote, the measure against which the two-thirds threshold is determined refers only to the number of votes cast, not the number of votes that could be cast if everybody voted.

According to Robert's Rules, a two-thirds vote is required:

- To suspend or change a rule already adopted
- To close or limit debate on a motion
- To prevent the consideration of a motion
- To close nominations or polls

Crossing voting thresholds

Voting results can also be determined according to a number of different variations on the basic majority and two-thirds votes. These variations relate not only to the threshold numbers required, but also to the number of members to be counted in determining that threshold.

Majority (or two-thirds) of the members present and voting

The *majority vote* and the *two-thirds vote,* if expressed without further qualification, are votes based on the total votes cast. These terms are often expressed with the phrases "a majority of the members *present and voting*" or "at least two-thirds of the members *present and voting.*"

Majority (or two-thirds) of the members present

Sometimes by design (and often by mistake), a voting threshold is stated as "a majority (or two-thirds) of the members present." Making decisions based on the number of votes in relation to the number of members present is usually undesirable because it removes a member's right to remain neutral and it requires you to stop and count the number of members present in order to determine the result. If a member is in the room and chooses not to vote, his neutrality has the effect of a negative vote because his presence is counted when determining the result.

Majority of the entire membership

In some cases, permitting a question to be decided by a *majority of the entire membership* is just as protective of the rights of individuals as deciding that question by a *two-thirds vote.* Sometimes, this threshold is used as an alternative to a two-thirds vote in matters where no previous notice has been given. For example, a motion to rescind something previously adopted requires a majority vote with previous notice, or a two-thirds vote without previous notice, or a vote of a majority of the entire membership.

Plurality

A *plurality vote* is the most votes cast for any choice in a field of three or more. The candidate or option receiving the most votes in such a situation has a *plurality*. A plurality is not necessarily a majority, and because it can designate a winner that the majority of the members oppose, it should be avoided.

According to Robert's Rules, when a ballot has more than two choices, balloting must continue until one choice achieves a majority. If re-balloting isn't practical, such as when conducting a vote by mail, you really should use some form of preferential voting. (See the sidebar "Preferential voting" for more explanation.) A plurality never elects unless your bylaws authorize it.

Cumulative voting

Some types of organizations, especially ones prone to factionalism, want to ensure that minority factions can achieve at least a minimal representation on boards and committees. This is accomplished through *cumulative voting*. Using this approach, when several seats are to be filled, as on a board, each member may cast as many votes as there are seats to be filled; votes may be cast in any combination and for any number of candidates. For example, if five members were to be elected to the board, normally, you would cast one vote each for up to five candidates. Under cumulative voting, you could cast all five votes for one or more of the candidates, distributing your five votes as you please. Cumulative voting enables a faction to coordinate its voting to affect an election of some level of representation on the board. Although it violates a fundamental principle of parliamentary law because it allows members to transfer their votes, the method has its place. Still, it should be used judiciously and with a full understanding of its implications.

Handling tie votes

Some of the folks in your group may think that a tie vote must be broken by the vote of the presiding officer. But the solution isn't as simple as that. Because a tie vote isn't a majority, if your motion requires a majority vote, the motion is *lost* if it receives a tie vote. Therefore, a tie vote is as much of a decision as a majority vote in opposition.

The myth that the presiding officer votes to break a tie is only a partial truth. If the vote is by ballot, the presiding officer votes with everybody else, and a tie vote is either a lost motion or a failed election. If you're electing an officer, you must re-ballot until someone receives a majority.

However, if the vote is by voice, by rising, or by counted vote, the presiding officer properly casts his vote only after the results are known and if he desires that his vote should affect the outcome.

He may want to break a tie, causing the motion to pass; or make a tie, causing the motion to fail. Similarly, with a two-thirds vote, he may want to cause the motion to pass by adding his vote to reach the two-thirds threshold, or he may want to cause the motion to fail by adding to the minority to keep the two-thirds threshold from being met.

However, if he doesn't want to change the outcome, the presiding officer shouldn't vote at all; by reserving his vote, he preserves the appearance of impartiality while presiding. That's infinitely more important than casting a vote that makes no difference.

Chapter 9

Subsidiary Motions: Helping to Process the Main Motion

● ●

In This Chapter

▶ Perfecting a main motion with subsidiary motions

▶ Ranking subsidiary motions

▶ Knowing when to use the right motion and how to use it properly

● ●

*I*n a perfect world, when the chairman states your main motion and calls for the vote, people won't just say, "Aye!" Instead, they'll erupt in a loud and unyielding cheer, and your name and picture will be on the front page of the next day's newspaper, and you may even get elected president of the United States, or at least get a phone call from him.

In other words, in a perfect world, your main motion is the perfect idea at the perfect time, stated in such a perfect way that no one can disagree with it.

But it's not a perfect world, and you're not always the one making the motions. So when somebody else comes up with a real dinger of an idea, the closest thing to perfect you have is a small-but-powerful assortment of tools from Robert's Rules that will help you take a sad song and make it better.

Disposing of a Main Motion

One sure thing in the world of meetings is that sooner or later, all motions are *disposed of*. No, that doesn't mean they're thrown out. (Well, some of them are, but that's not how we use the term here.) *Disposing* of a motion simply refers to making some decision about the motion so you can move on to the next item of business — in other words, it's the end result of all the talk.

The *subsidiary motions* are the tools you use to help dispose of the main motions in your meetings.

For example, somebody in your volunteer fire company moves "to buy a new fire truck." During discussion, it becomes clear that the color can affect the price, and you don't want to make a decision (and thus dispose of the main motion) until you decide on the color. So, you move to insert the word "green" before "fire truck," because you know the Hot Shot Fire Truck Catalog offers one on sale because nobody buys green fire trucks much anymore.

But before the group can dispose of the subsidiary motion to *Amend,* Lax Luster moves to amend the amendment by striking out "green" and inserting "red" instead. Unfortunately, your presiding officer Chief Slow Pitch (who hasn't read Robert's Rules anyway) is getting confused.

But all is not lost, because Ben Dare (the member who usually drives to the fires) wants a new fire truck, and he wants the right one at the right price. He knows that the group needs to dispose of Lax's amendment before it can work on your amendment, and the group has to dispose of your amendment before it can get back to the original question of whether to buy a fire truck in the first place.

Ben also knows that there's not enough time to discuss the issue any further in this meeting, so he moves to *Refer* (a really handy subsidiary motion for complicated or time-consuming motions) the main motion and the pending amendments to a committee comprised of himself, you, and Lax, with instructions that the committee report its recommendations next month. The motion to refer passes, and *voilà* — not only have you disposed of the motion to refer, you've also disposed of (temporarily) the main motion and two subsidiary motions (the pending amendments). Now you can move on to the next item of business.

Arriving at a final disposition for a motion can (and often does) require one or more subsidiary decisions. Hence, Robert's Rules establishes the term *subsidiary motions.*

Any or all of the things specifically related to a motion itself are dealt with in an orderly manner through the use of the *subsidiary motions.*

The subsidiary motions (listed in order of rank, from lowest to highest) are

✔ Postpone Indefinitely

✔ Amend

✔ Commit or Refer

✔ Postpone to a Certain Time (or Definitely)

✔ Limit or Extend Limits of Debate

✔ Previous Question

✔ Lay on the Table

Table 9-1 shows the most common use for each subsidiary motion. I discuss each of the subsidiary motions in more detail later in this chapter.

Table 9-1	Common Uses for Subsidiary Motions
If You Want to ...	*Then Use ...*
Avoid taking a direct vote on a motion	Postpone Indefinitely
Change the wording of the motion	Amend
Have a committee discuss a motion in detail and come back with a recommendation	Commit or Refer
Discuss a motion later in the meeting, or maybe put it off until your next meeting	Postpone to a Certain Time (or Definitely)
Provide for a certain amount of time for discussion of the motion, either for the subject matter or for subject matter or for each speaker	Limit or Extend Limits of Debate
End debate on the motion and vote now	Previous Question
Stop dealing with the motion temporarily to allow something of an urgent nature to be done immediately	Lay on the Table

Ranking the Subsidiary Motions

Each subsidiary motion has a specific purpose, and each has a rank, or a specific place in the order of things. They're outranked only by the *privileged motions,* which I cover in Chapter 10.

postpone = kill
amend = change
refer - be considered by committee

The established ranking of subsidiary motions is really very logical. For example, it doesn't make any sense to move to *postpone indefinitely* (kill) a motion, when a motion to *amend* (change the motion) might make it better. But if a motion to *amend* is currently being discussed, it makes perfect sense to consider referring the entire subject matter to a committee (motion to *commit or refer*).

To illustrate, suppose your local duck-lovers club is considering a motion to petition the post office to issue a stamp commemorating the Pea-brained Coot. But Minnie Mutter thinks having a stamp for a Pea-brained Coot is so stupid that she wants to drop the idea altogether. So, she moves to *postpone indefinitely* (kill) the main motion. But you think the idea may fly if you change the motion to promote the Flap-billed Quacker instead of the Pea-brained Coot. So, you offer an amendment to strike out "Pea-brained Coot" and insert "Flap-billed Quacker." Thanks to the *order of precedence* of subsidiary motions, Minnie's motion to *postpone indefinitely* has to go on hold until your amendment is considered because the amendment might remove or resolve Minnie's problem with the motion.

However, Gordy Flackflinger thinks both are birdbrained ideas; he jumps in before the vote on your amendment and makes a motion to *refer* the whole stamp motion to a committee to work out just which duck's head should go on a stamp and then come back next month with a recommendation. Again, because of the ranking of the motion to commit, Flackflinger's motion to *refer* takes precedence over your motion to *amend*.

Robert's Rules provides you with an orderly approach to handling the subsidiary motions by assigning them a relative rank, or *order of precedence,* which is shown in Figure 9-1. Each of the subsidiary motions is listed in order from highest rank to lowest rank. As you can see, all of them outrank the main motion, which has the lowest rank of all. This means that *voting on the main motion is only in order when no subsidiary motion remains to be decided.*

As Figure 9-1 depicts, when a motion is being considered, the motions before it on the list are out of order until the one being considered is disposed of. However, those above the motion in question can be moved and considered no matter what's pending in the lower ranks.

In the following sections, I discuss the seven subsidiary motions and the function of each in more detail.

			Can Interrupt	Requires Second	Debatable	Amendable	Vote Required	Can Reconsider
S E C O N D A R Y	**P R I V I L E G E D**	Fix the Time to Which to Adjourn		S		A	M	R
		Adjourn		S			M	
		Recess		S		A	M	
		Raise a question of privilege	I				Chair decides	
		Call for Orders of the Day	I				Chair decides	
M O T I O N S	**S U B S I D I A R Y**	Lay on the Table		S			M	Neg. Only*
		Previous Question		S			2/3	R*
		Limit or Extend Limits of Debate		S		A	2/3	R*
		Postpone Definitely		S	D	A	M	R*
		Commit (or Refer)		S	D	A	M	R*
		Amend		S	D*	A*	M	R
		Postpone Indefinitely		S	D		M	Affirm. Only
Main Motion				S	D	A	M	R

* See text for exceptions   M = Majority vote

Figure 9-1: Motions table listing subsidiary motions according to rank.

Let's Vote but Say We Didn't: Postpone Indefinitely

The subsidiary motion to *Postpone Indefinitely* can help you avoid uncomfortable decisions because its adoption means that your group has agreed not to decide. The adoption of postpone indefinitely says it's better not to decide than to decide one way or the other. It kills the motion for the time being, and the motion can't be brought up again in the same meeting.

Getting out of sticky situations

At a meeting of an educational organization I attended some years back, one of the members was trying to get the members to pass a resolution calling on the legislature to enact a mandatory continuing-education requirement into state law.

Every member of the organization was a believer in continuing education. They even paid dues to get good prices on the educational programs offered by their association. But there was great variance of opinion on just how much everybody wanted the *legislature* to impose a particular requirement on them. The resolution was very controversial because association members were all over the parking lot on the issue. Only one thing was certain: If the resolution in support of mandatory continuing education passed, the association could lose half its membership. And if the resolution failed, it would imply the association was against continuing education even though it certainly was not.

In this situation, it wasn't the motion to postpone indefinitely that got everyone off the hook. Instead of using that motion, the members just argued for an interminable period of time, went through all sorts of appeals on rulings of the chair, and ultimately avoided making a decision one way or the other only because the meeting adjourned with no meeting scheduled soon enough for the issue to become unfinished business in a later meeting (see Chapter 5).

There's a lot of truth in the idea that hindsight is always 20-20. I'm sure now that if I had made the motion to postpone indefinitely, it probably would have passed and the meeting would not have been so frustrating for either side. I've tucked this story away in my "If-I-knew-then-what-I-know-now" file so that I can benefit from the experience.

After its adoption, the motion to postpone indefinitely can be reconsidered. And if it's reconsidered and then *fails,* the main motion that it "killed" is again as alive as Jason was in *Friday the 13th, Part 2,* when he sprang forth again to stalk unsuspecting campers. See Chapter 11 for information on the motion to reconsider.

Using the motion to postpone indefinitely

Have you ever been in a meeting where a motion was made proposing an idea that sounded just fine on the surface, but was later found to be problematic (to put it nicely)? Or worse, you were embarrassed to even have to consider it, much less vote on it?

This kind of uncomfortable situation often occurs when you're faced with a motion to express an opinion in the name of the organization and the subject matter is controversial. A decision one way or the other could send the wrong message or even cause a split in the organization! The purpose of the subsidiary motion to postpone indefinitely is to diffuse potentially damaging motions.

Make the motion to postpone indefinitely by simply rising, being recognized by the chair, and saying, "Mr. Chairman, I move to postpone the pending motion indefinitely." (And just hope that your presiding officer doesn't ask you how in the heck he's supposed to know when you want to get back to the question if you're so vague!)

 The motion to postpone indefinitely is a great tool for strategists. If you're opposed to the main motion, you can test the strength of your allies in opposition without risking the adoption of the main motion. Because debate on the motion to postpone indefinitely can go into the merits of the main motion, you can speak again even if you've exhausted your right to speak on the main motion. And if the motion to postpone indefinitely passes, you've effectively killed the motion for the present session. And if it fails, you're just back to the debate on the main motion.

Six key characteristics of the motion to postpone indefinitely

A motion to postpone indefinitely

- Can't interrupt a speaker who has the floor
- Must be seconded
- Is debatable (Debate isn't restricted to the pros and cons of postponing indefinitely, but may go into the merits of the main motion.)
- Can't be amended
- Requires a majority vote for adoption
- Can be reconsidered if adopted

I Wanna Make a Change: Amend

The motion to *Amend* is perhaps the single most-used subsidiary motion. Use this motion whenever you want to change the wording of the motion under consideration. You can use it to make a good idea better or a bad idea more palatable. Amendments are really at the heart of the process of perfecting motions before a final vote, and the importance of understanding the basics of amending can't be overstated.

Amending the amendment

Amendments can be amended, but amendments to amendments cannot be amended (whew!) because, well, that could just go on forever and we'd all have smoke pouring out of our ears. If you don't believe me, just reread the first sentence in this paragraph. Even the explanation is complicated!

A motion to amend a pending main motion is called a *primary amendment,* or an *amendment of the first degree.* A motion to amend a pending amendment is called a *secondary amendment,* or an *amendment of the second degree.*

Although they are not amendable, secondary amendments are subject to all the rules for amendment.

If an amendment is adopted, the motion it's applied to changes. However, the amended motion itself is not adopted until the motion, as amended, is voted on and passes. If a motion to amend fails, the original motion is not changed in any way.

The subsidiary motion to amend is applicable to *pending* motions only. It can't be used to amend things such as bylaws, agendas, policies, or other motions that have already been decided. In those cases, the proper motion is to *Amend Something Previously Adopted,* which I cover in Chapter 12.

Most of the time, amendments are what bog down meetings because there's just so much to know. The section on amendments in *Robert's Rules of Order Newly Revised* is the longest section in the book, thanks to all the nuances and variations on basic forms of amendment. But a basic understanding of the forms of amending motions discussed here will give you the foundation you need to build your understanding. I encourage you to read this section with an eye on understanding the basic rules and forms and make it your practice to offer appropriate amendments in good form every chance you get. Practice makes perfect, and by learning to amend motions, you will help your group adopt motions that are clear, concise, and accomplish precisely what your group intended.

Six key characteristics of the motion to amend

A motion to amend:

✔ Can't interrupt a speaker who has the floor

✔ Must be seconded

✔ Is debatable if the motion to which it is applied is debatable (Permissible debate is restricted to the pros and cons of the amendment, and not to whether the main motion has merit.)

✔ Can be amended, but only one amendment to an amendment can be considered at any one time (See the sidebar "Amending the amendment.")

✔ Requires a majority vote for adoption, even if the main motion requires a different vote for its adoption

✔ Can be reconsidered

Amending by the book

One big rule for using amendments is this: An amendment must be relevant (or, as Robert's Rules describes, "germane") to the motion it seeks to amend.

For example, a fire department council member can move to amend a motion to buy a green fire truck by striking out "green" and inserting "red." But it's not germane to amend the motion by adding, "and send out for pizza" to the end. (Some firemen I know would consider that perfectly germane, and although the chairman at the meeting probably wouldn't, it *is* possible to appeal the chair's ruling and by majority vote declare the amendment germane.)

Another important rule to remember is that an amendment that does nothing but make the motion a rejection of the original motion is not proper and not in order.

For example, suppose the pending motion is to endorse the incumbent mayor's candidacy for re-election. A motion to insert "not" before "endorse" would be out of order. If your group wants to "not" endorse him, they must simply reject the motion. However, this rule does not prohibit the amendment to strike out "endorse" and insert "oppose" in its place. While this change rejects the notion of supporting the incumbent, it goes beyond merely "not" doing something and instead proposes doing something else!

Amendments are out of order when they place before the meeting a question that has already been decided in some way. For example, if you've defeated, postponed, or referred to a committee a motion to "buy a fire truck," and you're now discussing a motion to "buy a pizza," it's not in order to move to amend the motion to buy the pizza by striking out "pizza" and inserting "fire truck."

Basic forms of amendments

Amendments enable you to affect changes to pending questions in the following four ways:

- ✔ By *inserting* (or *adding,* if placing at the end) words, sentences, or paragraphs
- ✔ By *striking out* words, sentences, or paragraphs
- ✔ By *striking out and inserting* words (with the words inserted replacing the words struck out)
- ✔ By *amending by substitution* (a form of strike out and insert applied to paragraphs or entire motions)

Each amendment form is distinct and subject to its own unique considerations. In the following sections, I outline the considerations particular to each form. But one consideration is true for all of them: It is not in order to amend one form of amendment into another form.

For example, suppose an amendment is offered to insert words to a motion. It only complicates your life to try to amend the amendment into a motion to strike out words. If you're in a situation where that seems like the thing to do, encourage the group to defeat the first amendment (to insert words) and consider another amendment to accomplish the desired result.

Insert or add words, sentences, or paragraphs

Your neighborhood association is discussing a motion made on the recommendation of the building and grounds committee "that the association repave the parking lot around the clubhouse." Everyone seems to be concerned about how much the project will cost. The committee reports that they have obtained three estimates; they think the highest priced estimate is probably too much, and they believe that the lowest bid came from a company with a questionable reputation. You can tell from the discussion that everyone's in favor of repaving the lot, and that they probably will want to go with the middle bid. So, you decide to help the group cut to the chase by offering an amendment to the main motion.

You rise, address the chair and are recognized, and say, "Mr. Chairman, I move to insert the words, 'accept the bid of the ABC company to' after 'association' and before 'repave' so that if the amendment is adopted we would be voting on a motion 'That the association accept the bid of the ABC company to repave the parking lot around the clubhouse.'"

Your motion is a *subsidiary motion to amend* a main motion by *inserting* words; it is a *primary* amendment (an amendment of the first degree) being applied directly to a main motion.

After you have inserted or added words, you're not allowed to amend them by striking them unless you employ the motion to reconsider. (See Chapter 12 for details on the motion to reconsider.)

Strike out words, sentences, or paragraphs

At a board meeting of your service club, a motion is before the group to "make donations of $100 each to the Perfect Petunia Society, the Little Miss Muffet Pageant, the Mad Hatter's Artsy Crafts Fund, and the Four Corner Hammer Dulcimer Race Car Rally Fund."

You heard on the news last night that the manager of the Mad Hatter's Artsy Crafts Fund is under investigation stemming from allegations that he stuffed the hats with cash from the fund, loaded the hats up into his old footlocker, and bought a ticket to ride. You think that the group should wait and see what happens to him before making that donation. But you're okay with the other proposed donations.

So you rise, address the chair, and when recognized, offer the following amendment: "Mr. Chairman, I move to amend the motion by striking out the words 'the Mad Hatter's Artsy Crafts Fund.'"

Your motion is a *subsidiary motion to amend* a main motion by *striking out words;* it is a *primary* amendment (an amendment of the first degree) being applied directly to a main motion.

The motion to amend by *striking out* can itself only be amended by striking out words from the primary amendment. This is one of those rules that sounds arbitrary, but it is really only logical because when you offer a primary amendment to strike out words, you're applying it to existing words with the purpose of removing them from a main motion. Inserting words to be struck out is impossible because you can't strike out what's not already there. Additionally, keep in mind that striking out words from an amendment to strike out words simply leaves the words back in the original motion.

A motion to amend by striking out words always refers to consecutive words. In the example set up in this section to strike out "the Mad Hatter's Artsy Crafts Fund," it wouldn't be in order to also try to strike out the word "each" after "$100" in the same amendment. If you want to do that, you'll have to offer a separate amendment.

Creating the perfect substitute

A motion to *substitute* is nothing more than a primary amendment to a main motion. Therefore, secondary amendments (amendments to an amendment) are not only possible but very common.

The amendment process generally is known as *perfecting* the motion. So when you have a substitute motion (a primary amendment), it is through secondary amendments that you further perfect the main motion and also perfect the substitute. Only when each has been opened to further amendments and everybody is ready to make a decision is the vote taken on whether to substitute the new motion for the original one.

The chairman decides which of the two motions to perfect first. He calls first for amendments on either the original motion or the substitute, and when the members are finished making changes to one, he opens the floor to amendments on the other.

When all secondary amendments have been made to each of the two, the chair then puts the question on the motion to substitute. If the majority votes in favor of the motion to substitute, it becomes the new main motion.

Because this is the same as having struck out and inserted entire paragraphs, the only amendment that can be made to the new motion is to add to it, just as would be true for any part of any motion where a word (or words) is struck out and replaced with different language.

If the majority is opposed to the motion to substitute, it fails, and the original motion, as amended during the process of perfecting both motions, remains as the main motion on the floor.

In either case, the main motion is then subject to further debate and amendment.

If all these strikes make you feel like you're in a bowling alley or at a baseball game, don't feel like you're alone in your confusion. Just think about it piece by piece — and trust me when I tell you that this is one of those rules where the less said, the better.

Oh, all right. Here's an example.

Suppose the motion at hand is to send membership invitations to John Green, Fred Black, Red McTavish, and Henrietta Violetta. But you don't like anybody but Henrietta. So you move to strike out the words "John Green, Fred Black, Red McTavish, and," which, if adopted, leaves only Henrietta on the list.

But I like Fred and Red and only want to see John excluded, so I move to amend your primary amendment by striking out (from your proposed amendment) "Fred Black, Red McTavish, and."

If my secondary amendment — to strike out the names in your primary amendment — passes, then your amendment is left as an amendment only to strike out "John Green."

To help clarify why you can't insert words in a motion to strike out, just consider how little sense it would make for me to move to insert "Finkley McFlatbush" between "John Green" and "Fred Black" in your primary amendment. I can't add Finkley's name to the strike out list if he isn't anywhere in the main motion in the first place!

Strike out and insert words

Often, changing something requires more action than just adding words or removing them. Sometimes you need to replace one word (or group of consecutive words) with another.

For example, suppose you're in a board meeting of your professional association and one of the members moves to "Authorize the executive director to buy a new computer for the bookkeeper."

You've been around a while, and you know the bookkeeper has been complaining, but not about his computer. Actually, his complaints have to do with the computer's outdated software.

So, you rise, address the chair, and when recognized, offer the following amendment: "Mr. Chairman, I move to amend the motion by striking out the word 'computer' and inserting the words 'accounting software package.'"

Your motion is a *subsidiary motion to amend* a main motion by *striking out and inserting words;* it is a *primary* amendment (an amendment of the first degree) being applied directly to a main motion.

Amend by substitution

The *amendment by substitution* is a special form of "strike out and insert" applied to paragraphs or entire motions.

People sometimes use the term "substitute motion" when it comes to amending an entire motion by substitution, but I've found that if you can avoid that term in favor of "amend by substitution" or "motion to substitute," then you can use this important form of amendment correctly and effectively.

The purpose of amending by substitution is to make several changes in the way something is stated without having to rewrite the motion one amendment at a time. Simply say, "I move to substitute the following for the motion currently under discussion . . ." and offer your changes in completely revised language.

When an amendment by substitution is proposed, both the original motion and the substitute can be amended before a decision is made on the motion to substitute.

Suppose a motion is on the floor that "the chair appoint a committee of four members to study the feasibility of purchasing an office building for the association headquarters, and to report back to the members at the next meeting."

Now, let me color in the background. The motion comes from a friend of the president, who is gung-ho to "invest" the surplus fund money by purchasing a building his brother-in-law has for sale. The association has the money, but concern abounds about the wisdom of the president's "investment" proposal.

You think the membership (and not the probably-biased chairman) is best suited to choose committee members to look into how the association's funds should be invested. An office building may be a good investment, but you and others think other investments may be more lucrative, considering that the association's offices are currently housed in rent-free space provided by a friend of the organization.

So, instead of chopping away at the motion on the floor, you write up a motion to substitute, and you rise, address the chair for recognition, and when recognized, say, "Mr. Chairman, I move to substitute the following for the motion currently under discussion, 'That we elect a committee of six members to recommend a plan for investing the association's surplus funds, and that the committee report its recommendations as soon as possible, but no later than at the regular meeting three months from now.'"

Your motion is a motion to *substitute,* or to *amend by substitution,* and is nothing more than a primary amendment to a main motion. And even though its adoption will make major changes to the original proposal, it's really no different from a motion to strike out the pending motion and insert another motion in its place.

Adopting the motion to substitute does not adopt what it proposes. The adoption simply replaces the original motion with a new motion.

Let's Send It to Committee: Commit or Refer

For all but the most simple and direct of motions, everyone's interests may be best served by referring a motion to a committee instead of spending a lot of meeting time on discussion of the subject. When a number of details need to be worked out and the motion needs to be discussed much more informally or at greater length than is possible in a regular meeting, refer the motion to a committee, or perhaps to the executive board of your group by adopting the subsidiary motion to *Commit.*

Using the motion to commit

It's a simple process, but before you make the motion, you need to give it a little thought and ask yourself these questions:

- ✔ **Which committee are you referring the motion to?** A standing committee? A special committee dealing solely with this motion? (You can find a complete discussion of committees in Chapter 16.)

  Include the committee details in your motion. For example, you may say, "I move to refer the motion to the Recreation Committee," or "I move to refer the motion to a committee of six to be appointed by the president," or "I move to refer the motion to a committee comprised of the officers."

- ✔ **What do you want the committee to do?**

  You should at least give the committee an instruction on when to report, but you can be as specific as you want. A specific instruction may be, ". . . to consider and recommend the time and place of the picnic and report back to the membership next month," or you may just refer the motion with the instruction, ". . . to report its recommendations at the next meeting."

The motion to commit should be used more often than it is because it provides the opportunity to take as much time as is possible and necessary to gather information or consider alternatives before a final decision is made. If you want to have good meetings where most of the decisions are quick and easy, use committees to hash out the details and come to the assembly with well thought out proposals.

This section discusses the motion to commit as a *subsidiary motion,* but you can create a committee even when no motion is pending. When you do that, this motion takes the form of an *incidental main motion,* and when used in that manner, it is governed by the rules for incidental main motions and not subsidiary motions. I discuss incidental main motions in more detail in Chapter 6.

Delegating authority to a committee

If a decision needs to be made before the membership can meet again, you can appoint a committee *with power,* giving it the authority to act for the membership without further membership approval. However, a committee with power must not exercise any more power than what was authorized, and the committee's authority cannot exceed the power of the body that appointed it.

For example, if the body appointing the committee is the board, then the board may not empower the committee to do anything it (the board) could not do on its own.

Six key characteristics of the motion to commit

A motion to commit

- Can't interrupt a speaker who has the floor
- Must be seconded
- Is debatable (Permissible debate is restricted to the pros and cons of making the referral and not to whether the main motion has merit.)
- Can be amended, specifically the committee selection details and any instructions given to the committee
- Requires a majority vote
- Can be reconsidered if adopted and the committee has not begun its work (If the group wants to terminate the committee's involvement with the subject after it has begun its work, the proper motion is to *Discharge a Committee.*)

Let's Deal with This Later: Postpone to a Certain Time (or Definitely)

Although it pains me to admit it, in some ways real life and meetings aren't all that different. Sometimes you just need to put things off.

I've attended more meetings than I can count, and I've found that groups don't always have all the information they need to reach a decision. As a result, continuing consideration of particular motions becomes very difficult.

Maybe you've been in a meeting and realized that some motion is taking up time better spent on something else. You know a decision needs to be made, but it doesn't need to be made at that moment, and other things need to be taken care of before the meeting adjourns. Or perhaps it's officer-election night, but the bridge across the river (where most of the members live) is out and you have barely enough members to make a quorum. Holding your election under these circumstances is unthinkable.

The motion to *Postpone to a Certain Time (or Definitely)* gives you a chance at having better luck the next time around. It doesn't kill the motion — it simply reschedules its consideration.

Using the motion to postpone to a certain time

Moving to postpone a pending main motion to a definite time is very easy. You just need to decide when you want to readdress the postponed motion. After obtaining recognition from the chair, you present your motion to postpone in one of the following ways, depending on when you plan to resume the discussion:

- ✔ **Later in a current meeting:** "Mr. Chairman, I move to postpone the pending motion until 8:30 tonight."

- ✔ **Another day in a session of more than one day:** "Mr. Chairman, I move to postpone the pending motion until the meeting tomorrow afternoon."

- ✔ **Next regular meeting:** "Mr. Chairman, I move to postpone the pending motion until our next regular meeting."

- ✔ **Future event:** "Mr. Chairman, I move to postpone the pending motion until after our speaker gives his presentation."

Limiting the time of postponement

Without limits on the time you can move back consideration of a motion, you could postpone something until two weeks before Bill Gates runs out of cash, killing the discussion as dead as the motion to postpone indefinitely. The idea behind postponing to a certain time is to afford yourself the luxury of a little more time before you act on a motion. Not to kill it.

Postponing to the next regular meeting

A motion to postpone definitely can't move consideration beyond the next regular meeting. The postponed motion is then taken up as *unfinished business* unless a special provision is made to make it a *special order of business,* or *the* order of business for a particular meeting. (Refer to Chapter 5 for a discussion of unfinished business.)

Postponing to a later meeting in a session

If the organization meets less often than quarterly, then the main motion can't be postponed beyond some time in the current session, which may be the current meeting only, or possibly could cover a few days in some cases. (See Chapter 3 for specifics on the differences between a meeting and a session.) In such a case, however, the motion may be referred to a committee to report back at the next meeting.

Postponing to a time later in a meeting

A motion postponed to a time later in the same meeting can't be considered before that time.

Postponing to a time before the next regular meeting

Sometimes a postponed motion needs to be decided before the next regular meeting. In this case, you provide for an adjourned meeting by using the privileged motion to *Fix the Time to Which to Adjourn* and postpone the pending motion until then. Chapter 10 contains a rundown of this type of privileged motion and how to use it properly.

Six key characteristics of the motion to postpone to a certain time

A motion to postpone to a certain time (or definitely)

- ✔ Can't interrupt a speaker who has the floor
- ✔ Must be seconded
- ✔ Is debatable (Permissible debate is restricted to the pros and cons of postponement only. Debate may not go into the merits of the main motion.)
- ✔ Can be amended, specifically the details of the time to which the postponement is made and whether it should be made a special order (You can find details about special orders in Chapter 5.)
- ✔ Requires a majority vote
- ✔ Can be reconsidered if adopted (If the motion to postpone definitely fails, the motion can be reconsidered as long as no material debate has progressed on it. If no additional debate has occurred, the reconsideration vote is bypassed, and the motion just needs to be renewed.)

How Long Can This Go On? Limit or Extend Limits of Debate

Robert's Rules allows a member to speak in debate twice on each motion — with up to ten minutes per speech! Even for small boards, that kind of rule can make for some l-o-o-o-ng meetings, especially if you're unlucky enough to have more than one know-it-all and an antagonist or two in your group. If you've got a hot debate and even one or two members who like to argue (or who otherwise like to impress you with their verbiage), then you could be pulling an all-nighter. But don't panic just yet. You can use the subsidiary motion to *Limit Debate* and do just what the name implies.

In my experience, the motion to limit debate is usually used when time is short and debate is likely to be lengthy.

But many groups have adopted special rules of order (see Chapter 2) to limit the time allowed for speeches. If your group has this kind of special rule, you use the motion to *Extend the Limits of Debate* when a proposal really needs a thorough hearing and the rule hinders your need to discuss it at length.

Using the motion to limit or extend limits of debate

A motion to limit or extend limits of debate affects a change in your adopted rules for debate in several different ways. Some of its more common uses are

✔ **To shorten, or lengthen, the maximum time members (or a single member) may speak in debate.**

"Madam President, I move that the discussion on this motion be limited to two minutes per member, per speech."

"Mr. Chairman, I move that the members each be allowed an automatic two-minute extension per speech."

"Mr. President, I move that Mr. Wise's time be extended five more minutes."

✔ **To set the number of times a member may speak.**

"Madam Chairman, I move that no member be allowed to speak more than once on this motion."

✔ **To set the total number of speeches each for and against the motion, and to set the maximum length for each speech.**

"Mr. President, I move that discussion be limited to two speakers for and two speakers against this motion, not to exceed three minutes per speech."

✔ **To define the total time allotted for discussion, or to define the time after which debate will be closed and voting will take place.**

"Madam Chairman, I move that we limit discussion on this motion to a total time of 20 minutes."

"Mr. Chairman, I move that at 9:00 p.m. we close all debate on this subject matter and proceed at that time to vote."

Additional information

The motion to limit or extend the limits of debate

✔ Isn't allowed in committees

✔ Can't be used to bring an immediate close to debate (If you want to stop debate and vote, the proper motion is *Previous Question,* which is describer later in this chapter.)

✔ Can generally be applied to any debatable motion or series of debatable motions, and if adopted, is termed an *order* limiting (or extending) debate (When it expires, the *order* is said to be *exhausted.*)

✔ Is often adopted by unanimous consent, but if a vote is required, its adoption requires a two-thirds (rising) vote

---

Saving time: Changing the default rule

To my clients who use Robert's Rules, I like to suggest that they consider adopting a *special rule of order* (see Chapter 2) to shorten the time a speaker may hold the floor from ten minutes per speaker and two speeches per motion to something a little less.

Some groups, such as those who have monthly meetings of 20 to 30 members, just adopt a special rule that limits speeches to three minutes instead of ten. Other groups with larger numbers may have a special rule that permits only two or three speakers for and two or three against any main motion, with a short fuse (two-, three-, or five-minute limit) on each speech.

I can't begin to tell you how much time you save with a special rule of order on this issue. You can always extend these limits with a two-thirds vote when you need to. But by establishing a special rule of order, your group will find that debate will be more concise, less redundant, and (most importantly to some) much less inclined to wear your nerves thin.

This section discusses this motion as a *subsidiary motion,* but you can change the default limits of debate for a meeting (or part of it) when no motion is pending. When you do that, this motion takes the form of an *incidental main motion* and, when used in that manner, it is governed by the rules for incidental main motions and not subsidiary motions. I discuss incidental main motions in more detail in Chapter 6.

Six key characteristics of the motion to limit or extend limits of debate

A subsidiary motion to limit or extend the limits of debate

- Can't interrupt a speaker who has the floor
- Must be seconded
- Isn't debatable
- Is amendable, but amendments are not debatable
- Requires a two-thirds vote (but is often adopted by unanimous consent)
- Can be reconsidered if adopted (However, the motion to reconsider is not debatable. Reconsideration of a failed subsidiary motion to limit or extend the limits of debate is in order as long as no material debate has progressed on the motion. If additional debate has occurred, a reconsideration vote is not necessary. The motion to limit or extend limits of debate just needs to be renewed.)

Let's Shut Up and Vote: Previous Question

How many times have you come home from a meeting exhausted because so much time was spent, as the saying goes, beating a dead horse? How can people find so many different words to repeat the same argument *ad nauseum?* If you can't count high enough to answer the first question, and if you're just rolling your eyes back in familiarity of the second, then *Previous Question* is the subsidiary motion for you.

Putting the damper on debate

Although the name doesn't quite speak for itself, the previous question is simply a motion to end debate, allow no further discussion or subsidiary motions (except *Lay on the Table,* which outranks it) on the pending question (or series of questions, if, for example, a motion to commit or an amendment is pending), and take the vote on all pending motions.

Previous question is one of the easiest subsidiary motions to use because it's not debatable, making it a quick decision. Because adopting it terminates members' rights to speak or hear more information, the previous question requires a two-thirds vote. But very little can interrupt it, and when used properly, this motion can really save you and your group a lot of time. Why? Because if two-thirds of voters are ready to stop debate and vote on the pending motion (or motions), it's probably pointless to keep on with the debate.

Using previous question to stop debate and vote immediately

Despite its ease of use, previous question is one of the motions that winds up being handled incorrectly. (See the sidebar "Misusing the previous question" in this chapter.) Members can't just call out "Question!" and expect the presiding officer to close debate on their demand.

The previous question is a motion to close debate that can only be made by someone who has been recognized by the chair. And it requires a two-thirds vote.

You start the process by first obtaining recognition by the chair. For example, "Mr. Chairman, I move the previous question on the motion 'to buy *Robert's Rules For Dummies* for our president.'" The chair states the question and calls for the vote. If two-thirds are in the affirmative, debate stops and you vote on whether to buy *Robert's Rules For Dummies* for your president.

If the previous question isn't adopted, you continue with debate until the cows come home, or until nobody has anything else to say, whichever comes first.

The previous question may be ordered on the pending question or on a series of pending questions.

Misusing the previous question

Surely you've attended many meetings in which some impatient soul shouts, "Question!" or "I call the question!" To your dismay, you then hear the presiding officer respond almost automatically with, "The question has been called. All those in favor of buying *Robert's Rules For Dummies* for your president will say 'Aye.'"

If only the members and the presiding officer would stop to think, they would realize that no respectable book on parliamentary procedure permits one person to unilaterally stop debate by making a demand!

Still, it happens all the time. But ordering the previous question properly requires two-thirds of the members present and voting to decide to end debate.

The right to be heard can't be taken away from a minority that wants to keep on talking until more than twice as many members are ready to shut up and vote.

For example, the immediately pending motion may be a proposed amendment to a main motion. If, during debate on the amendment, the previous question is moved without qualification, the decision before the group is whether to stop debate and vote *on the pending amendment*.

However, if the previous question is moved and adopted for the entire series of pending motions, a vote is taken immediately on the pending amendment and then on the main motion (as amended).

Six key characteristics of the motion previous question

The subsidiary motion previous question (to end debate)

- Can't interrupt a speaker who has the floor
- Must be seconded
- Isn't debatable
- Isn't amendable, except as to whether it applies to the immediately pending motion or to an entire series of pending motions, such as pending amendments to a pending main motion
- Requires a two-thirds vote

> ✔ Can be reconsidered if adopted, but only if no part of the
> adopted order for the previous question has been executed (If
> previous question fails, reconsideration is in order as long as
> no material debate has progressed on the motion or motions
> to which it was applied. If additional debate has occurred, a
> reconsideration vote is unnecessary. The previous question
> just needs to be renewed.)

We Gotta Do This NOW: Lay On the Table

In yet another scenario from a meeting from you-know-where
(red hot, lots of fire), you've probably been in a meeting when that
fellow who thinks he knows everything there is to know about parliamentary procedure tries to kill a motion he opposes by saying,
"I move to table!" Well, that may work in a legislature, but under
Robert's Rules, the subsidiary motion to *Lay On the Table* refers to
temporarily setting aside a pending motion (or a series of pending
motions) to take care of something else deemed urgent.

The motion to lay on the table is, in fact, less about the business
being discussed than about the assembly needing to handle something else immediately. And although the motion is just a temporary
disposition of the pending business, no time is taken to decide in
advance when to get back to the motion being laid on the table.

Using the motion to lay on the table

When something urgent comes up that requires the immediate decision by the assembly to set aside a pending motion, the motion to
lay on the table is in order.

After you're recognized by the chair, you say, "Madam President,
because our speaker has arrived, I move to lay the pending motion
on the table."

Making the motion is really that simple. If the circumstances don't
clearly indicate why the motion is being made, the chair should
ask what makes the motion appropriate.

It's never in order to use the motion to lay on the table to kill a
motion or to delay its consideration.

If the motion is made with improper intentions, the presiding officer should simply clarify the motion based on the maker's intent and put the question not on *Lay on the Table* but on *Postpone Indefinitely* or *Postpone to a Certain Time,* as the case warrants.

Anything pending when the motion to lay on the table is adopted goes to the table, too. So, if a motion being laid on the table has a pending amendment, or a pending motion to commit, or is even under an order for the previous question, then everything associated with the pending main motion goes to the table. And when the motion is taken from the table, it appears before the group in the same state as when it was laid on the table.

If the motion laid on the table isn't taken from the table (see Chapter 12) by the next regular meeting, it evaporates quicker than hot water in you-know-where!

Six key characteristics of the motion to lay on the table

The subsidiary motion to lay on the table

- ✔ Can't interrupt a speaker who has the floor
- ✔ Must be seconded
- ✔ Isn't debatable
- ✔ Isn't amendable
- ✔ Requires a majority vote
- ✔ Can't be reconsidered if adopted because the motion to take from the table is easier to use for that purpose (reconsideration is permitted if lay on the table fails, as long as no material debate has progressed on the motion or motions to which it was applied. If additional debate has occurred, a reconsideration vote is unnecessary. The motion to lay on the table just needs to be renewed.)

Chapter 10

Privileged Motions: Getting Through the Meeting

*Q*uite often, meetings are interrupted by issues that are unrelated to the motion being discussed but that require immediate decisions. For example, your group may agree on a schedule for the business of the evening and then find that something is taking more than its allotted time and you want to get back on schedule. Or perhaps a problem develops that affects the comfort of the group. Or you may just want to take a short break, or even quit, go home, and finish your discussions later.

When one of these situations arises, *privileged motions* help you take care of the problem and get on with your business.

Any or all things specifically related to the meeting itself or to the comfort of members in attendance are dealt with in an orderly manner through the use of *privileged motions*. They're called *privileged* because even when other business is pending, the real needs (regarding time, comfort, or other special needs) of the people in the meeting are considered important enough to be dealt with immediately.

The privileged motions (listed in order of rank, from lowest to highest) are

- ✔ Call for Orders of the Day
- ✔ Raise a Question of Privilege
- ✔ Recess
- ✔ Adjourn
- ✔ Fix the Time to Which to Adjourn

Table 10-1 shows the most common use for each privileged motion. I discuss each of the privileged motions in more detail throughout this chapter.

Table 10-1	Common Uses for Privileged Motions
If You Want to ...	*Then Use ...*
Get the meeting back on schedule	Call for Orders of the Day
Deal with something affecting the comfort of the group, or even that of a single member	Raise a Question of Privilege
Take a short break	Recess
End the meeting	Adjourn
Continue the current meeting on another day	Fix the Time to Which to Adjourn

Ranking the Privileged Motions

Each privileged motion has a specific purpose, and each has a rank or a specific place in the order of things. Privileged motions outrank *subsidiary motions,* which I cover in Chapter 9.

The established ranking of privileged motions is really very logical. For example, it doesn't make any sense to move to *Recess* (take a short break) when a privileged motion to *Adjourn* (end the meeting) is under consideration. And yet if the motion to adjourn is on the floor, it's possible that members may want to establish a continuation of the current meeting rather than just end everything until the next regular meeting.

TIP

Robert's Rules provides you with an orderly approach to handling the privileged motions by assigning them a relative rank, or *order of precedence,* which is shown in Figure 10-1. Each of the privileged motions is shown in order from highest rank to lowest. As you can see, these motions even outrank the *subsidiary motions.*

As Figure 10-1 depicts, when a motion is being considered, the motions below it on the list are out of order until the one being considered is disposed of. However, those motions above the motion in question can be moved and considered no matter what's pending in the lower ranks.

In the following sections I discuss the five privileged motions and cover the function of each in more detail.

			Can Interrupt	Requires Second	Debatable	Amendable	Vote Required	Can Reconsider
S E C O N D A R Y	**P R I V I L E G E D**	Fix the Time to Which to Adjourn		S		A	M	R
		Adjourn		S			M	
		Recess		S		A	M	
		Raise a question of privilege	I				Chair decides	
		Call for Orders of the Day	I				Chair decides	
M O T I O N S	**S U B S I D I A R Y**	Lay on the Table		S			M	Neg. Only*
		Previous Question		S			2/3	R*
		Limit or Extend Limits of Debate		S		A	2/3	R*
		Postpone Definitely		S	D	A	M	R*
		Commit (or Refer)		S	D	A	M	R*
		Amend		S	D*	A*	M	R
		Postpone Indefinitely		S	D		M	Affirm. Only
Main Motion				S	D	A	M	R
*See text for exceptions							**M = Majority vote**	

Figure 10-1: Motion table showing privileged motions according to rank.

This chapter discusses these motions in their privileged form. But these motions can also be made as incidental main motions, and when used in that manner, the rules relating to their order of precedence and privileged status change. I discuss these changes in more detail in Chapter 6.

Let's Get Back on Schedule: Call for Orders of the Day

Your time is important. So is that of other members. Your meeting has a purpose and a goal of taking care of the group's business within a specific time frame. Meeting time is the time to get down to business, make decisions, and go home.

Recognizing the value of your time, Robert's Rules gives you a special motion to use to keep things running on schedule. If you're in a meeting and see that the adopted agenda (or program, or order of business established by rule) isn't being followed, or if the time has arrived for an item of business and the chair continues other pending business, you can insist that the schedule be followed.

In such a situation, the privileged motion to *Call for Orders of the Day* is just what you need. With this motion, the demand of a single member requires the group to resume the scheduled business immediately, unless the members decide otherwise by a two-thirds vote.

This motion is not permitted in a committee of the whole (see Chapter 3).

Using the motion to call for orders of the day

There are two situations in which using a call for orders of the day is appropriate:

- ✔ When the time is reached for a particular item of business to be discussed but other business continues

- ✔ When, for some reason, business isn't being taken up in the proper order

The privileged motion call for orders of the day is made by simply rising and saying, "Mr. Chairman, I call for the orders of the day." You may also say, "Madam President, I demand the regular order be immediately resumed."

Even if someone else is speaking, you can interrupt to make this motion because the privilege of the group is to be able to follow its schedule.

Your presiding officer is responsible for keeping the meeting on track, and when this motion is made, his duty is to proceed immediately to the proper item of business.

The chair responds to the member calling for orders of the day by saying, "Orders of the day are called for" and proceeding to announce the proper current item of business.

Setting aside the orders of the day

If the presiding officer or one of the members thinks that it's likely the members would rather continue the business currently before them, they can make that decision by a two-thirds vote as follows:

- ✔ The chair, instead of proceeding immediately to the scheduled item of business, can inform the assembly of the item of business that is in order and ask whether the members wish to move on to that item. The members can choose to continue with the currently pending business by a two-thirds vote in the negative.

- ✔ A member can simply move that the time for consideration of the currently pending business be extended, or that the rules be suspended (see Chapter 11) and a particular matter be taken up. Either way, the motion requires a two-thirds vote in the affirmative.

Six key characteristics of the motion to call for orders of the day

The motion to call for orders of the day

- ✔ Can interrupt a speaker who has the floor
- ✔ Doesn't need to be seconded
- ✔ Isn't debatable
- ✔ Can't be amended
- ✔ Requires enforcement on the call of any member unless the members, by a two-thirds vote, decide to continue with the currently pending business
- ✔ Can't be reconsidered

It's Cold in Here: Raise a Question of Privilege

Lots of things happen in meetings that keep members from being comfortable or able to concentrate on the business at hand. A good illustration of such disturbances is in a scene from the movie *A Beautiful Mind.* In one classroom scene, the jackhammers are so loud as to render it impossible to hear the teacher, and it's too hot to close the window and muffle the noise. An attractive student successfully gets the construction crew to stop their jackhammering, and the class is able to proceed in a quiet, but well-ventilated, classroom.

Such is the nature of meetings. Air conditioners are set too low or too high, there's noise out in the hall, or a group of members are abuzz about something and you can't hear the discussion. Anything that affects the comfort of the assembly can be dealt with on the request of one member who raises a question of privilege.

More often than not, the motion to *Raise a Question of Privilege* is made to solve some immediate problem of particular and immediate annoyance to the group. But this motion covers other situations, too.

The two types of questions of privilege are

- **Those dealing with matters affecting the entire group.** Examples of these include the physical comfort of members, questions about the organization, questions about the conduct of its officers or employees, questions about the accuracy of published reports, and so on.

- **Those dealing with matters affecting an individual.** An example of this type is an inaccurate report of something said or done by a member.

Using the motion to raise a question of privilege

There you sit, seventh row from the back in a small and crowded meeting hall. The meeting of the Association of Seersucker Beanbag Manufacturers is underway, and an important motion is being debated. Some bonehead is out in the hall talking about his recent foot surgery, and you're not only disgusted, you're also unable to concentrate on the debate.

What to do? Easy! Raise a question of privilege! Stand up and (interrupting the current speaker because you just don't want to miss anything more of what's being said) say, "Mr. Chairman, I rise to a question of privilege affecting the assembly. There is a loud disturbance coming from the hall and a large number of us cannot hear or concentrate on the discussion."

The chair may respond, "Will the bonehead in the hall please shut up and take his foot with him?" No, sorry — I'm just kidding. That's probably what he would like to say, but as I discuss in Chapter 7, the chair must avoid getting personal and stick to the issue at hand.

What the chair really should say is, "Will someone please ask the members in the hall to remove the conversation from the doorway, and please close the doors to the hall?"

The privileged motion to raise a question of privilege is one of those motions that rarely involves more than just a decision by the chair. It may be used to introduce a motion that needs to be decided by the group, and the need to decide is immediate.

Suppose you're in a board meeting, and the executive director and two committee chairmen, none of whom are board members, are present. The executive director has just finished her report, and serious problems with her job performance are apparent.

You want to make a motion to consider her continued employment at a change in salary, and you believe only the board members should be in the room when you make the motion. So, you raise a question of privilege relating to the assembly in order to decide immediately whether or not to go into executive session and consider your motion.

The question of whether to go into executive session and take up your motion immediately is the question of privilege; the motion you make concerning the executive director is just a main motion whose immediate consideration is made possible by raising the question of privilege.

It's really rare that anything other than a motion affecting the physical comfort of the members in a meeting is properly used as a privileged motion (which can interrupt pending business). The other examples I provide in this section are most often handled as incidental main motions, which are the same motions except that they're made while no other business is pending. (I discuss incidental main motions in Chapter 6.)

Six key characteristics of the motion to raise a question of privilege

The motion to raise a question of privilege

- ✔ Can interrupt a speaker who has the floor, but only if the motion's object would be lost by waiting. Otherwise, the motion can interrupt pending business.

- ✔ Doesn't need to be seconded, but if the solution to the problem being addressed requires another motion, then that motion needs to be seconded

- ✔ Isn't debatable, but if raising the question requires another motion, then that motion is debatable

- ✔ Can't be amended, but if raising the question requires another motion, then that motion is amendable

- ✔ Is decided (ruled on) by the chair

- ✔ Can't be reconsidered if it's the chair's decision (ruling)

Let's Take a Break: Recess

No, it's not time to go out to the playground and climb the jungle gym. Well, maybe it feels like time for that kind of recess, but that's not likely to happen unless you're in class and this is your parliamentary procedure textbook. Recess in this sense usually only refers to taking a break in the middle of a meeting. But I promise you that the feeling is the same. Recess is *recess!*

Well, almost. *Recess,* like other privileged and subsidiary motions, also has a form for use as an incidental main motion (see Chapter 6) and has a few different rules if it's made when nothing else is pending and the group wants to take a short break.

But the *privileged* motion to recess is made to consider whether or not to take a short break *immediately while another motion is pending,* and it can interrupt just about anything under consideration other than one of the privileged motions concerning adjournment.

A recess doesn't close a meeting. When you reconvene from the recess, you take up business right where you left off.

Using the motion to recess

I can't remember any time in my career, either as a member or as a parliamentarian, when a motion to take a recess failed. About the only time it may not go through is when somebody trumps the motion with a motion to adjourn.

The motion to recess provides for a short break in the proceedings, and the privileged motion is one that's used to get a recess immediately, even while you're in the middle of something. It can be used strategically to allow an opportunity for a caucus or simply so you can step outside for a breath of fresh air.

Because a motion to recess can't interrupt a speaker, you're required to wait for recognition by the chair. But the form is simple: "Madam Chairman, I move that we take a 15 minute recess," or "Mr. President, I move we take a recess until 3 p.m.," or "I move we recess until reconvened by the chair."

Unless your meeting is holding everyone rapt in enjoyment of the discussion, calls of "second" are likely to erupt from all corners of the room (and from the middle and sides, too!). Unless it appears that the motion to recess may meet objection or perhaps an amendment to deal with the length of the recess, the chair can usually obtain general (or unanimous) consent (see Chapter 8). If objection arises or an amendment is offered, a voice vote is the way to go.

To resume business as usual, the chair calls the meeting back to order by saying something like, "The recess is ended and the meeting will please come to order."

That's it. You're back — refreshed, reenergized, regrouped, and ready to proceed.

Six key characteristics of the motion to recess

The motion to recess, as a privileged motion,

✔ Can't interrupt a speaker who has the floor

✔ Must be seconded

✔ Isn't debatable

✔ Is amendable with respect to the length of the recess, with no debate permitted on such an amendment

✔ Must have a majority vote

✔ Can't be reconsidered

Let's Get Outta Here: Adjourn

Those magic words, "I declare the meeting adjourned!" Who doesn't love 'em? Most of the time, nobody. In fact, as great as meetings can be when conducted by effective leaders who know what they're doing, adjourning is probably only *bad* news when your great idea is on the floor, is close to being adopted, and the opposition uses the motion to *Adjourn* to successfully close the meeting.

Needless to say, I'm convinced it's one of the world's most favorite motions. You just can't have a successful meeting without it!

By the time the motion to adjourn is even close to coming up, you and a few of the others in your meeting may already be making your way to the door. But some things can happen that you may not want to miss, so you may be doing yourself a big favor by hanging around long enough to actually hear the presiding officer declare the meeting adjourned.

Between the time the motion to adjourn is adopted and the chair declares the meeting adjourned, any one or more of the following actions are permitted and in order:

✔ Providing information about business requiring attention before adjournment

✔ Making important announcements

✔ Giving notice of a motion to reconsider a vote that took place at the meeting

✔ Moving to *Reconsider and Enter on the Minutes* (see Chapter 12) in connection with a vote that took place at the meeting

✔ Giving notice for any future motion that requires previous notice to be given at a meeting

✔ Moving to set the time for an adjourned meeting

In some situations, adjournment can take place without a motion. One is when the hour adopted for adjournment has arrived. At that time, the chair announces the fact, and unless you or someone else is pretty quick to move to set aside the orders of the day, the meeting may be adjourned by declaration.

Another instance in which adjournment doesn't need a motion is when some emergency or immediate danger makes hanging around for a vote a really knuckle-brained thing to do. For example, if there's a fire, your presiding officer should just break the glass to set off the alarm, and then declare the meeting adjourned to meet again at the call of the chair.

The other (more common) scenario in which adjournment can happen without a motion is when you've reached the end of the agenda. In that case, the chair may just ask whether there's any more business; if you don't speak up to make that motion you've been thinking about, and if no one else speaks up, the presiding officer can declare the meeting adjourned. Everybody can go out for coffee and beignets (I'm in Louisiana, and we love those little fried, square donuts!) before going home after the meeting.

A meeting isn't adjourned until the chair *declares* it adjourned, no matter how loud the "ayes" ring out when the vote is taken.

Using the motion to adjourn

The motion to adjourn is straightforward and simple. It comes in three basic forms:

✔ **Adjourn now:** "Madam President, I move to adjourn."

   Adoption of the motion closes the meeting. At the heart of everyone making this motion is the bleeding desire to fold it up and go home! This form of the motion is *always* privileged, meaning that even when nothing else is pending, the motion to adjourn must be immediately disposed of by direct vote, unless the higher ranking motion to *Fix the Time to Which to Adjourn* is made. (I discuss that motion in the final section of this chapter.)

   This form of adjourn is the only way in which the motion may be used as a privileged motion (meaning it can be made while other business is pending).

✔ **Adjourn to continue the meeting later:** "Madam President, I move to adjourn to meet again tomorrow at 8 a.m."

   This form sets up a continuation of the current meeting. Tomorrow's meeting is called an *adjourned meeting* or an *adjournment of* the current meeting. At the heart of everyone making this motion is the same bleeding desire to get away from it all until they're dragged kicking and screaming back, being required by duty to continue an unfinished agenda.

> ✔ **Adjourn sine die (without day):** "Mr. Chairman, I move to adjourn sine die."
>
> This form adjourns the assembly completely and is used to end the final meeting of a convention of delegates.

Although the second two forms are not *privileged* (meaning they're only in order as *main motions* and can only be made when no other business is pending), the rules of procedure are otherwise the same.

Six key characteristics of the motion to adjourn

The privileged motion to adjourn

> ✔ Can't interrupt a speaker who has the floor
>
> ✔ Must be seconded
>
> ✔ Can't be debated
>
> ✔ Can't be amended
>
> ✔ Must have a majority vote
>
> ✔ Can't be reconsidered, but can be renewed if any business has gone forward after a motion to adjourn has failed

If the motion specifies when adjournment will occur or sets a future time to which the group will adjourn as a continuation of the current meeting, that aspect of the motion can be amended and debated.

Let's Go Home and Finish Another Day: Fix the Time to Which to Adjourn

The last of the privileged motions on the list, the motion to *Fix the Time to Which to Adjourn,* is the one that can be made at just about any time no matter what else is before your meeting.

It may become clear at some point in the meeting that you need more time if you're to get everything accomplished that you intended. And you don't want to wait until the next regular meeting to finish things up. You may be dealing with elections or just an overloaded agenda. You may not even have another regular meeting scheduled for a long time. When you find yourself in this situation, the thing to do is to provide for an adjourned meeting.

An *adjourned meeting* refers to a meeting that continues the same order of business, or agenda, that wasn't concluded in an earlier meeting. It's a separate meeting in one sense, but it's technically a continuation of the same meeting. The adjourned meeting is used mostly to take care of important business that should not (or must not) wait until the next regular meeting, but that can't go forward in the current meeting due to lack of enough time (or perhaps a lack of enough people to have a quorum). (Flip back to Chapter 4 for a thorough discussion of quorum.)

Using the motion to fix the time to which to adjourn

As soon as you realize that the work ahead of you is likely to consume more time than you have, the time is right to offer the motion to fix the time to which to adjourn. It's privileged when it's made while other business is pending, and because it's the highest ranking motion, it takes precedence over just about everything, including a pending motion to adjourn. That last little inclusion is great because it gives you or other judicious members of your organization one last chance to keep your good ideas alive and within reach of the membership before the next regular meeting. This means a lot in the case of a group that only meets quarterly (or even less often).

This motion is introduced by saying, "Mr. Chairman, I move that when we adjourn, we adjourn to meet again next Tuesday night at 6 p.m. at the clubhouse." Or, if you need to keep some options open, say something like ". . . to meet next week on the call of the president."

Among the more common situations when this motion is used is when a motion is made that would benefit from having an evening to itself. In this situation, the motion to fix the time to which to adjourn is made as a way of postponing the motion until there's enough time to handle it properly. Or if you're running out of time, this privileged motion may be made to set up the time for an adjourned meeting just before making a motion to adjourn.

When you're faced with a lack of quorum (enough people to legally hold the meeting), fixing the time to which to adjourn gives you another chance to have the meeting that should have gone forward on the original date but couldn't due to poor attendance.

Six key characteristics of the motion to fix the time to which to adjourn

The privileged motion to fix the time to which to adjourn

- ✔ Can't interrupt a speaker who has the floor
- ✔ Must be seconded
- ✔ Can't be debated
- ✔ Can be amended only as to the date, hour, and place; such amendments cannot be debated
- ✔ Needs a majority vote
- ✔ Can be reconsidered

Chapter 11

Incidental Motions: Dealing with the Questions of Procedure

As you go through your day, you probably have some well-established routines that get you from one thing to another. You get up, you have some coffee, and you get ready for the day ahead. You go to work, school, or otherwise go about your life. You come home, you relax, and maybe do a little work in the yard. If you have time, you may read, study, watch a little TV, or do a little surfing on the Web. Soon enough, you tire, you retire, and tomorrow you do it all over again.

You may have your daily routine figured out, but you still have a lot of decisions to make about how to do the different things you do. Are you going to cook your breakfast or stop at the Greasy Spoon? Will you have your eggs sunny side up or scrambled? How are you getting to work? Will you drive, walk, or take the bus?

You make some decisions every time you deal with a particular situation, like deciding what to have for breakfast. Other times, you make a decision and stick with it until you make a change, like figuring out how you'll get to work. No matter what the big picture is, you have to make decisions just to be able to move from one thing to the next. It's not just about the main goals — the decisions you make to reach those goals are just as important. The same philosophy applies to meetings and the ways in which decisions are made.

Defining Incidental Motions

In your meetings, your group often needs to decide how to proceed in handling your business. Should you vote by ballot? Is the chairman correct? Is there enough money in the treasury? Can your group say "Yes" to part of a motion and "No" to another part? Should your group even be talking about this? Also, when it comes to arriving at group decisions, it matters very much if things aren't handled correctly or in the manner agreed to by all, when improper handling results in the compromise of the rights of one, some, or all of the members.

Robert's Rules takes into account the need for members to make these kinds of decisions — to insist on strictly following the rules, to relax the rules for a special reason, or to decide to handle something in a particular way. These decisions are made by the introduction and consideration of what are called *incidental motions*. These motions help your group (or your presiding officer) decide a question about whether something is being done correctly, whether to get more information, or how to handle some aspect of the pending business.

The term *incidental motion* refers to any of the motions described in this chapter when they're made in direct connection with a motion to be introduced, a pending motion, or a motion that has just been pending. But when any of the motions described in this chapter are made as *main motions,* they're called *incidental **main** motions,* and even though the purpose is pretty much the same as described below, the rules for using them are a little different. Check out Chapter 6 for the rules regarding main motions.

Using Incidental Motions

The incidental motions in Robert's Rules cover most anything that can come up when you're in your meeting. They are

- ✔ Point of Order
- ✔ Appeal the Ruling (decision) of the Chair
- ✔ Suspend the Rules
- ✔ Object to Consideration of the Question
- ✔ Division of the Question
- ✔ Consider Seriatim (by paragraph)

✔ Division of the Assembly

✔ Motions Related to Method of Voting and the Polls

✔ Motions Related to Nominations

✔ Request to Be Excused from a Duty

✔ Parliamentary Inquiry

✔ Point of Information

✔ Request for Permission to Withdraw or Modify a Motion

✔ Request to Read Papers

✔ Request for Other Privilege

Table 11-1 lays out exactly which motions you use depending on what you're trying to accomplish in your meeting. Each of these motions is discussed in detail in the following sections.

Table 11-1   Common Uses for Incidental Motions

If You Want to . . .	Then Use . . .
Enforce the rules	Point of Order
Overrule a decision of the chair	Appeal
Do something that violates a rule	Suspend the Rules
Avoid any consideration of a main motion	Object to the Consideration of the Question
Divide a motion into separate parts for debate and vote	Division of the Question
Discuss a long motion part by part before voting on the whole	Consideration by Paragraph
Question the result of a voice vote	Division of the Assembly
Take a vote other than by voice, or open or close the polls	Motions Related to Method of Voting and the Polls
Designate a method for taking nominations, or open or close nominations	Motions Related to Nominations
Avoid a compulsory obligation of membership or office	Request to Be Excused from a Duty
Ask a question about procedure	Parliamentary Inquiry

(continued)

Table 11-1 *(continued)*

If You Want to . . .	Then Use . . .
Ask for information pertaining to a motion on the floor	Point of Information
Withdraw or change a motion already stated by the chair	Request for Permission to Withdraw or Modify a Motion
Read something to the assembly	Request to Read Papers
Speak or make remarks when no business is pending	Request for Other Privilege

Hey, We're Not Doing This Right: Point of Order

The situation is inevitable: An important rule is ignored, or overlooked, or just plain broken, and one or more members wind up with the short end of the stick. Any self-respecting book on rules will provide a rule that says any member who notices a breach of the rules has a right to call immediate attention to the fact and insist that the rules be enforced. Robert's Rules provides for this type of situation by giving us the procedure for raising a *Point of Order*.

Rising to a point of order

You're sitting there in your meeting waiting for the right moment to rise and get recognition of the chair (in this case, the president) to speak against the stupid idea that your service club supports a proposition to increase the local sales tax. All of a sudden somebody in the back of the room shouts "Question! Question! I call for the question!" and the president says, "The question has been called for. We'll stop discussion now and vote!"

You're dumbfounded. You thought your president knew by now that one member can't end debate by hollering out "Question!" You know the rules for ending debate are explained in *Robert's Rules For Dummies* (right there in Chapter 9, where I discuss the subsidiary motion *Previous Question*), and, after all, your club just bought a copy for your president. But unfortunately, he hasn't read it yet.

So, if you want to have your say on the issue, you have to stop the president from ending debate on the demand of this one member, and at least get him to put a vote to the members on whether to end the debate. You rise — quickly, mind you, even if you interrupt a speaker, or you'll be too late — and say, "Point of order, Mr. President!" or "Mr. President, I rise to a point of order!"

Stating your point

The presiding officer says to you, "The member will state his point of order," and in this case you say, "Mr. President, the member did not obtain recognition of the chair, nor did his motion to end debate have a second, and we did not vote on whether we're ready to end debate."

Ruling of the chair

Now, if you're lucky and the president isn't trying to short-circuit the debate, he says "The point is well-taken, and the previous question (or motion to end debate) is not before the membership. Is there any further discussion on the motion to endorse the sales tax increase?" You can then obtain recognition of the chair and proceed to speak against the idea.

You may be unlucky, though, and the president may simply rule your point well-taken, ask for a second to the previous question, and then take a rising vote on whether to end debate. If two-thirds of the members vote to end debate, then your point may be well-taken, but the group is still tired of all the talk. However, because your president clearly doesn't even know how to deal with previous question, he may say, "The point is not well-taken, and I'm tired of all this talk." (If he does this, you'll be glad to know about your right to appeal, which I discuss in the next section of this chapter.)

A point of order can be raised at any time when any member notices a violation of the rules. The chair's duty is to make a decision, called a *ruling,* on the point of order. He may need to check the rules or the bylaws, or ask the parliamentarian for advice, but in any case, a point of order is usually ruled on in one of two ways: The point is declared either "Well-taken," or "Not well-taken," and a short explanation of the ruling is given.

When the chair is in doubt

Sometimes, however, the point being raised is not as clear as whether the motion to end debate is being handled correctly. The point of order may, for example, be that a proposed amendment is not germane to the main motion. In that case, the chair may reasonably bc in doubt (or may just prefer to let the assembly decide the point in the interest of harmony). If that's the case, he responds, "The chair is in doubt on the member's point. All those who consider the amendment germane will say aye . . . Opposed, no . . . The ayes have it and the amendment is germane."

Beating the clock: Timely points of order

If you believe the rules aren't being followed, you need to speak up fast because points of order are subject to timeliness requirements. With few exceptions, if you let a breach of the rules pass without saying something when it occurs, you lose the opportunity to object. Parliamentarians like to call this the "You snooze, you lose" rule!

Reserving a point of order

If you think a motion may be out of order but you can't be sure until the motion is made and stated by the chair, you can *reserve a point of order*. After the motion is made, you have to either press the point or withdraw it. You can't wait until some debate has occurred. If you do, then the chair doesn't have much choice but to rule your point of order as "Not well-taken."

Raising your point of order before it's too late

To raise a point of order correctly, you must raise it at the time the breach of order occurs. That's pretty straightforward. If some motion is out of order, if the vote is not taken correctly, or if the procedure is breached, you must raise the point of order at that time or else you're out of luck. No second-guessing after the meeting is allowed. Not even for votes! If you want to raise a point of order about the conduct of a vote, you must do it before the next item of business is introduced, or no matter what, the results declared by the chair must stand.

Exception for the continuing breach

The timeliness requirement carries a big exception that centers on what's called a *continuing breach* of the rules. If the violation of the rules involves one of the following situations, a point of order can almost always be raised at any time:

- ✔ Adoption of a motion that violates your bylaws

- ✔ Adoption of a motion that conflicts with a previously adopted motion, unless the vote was by the margin required to *Amend or Rescind Something Previously Adopted* (see Chapter 12)

✔ Violation of procedural rules in any law governing your organization

✔ Anything done in violation of a fundamental principle of parliamentary law, even if agreed to unanimously, such as the rules that

- Allow only one question to be considered at a time

- Limit the right to vote to members present at the time the voting occurs in a legal meeting

✔ Anything done in violation of a rule protecting rights of absentees or individual members, such as

- Quorum requirements

- Requirements for previous notice

- Rules requiring a secret ballot vote

- Preventing a particular member from having full rights to participate in a meeting except after proper disciplinary proceedings (or under provisions of properly adopted motions to limit debate, close the polls, and so on)

Six key characteristics of the motion point of order

A point of order

✔ Can interrupt a speaker who has the floor

✔ Doesn't need to be seconded

✔ Isn't debatable

✔ Can't be amended

✔ Is decided by the chair

✔ Can't be reconsidered

Sorry, Madam President, But I Disagree: Appeal

Even the most highly studied, best prepared, and extremely popular presiding officer can make mistakes, and when one of those mistakes involves a ruling on a matter of parliamentary procedure, any two members can require that the ruling be decided by the membership through the process called *Appeal*.

The appeal of the motion to appeal

Robert's Rules says that disagreeing with the chair is no different from disagreeing with a member in debate, and you're given a way to do it without getting personal. In fact, if you don't appeal from the decision of the chair, Robert says you don't have any right to criticize the ruling! Knowing how to use this incidental motion is important in case the chair doesn't make the correct ruling on your point of order. And the chair needs to know how to use it as well because it's often the best way out of a sticky wicket!

Appealing (from) the ruling of the chair

When a presiding officer makes a ruling and a member disagrees, the proper thing to do is to rise and say, "Madam President, I appeal from the ruling of the chair." If another member seconds the appeal, the procedure is rather simple: Madam President puts the question to the members, who decide whether to sustain her ruling. But under Robert's Rules, the presiding officer gets to speak first and last in any discussion about the appeal or her decision.

It doesn't matter whether the ruling is on a point of order made by a member or the ruling is made simply because the presiding officer recognizes that some procedure or motion is not in order. Her job is to rule on parliamentary procedure to keep things moving along and to assure that the rights of the minority aren't trampled.

So when you move, for example, to amend a motion to spend $500 to have a picnic on the Fourth of July by striking out "picnic on the Fourth of July" and inserting "buy the secretary a new desk," the chair may very likely rule your amendment "out of order" because she decides it isn't germane to the original motion. When she rules your motion out of order, she's expected to explain her ruling. In this case, she makes the ruling because she considers the main motion to be about having a social event and not about buying furniture.

But you're not focusing on the picnic. You're thinking about the $500, and you think that if the group spends $500, it should be on the secretary's desk. And maybe in place of the picnic you can have a watermelon roast sometime during the summer where everybody brings their own watermelon (and less money is spent).

Your option, then, is to say, "Madam President, I appeal from the ruling of the chair." If your appeal has any support, someone will second it, and you're on!

Because the motion to *Amend,* on which the ruling was made (and from which you're appealing), is debatable, you can seek recognition to speak to your appeal. You explain that your amendment is

germane to the spending of the money, and that's why you appeal.
You ask the members, when deciding whether to sustain the decision of the chair, to consider that this amendment is completely
germane to a question on spending $500.

Stating the question on the appeal

The chair thanks you and, realizing that it's no big deal (this isn't
about her being right, it's about what the members want), wel-
comes the opportunity to let the members decide. She puts the
question to the membership by saying, "Shall the decision of the
chair be sustained?"

Deciding the appeal

If the members agree with the ruling of the chair, then they vote
"Yes" to *sustain the decision* of the chair. If they want to consider
your amendment, then they vote "No" and *overrule* the chair. If
they sustain the chair's ruling, then your amendment is out of
order. Otherwise, your amendment is in order, and the chair is
expected to entertain discussion on the amendment. The appeal
doesn't decide whether the amendment is adopted, only whether
it's in order to come before the membership.

Applying the motion to appeal

An appeal can only be applied to a *ruling* of the chair, not to an opinion, such as is a response to a *parliamentary inquiry* (discussed later
in this chapter). Nor is the declaration of the result of a vote subject
to an appeal. To challenge the result of a vote, you call for a *Division
of the Assembly* (discussed in the section "I'm Not So Sure the Ayes
Really Have It: Division of the Assembly," later in this chapter).

Six key characteristics of the motion to appeal

An appeal from the ruling of the chair

- ✔ Can interrupt a speaker who has the floor
- ✔ Needs to be seconded
- ✔ Is debatable unless the immediately pending question is not
  debatable
- ✔ Can't be amended
- ✔ Requires a majority vote to overturn the decision of the chair
- ✔ Can be reconsidered

We Can't Let That Stop Us: Suspend the Rules

When I was a junior in high school (way back in the middle of the twentieth century), my English teacher asked me to take some photographs to the yearbook sponsor's classroom during a class period. It was against the rules to be in the hall during class periods, but the teachers could suspend that rule by giving a hall pass. If I got stopped and questioned by another teacher or a hall monitor, I just showed my hall pass, and they let me continue on my mission.

In your organization's meetings, sometimes you need to take care of some business that would normally violate your rules. When the circumstances warrant an exception, and if making the exception won't violate the bylaws or compromise the rights of absentees or of a minority of the size the rule was designed to protect, then the incidental motion to *Suspend the Rules* is your hall pass.

Using the motion to suspend the rules

The motion to suspend the rules is often used in conjunction with the motion to do whatever it is you're trying to do that is against your rules. Because the adoption of the motion (requiring a two-thirds vote) would certainly be followed by a vote to do that for which the rules were suspended, the motion to suspend the rules isn't considered a violation of the "one question at a time" principle of parliamentary law (see Chapter 3).

Suppose you want to have a professional parliamentarian preside at one of your meetings in which a very divisive issue, like whether to fire your executive director, is on the agenda. Your rules, however, require the president to preside at all meetings. But the president has strong feelings about the issue and just can't do the job impartially. You can't have somebody else preside without breaking your rules. What can you do?

If you can get two-thirds of the members present and voting to approve a suspension of the rules, you can have the parliamentarian handle the meeting. The motion is made by saying, "Mr. President, I move that we suspend the rules and authorize the parliamentarian to serve as presiding officer for the meeting." If the motion receives a second and can muster a two-thirds vote, then the rules are suspended and your parliamentarian can preside over the meeting.

Sometimes the motion to suspend isn't combined with the motion it affects because it's not so clear that the original motion will pass even if the suspension of the rules to consider it is authorized. This situation is illustrated by a common application of suspend the rules when something is taken out of its regular place on your agenda.

For example, take the meeting example set up earlier in this section, in which the parliamentarian has been placed in the chair. Everybody is ready to get on with the debate on the controversial issue, but on the agenda, it's way down in unfinished business. Nobody really cares about the committee reports right now. So, to get started on the hot item, somebody has to move that "We suspend the rules and take up the question on firing the executive director." With a second to the motion and a two-thirds vote, you can move right into debating the fate of your executive director.

If I were your parliamentarian–presiding officer, I may even get straight to that point by *assuming the motion* (see the sidebar "Assuming a motion") and *asking for unanimous consent* (see Chapter 8). That's every bit as good as having a motion, a second, and a two-thirds vote!

In this case, suspension of the rules to consider the question doesn't mean you've decided to fire the executive director. It just allows you to skip all the routine business normally on your agenda and go right to the big debate.

Knowing when you can't suspend the rules

I have a friend who says that you may as well not have rules if you can suspend them anytime you need to. But really just the reverse is true: Unless you provide a rule to allow you to make exceptions, you probably wouldn't want to have any rules at all.

But my friend is right in one respect — some rules *cannot be suspended*. They are

- **Constitution and bylaws:** Your bylaws are a contract between members, and they can't be suspended no matter how great a vote to suspend them might be, nor can they be suspended because the rule is just too inconvenient. The same goes for any procedural rules written into the laws governing the organization (such as state corporation laws).

However, if a bylaw provides for its own suspension, it can be suspended. This exception applies only if the bylaw is "clearly a rule in the nature of a rule of order" dealing with the "conduct of business in a meeting or the duty of officers in that connection." This exception is pretty limited, and professional parliamentarians generally say this exception doesn't permit anything in bylaws to be suspended except for changes to an order of business, permitting someone other than the president to preside, or permitting someone other than the secretary to take the minutes.

✔ **Fundamental principles of parliamentary law:** Such principles can't be suspended, even if a suspension is agreed to unanimously. Fundamental principles include those that

- Allow only one question to be considered at a time

- Limit the right to vote to members present at the time the voting occurs in a legal meeting

✔ **Rules protecting rights of absentees or individual members:** These rules include

- Quorum requirements

- Requirements for previous notice

- Rules requiring a secret ballot vote

- The right of any particular member to exercise full rights to participate in a meeting except after proper disciplinary proceedings (or under provisions of properly adopted motions to limit debate, close the polls, and so on)

Six key characteristics of the motion to suspend the rules

A motion to suspend the rules

✔ Can't interrupt a speaker who has the floor

✔ Needs to be seconded

✔ Isn't debatable

✔ Can't be amended

✔ Requires a two-thirds vote (But if you're suspending a rule protecting a minority less than one-third, then the rule can't be suspended if there is a negative vote as great as the number protected by the rule. A *standing rule* can be suspended by majority vote.)

✔ Can't be reconsidered

Assuming a motion

A presiding officer who knows when and how to *assume* a motion has a great time-saving tool in his arsenal.

Incidental motions sometimes lend themselves very well to this technique. When the chair detects that the members will follow some course of action that may well be moved, seconded, and stated by the chair, he saves a lot of time by assuming the motion and asking for general consent.

Examples of this presiding technique appear throughout this book. *Assuming a motion* is most often used when a particular item of business is already on the agenda. Examples include routine items like approving the minutes, or specific motions scheduled to come before the membership either by previous notice or by having been postponed to a certain time.

To assume a motion, you just assume it! For example, you simply say, "The question is on the approval of the minutes. Are there any corrections or additions?" Nobody has to make a formal motion. Assuming a motion is completely proper if it's clear that the motion is in order and is otherwise something that the membership intends to debate and decide.

Oh, Come On Now: Object to Consideration of the Question

Any original main motion that you just think is such a bad idea that it should never even be discussed is a fair target for *Object to the Consideration of the Question.* And this incidental motion is in order until the members begin to consider and debate the main motion.

After discussion begins, it's too late, no matter how lousy the idea. You can't stop it with this motion then. You can only kill the motion by moving to postpone indefinitely or by voting it down. In short, if you miss your chance to kill it by objecting to its consideration, you have to at least listen to the maker give his pitch because he's entitled to recognition to speak first to his motion.

Using the motion to object to the consideration

The following example is not the only situation in which this motion comes in handy, but it's one of those common scenarios that lends itself to describing the motion's use.

If you're an active member of an organization and participate regularly in its meetings, you've no doubt encountered Stumpy Neverstops. You know, the guy who shows up at every meeting making the same motion that gets argued and finally voted down. Every meeting, Stumpy batters the hull of his ship. Every month, he persists in introducing his motion, trying to get the group to do something it just doesn't want to do and isn't likely to want to do anytime soon.

After a few meetings like this, you're at your wit's end, and there's no end in sight because Robert's Rules allows Stumpy to make his motion again at every new meeting even if it failed at a previous meeting; and Stumpy knows no shame. Well, that can all end now. In the following sections, I tell you how to send Stumpy sailing around the reef in his lifeboat while you enjoy a calm sea for a change.

Objection initiated by a member

To use object to the consideration, get to your feet quickly (hopefully as soon as the undesirable motion rolls over the lips of the person offering it) and say, "Mr. Chairman, I object to the consideration of the question."

Because this motion decides whether to summarily dismiss a motion without consideration, it doesn't even need a second. The chair just responds with, "The member objects to the consideration of the motion. All in favor of considering the motion will rise. [pause] Opposed rise. There are two-thirds opposed to considering the motion and it will not be considered." It's all over, Stumpy. Sit down!

Finely tuned quick-draw skills help you out any time you need to use object to the consideration. If, for some reason, you need to apply this motion to a subsidiary motion (such as may happen if there's a motion you really want to discuss and you think that Stumpy's attempt to postpone or refer it to a committee for the third or fourth time is just a way to delay), you have to be even faster, because it's too late to object to consideration of a motion once bebate has begun, or if any subsidiary motion has been stated by the chair.

Objection initiated by the chair

If the chair has a good sense of members' limits when it comes to likely intolerance for some motions, he may want to offer (on his own initiative) the members the opportunity to object by saying, "It is the sense of the chair that the consideration of this question may have objection. Shall the motion be placed before you for your consideration?"

If a motion is outside the scope of the purposes of the organization, is in conflict with the bylaws, or is otherwise deemed out of order to be considered, then object to the consideration of the question is itself out of order. When this incidental motion is used incorrectly in this manner, it should just be treated as a point of order, with the chair ruling the motion objected to as out of order.

Six key characteristics of the motion to object to the consideration

An objection to the consideration of the question

- ✔ Can interrupt a speaker who has the floor (until debate has begun on the motion to which it is applied)
- ✔ Doesn't need to be seconded
- ✔ Isn't debatable
- ✔ Can't be amended
- ✔ Requires a two-thirds vote against consideration to sustain the objection
- ✔ Can be reconsidered only if the objection is sustained

Too Much in One Fell Swoop: Division of the Question

Sometimes a single motion is made that proposes several different things, each of which could stand alone as a separate motion. In one case, all the different things could be related and involve the same subject matter. In another case, they might be several unrelated actions made under the same motion. In either case, you may want to vote in favor of some of the things and against some others, but because everything is wrapped up in one main motion, the multiple-choice option is not available to you.

Or is it? Thanks to the incidental motion *Division of the Question,* you may be able to have some choice after all. If the individual proposals are related, you can move a division of the question, and if seconded and passed, you'll have created a series of individual motions for your group to consider. If the proposals are unrelated and are simply lumped together under the same motion, you can simply demand the division of the question — all by yourself — and the division has to be made.

For a motion to be divided, the parts have to be capable of standing on their own. A motion to purchase a television and give it to the school can't be divided because if you don't purchase the television, you can't give it to the school.

Using division of the question

The motion to divide the question is applicable in two unique situations.

On a single-subject motion

Suppose good ol' Stumpy (the guy who just can't let go of his brilliant ideas) makes it to your meeting again, and he has a brand-new motion that the group start meeting at his brother Bumpy's pizza place and that you be served the Stumpy Weekly Special Combo pizza with a tankard of Lucky Lagerbrau Ale.

Now, you're all for changing to meet at Bumpy's Pizzeria, but you would rather order your own selections from the menu. So you second the motion, and as soon as the chair states the motion, you move to divide the question: "Mr. Chairman, I move to divide the question to vote on where we'll meet, and then vote on the menu."

The chairman hears somebody say "Second" and thinks your motion is so darn reasonable that no one will object, so he says, "It's been moved and seconded to divide the question into two parts to first decide on a new meeting place, and then to decide on the menu." Then, he asks for general consent rather than taking a vote, and hearing no objection, he declares the motion divided and puts each question separately. You vote to meet at Bumpy's Pizzeria, and you wind up amending the second motion to provide for individual orders for lunch.

On a motion covering several unrelated items

This situation is often encountered when a committee reports recommendations on several different matters referred to it, and after presenting the report, the reporting member moves adoption of the recommendations contained in the report.

Suppose you're considering the report of the Dress Code Committee, and you hear all the different things they've recommended. Most are absurd, but you really think one recommendation is right on target! In this case, you can just rise and say, "Mr. Chairman, I call for a separate vote on the recommendation to buy Mr. Finkblossom a new bow tie." (Because you know that everything else the committee recommended is likely to go down the tube, you want to have at least *some* chance to help your membership chairman look a little better!)

In this scenario, the chair *must* take up that question separately. He may even get smart and divide out the other recommendations on his own motion by unanimous consent. But he doesn't have to. He just has to take a separate vote on the bow tie recommendation.

Six key characteristics of the motion division of the question

A motion to divide the question

- ✔ Can't interrupt a speaker who has the floor
- ✔ Needs to be seconded
- ✔ Isn't debatable
- ✔ Can be amended
- ✔ Requires a majority vote (but if the parts of the motion to which it is applied are unrelated, one member may demand the division of the question)
- ✔ Can't be reconsidered

Let's Go Over This Carefully: Consider by Paragraph

Your Bylaws Committee has finally finished its revision of the bylaws, and the special order of business for today's meeting is to consider the revision. You're interested in tweaking a couple of words here and there, and a few other folks have some last minute suggestions to improve readability and maybe clear up an ambiguity or two.

The proposed bylaws revision is about three pages long, and if you want to save time and avoid the confusion of skipping around the revision trying to deal with all the final edits, use the motion to *Consider Seriatim,* or *Consider by Paragraph.*

Using the motion to consider by paragraph

You can use this motion any time your parliamentary situation has you considering a long report or a motion with many parts and you want to be able to discuss and amend each part in a logical sequence before finally considering the document as a whole.

Moving for consideration by paragraph

In most situations where this procedure would be in order, it's pretty likely the chair will just handle the subject matter by seriatim (section by section) anyway. But if she doesn't, you can make the motion by saying, "Madam Chairman, I move to consider the bylaw revision by paragraph." The chairman will probably handle your motion by asking for unanimous consent, but it's just as proper for her to call for a voice vote.

Procedure for consideration by paragraph

Your group has come to the point in the meeting where it's time to consider whether to adopt the revision of the bylaws, and you've adopted the motion to consider it by paragraph.

In this case, the chairman of the Revision Committee presents the first section. The chair then asks for discussion or amendments on that section. The process for debate and amendment is then handled like it is for any other motion, and when you've finished with the first section, you move on to the next one.

After you've gone through the whole document and amended everything to your group's satisfaction, the chair opens the entire document to amendment. That's the group's final chance to make any more changes.

Then, just as with any main motion, you can debate and amend anything about the document. When you get to the point that nobody wants to make any more changes and everybody has had their say, the group votes on the amended revision and the chair announces the result.

Considering as a whole

Sometimes, the report or revision or whatever it is you're considering has been so overworked that the membership is really ready to just adopt everything the way it is; they don't really care to go through it by paragraph. In this case, the motion to consider by paragraph may fail, or if the presiding officer starts to consider by paragraph, somebody may move to *Consider as a Whole*. If such a motion passes, you just proceed directly with the vote on the report or revision as presented.

Whether or not you consider a motion by paragraph depends on the pleasure of the group. But seriatim (point by point) consideration is definitely the way to go if you intend to review the item as a group one last time before the final vote.

Six key characteristics of the motion to consider by paragraph

A motion to consider by paragraph

- ✔ Can't interrupt a speaker who has the floor
- ✔ Must be seconded
- ✔ Isn't debatable
- ✔ Can be amended
- ✔ Requires a majority vote
- ✔ Can not be reconsidered

I'm Not So Sure the Ayes Really Have It: Division of the Assembly

I've been in more meetings than I can count in which the oh-so-few opponents of a motion were able to shout their "No!" votes so loudly that, if you didn't know better, you'd think they were in the majority.

The side that hollers the loudest isn't always the majority; sometimes they fool the chairman and he says, "The noes (or ayes) have it and the motion fails (or passes)." If you doubt the result of the voice vote (or a vote by show of hands), then you have the right, as a single, lone member, to use the motion *Division of the Assembly* and demand that the vote be immediately taken by rising vote so everyone can see just which side is really in the majority.

Using division of the assembly

In any situation where you're in doubt of the result of a voice vote or a vote by show of hands, you should be quick to your feet and say (loudly enough to be heard by the chair), "Division!" or "I call for a division!"

Division on demand of a member

If a member demands a division of the assembly, then the presiding officer must immediately retake the vote: "All those in favor will rise. [pause] Be seated. All those opposed rise. [pause] Be seated." The chair then redeclares the result based on the rising vote.

If a member is still in doubt after the rising vote, he or she may move for a counted vote. But this motion requires a second and an affirmative vote of the membership to order the vote be counted. However, if the chair remains in doubt as to the result of a rising vote, he may proceed to order a counted vote on his own initiative.

Division on the initiative of the chair

The chair may not even wait for a call for a division. If he can't be sure of a majority based on the voice vote or show of hands, he may retake the vote by a rising vote by saying, "The chair is in doubt as to the result. Will all those in favor of the motion rise. [pause] Be seated. All those opposed rise. [pause] Be seated. Thank you. The affirmative is in the majority and the motion is carried."

Six key characteristics of the motion division of the assembly

A motion for division of the assembly

- ✔ Can interrupt a speaker who has the floor
- ✔ Doesn't need to be seconded
- ✔ Isn't debatable
- ✔ Can't be amended
- ✔ Requires no vote to be taken
- ✔ Can't be reconsidered

Deciding How to Decide: Motions Related to Methods of Voting and the Polls

There are several possible methods of voting other than by voice vote or rising vote, both of which are the usual methods of voting on motions (depending on the threshold required for a motion to pass).

Whenever you want to vote on a motion using another method of voting, you use a *Motion Related to the Method of Voting*. And whenever you want to specify when voting will take place, you use a *Motion Related to the Polls*.

Using motions related to voting and the polls

Motions related to the method of voting or the polls are in order as incidental motions anytime an election is pending or when a vote is about to be taken on a motion. They are incidental *main* motions if no other business is pending.

Selecting a method of voting

Often, as is the case with many incidental motions, the method for voting can be decided informally by general consent. A good presiding officer will sometimes simply call for a ballot or a counted vote. But if, for whatever reason, you want to use one of these forms or another voting method, such as a roll call or signed ballot, you can make the motion upon obtaining recognition by the chair.

If you want the vote to be by ballot, say, "Mr. Chairman, I move that the vote on this motion be by ballot."

The different methods of voting are discussed in Chapter 8.

Opening or closing the polls

Usually associated with balloting, the motion to close the polls is best left to be handled by the presiding officer, who, seeing that all who wish to vote have done so, declares the polls closed.

But if someone comes into the meeting who has not voted, and if the votes haven't been counted (and the results haven't been announced), it's perfectly permissible to allow latecomers to vote. But if the polls have been formally closed either by motion and vote or by declaration of the chair, then they can be opened only by majority vote (or unanimous consent) to permit the latecomers to cast their ballots. You can find important general information on voting in Chapter 8 and on elections in Chapter 14.

Sometimes a group's bylaws prescribe that a vote be by ballot. In this case, changing the form of voting is not in order because a member's right to secrecy can't be compromised even by the unanimous consent of all those in the meeting. Similarly, an election that's required to be conducted by ballot can't be held by a voice vote even if there's only one nominee or candidate because such a change compromises a member's right to cast a write-in vote.

Ballot voting obtains the truest expression of the will of your membership on a question, so when it's prescribed, it must be used.

Six key characteristics of motions related to voting and the polls

A motion related to voting and the polls

- ✔ Can't interrupt a speaker who has the floor
- ✔ Must be seconded
- ✔ Isn't debatable
- ✔ Can be amended
- ✔ Requires a majority vote (except for closing the polls, which requires a two-thirds vote)
- ✔ Can be reconsidered if it's a negative vote on a motion to reopen the polls

Coming up with Candidates: Motions Related to Nominations

There are several possible methods of taking nominations for the offices and positions elected by your membership. I cover these in detail in Chapter 13.

Whenever you need to specify a way to come up with nominees, as you probably will for situations not covered in your bylaws, you use a motion related to the method of nominations. And whenever you want to specify when nominations can be made, you use a motion to *open* or *close* nominations. Collectively, these motions are known as *Motions Related to Nominations*.

Using motions related to nominations

I cover the different methods for nominations as well as the procedures for opening and closing nominations in detail in Chapter 13. But the motion to specify a particular method for nominations or to open or close nominations is about as basic as it gets.

Method of nominations

This example is based on moving to have nominations by committee, but the form is essentially the same for any of the methods. You simply say, "Mr. Chairman, I move that the chair appoint a committee of three to consider and make recommendations on the replacement of Mr. Finkblossom, who has resigned as chairman of the Membership Committee." Whatever the nomination method you propose, just be specific.

Motions to open or close nominations

A motion to *open nominations,* when made by a member, is usually a motion to reopen nominations after they have been closed. (The chair usually just announces the opening of nominations at the appointed time when they are in order.)

A motion to *close nominations* is rarely made by members because it's never in order to make this motion as long as anyone wishes to make a nomination. Also, members rarely move to close nominations because whenever no further nominations are offered, the chair usually just declares, "Hearing no further nominations, nominations for the office of [name the office] are closed."

Six key characteristics of motions related to nominations

A motion relating to nominations

- Can't interrupt a speaker who has the floor
- Must be seconded
- Isn't debatable
- Can be amended
- Requires a majority vote (except the motion to close nominations, which requires a two-thirds vote)
- Can be reconsidered if it's a negative vote to close nominations

I Don't Want To Do This Anymore: Request to Be Excused from a Duty

Sometimes membership requirements involve more than just paying dues. You may be required to complete a service project, serve on a committee, or attend a minimum number of meetings to maintain your membership. If you're an officer or committee chairman, your bylaws probably define some very specific responsibilities and duties for you.

When it becomes difficult, or impossible, for you to fulfill an obligation imposed on you as a member, you can *Request to Be Excused from the Duty;* if the other members agree (and if the bylaws don't provide otherwise), then they can grant your request.

Using the request to be excused from a duty

If you want to be excused from a duty, you may ask for unanimous consent, or the request may be handled by motion and vote.

It's generally in order to make this request any time a motion is being considered that is connected with the duty you're expected to perform.

If you've accepted an office or other position of responsibility, such as that of a committee chairman, and you find yourself unable to properly perform the duties of your office, then you'll probably use this motion in the context of a resignation.

Resignation from office

A *resignation* is a form of request to be excused from duty, and the rules for resignation from office require you to not abandon your duties until your resignation has been accepted or until the members have had a reasonable opportunity to accept it.

Resignation from membership

Resignation from membership is also a form of this motion, but it can't be used to avoid obligations already incurred. If your dues are paid up, you can't be required to continue membership if you choose not to. But if you owe back dues, resignation doesn't relieve you of the obligation to pay amounts that you may owe, and the members aren't under any obligation to accept your resignation until you're current in meeting your obligation.

If you aren't in good standing and your resignation isn't accepted, then it's possible for additional charges to accrue against you.

Six key characteristics of the request to be excused from a duty

A request to be excused from a duty:

  ✔ Can interrupt a speaker who has the floor if the request requires immediate attention

  ✔ Must be seconded (but only if moved formally)

  ✔ Is debatable

  ✔ Can be amended

  ✔ Requires a majority vote

  ✔ Can't be reconsidered if it's an affirmative vote

Is It In Order To . . . ? Parliamentary Inquiry

You may have the sense that something isn't being done according to Hoyle, er, Robert, but you don't want to tip your hand or embarrass yourself by raising a point of order until you're sure. Or, you may want to understand the parliamentary situation better so you can decide whether to make a particular motion. Or, you may want to know the effect of the pending motion.

When you want to know the answer to these kinds of questions, or just whether something going on (or being contemplated) is in order, you should make a *Parliamentary Inquiry.*

Using parliamentary inquiry

To make a parliamentary inquiry, just stand up and state, "Madam President, parliamentary inquiry please."

And Madam President should stop and ask you for your question: "The member will please state his question." You may respond, "Madam president, is it in order to amend this amendment?"

Whatever you need to know, just ask. That's the parliamentary inquiry.

A parliamentary inquiry elicits an *opinion,* not a ruling, from the chair. Because of this, the chair's answer to a parliamentary inquiry is not subject to appeal.

However, if the member, having received the answer to his question, should then raise a point of order, the decision, or *ruling,* of the chair would be subject to appeal.

Six key characteristics of parliamentary inquiry

A parliamentary inquiry

- ✔ Can interrupt a speaker who has the floor
- ✔ Doesn't need to be seconded
- ✔ Isn't debatable
- ✔ Can't be amended
- ✔ Requires that no vote be taken
- ✔ Can't be reconsidered

I Need to Know More: Point of Information

You get to your lodge meeting and the Grand Prancing Reindeer has finished the Oblations to McGillicuddy ritual and moves the admission to the lodge of six new inductees. But you're a practical person, and you know that the admission ritual costs the lodge about $100 per person (to pay for the chocolate syrup and marsh-mallows for the inductees' candy-coating prior to their taking the oath, of course), and, well, before you vote, you want to know how much money is left in the treasury.

Whether it's asking for the cash balance or for some other critical information to help you understand something related to the business before your group (but not related to procedure), you can rise to a *Point of Information* by addressing the chair.

Using point of information

All points of information should be addressed to the chair or through the chair. In the example above, you rise and say, "O Great One, I rise to a point of information."

The Grand Prancing Reindeer replies, "The Young Buck will state his point." You say, "O Great One, your humble supplicant seeks to know how much fodder remains in the manger before voting on admitting the fawns into the barn."

In this case, you're really asking the Exalted High Grainkeeper (treasurer), but the correct form for the inquiry is to direct your question to the chair. So the chair would properly respond here with, "The Exalted High Grainkeeper will report the height of the grain in the bin."

In any event, the goal of this motion is to get information. When you have the information you seek, business can proceed.

Sometimes members think that a point of information is a procedure used to give information to the chair. That's just plain wrong — it would be a sneaky way to debate your point. If you really want to "give" information using this method, you at least have to arrange your information in the form of a question. In the example given above, your goal may be not so much to find out how much money is in the treasury as to inform the group that the ritual is expensive and costs must be considered. Either way, the point of information is about getting, not giving, information.

Six key characteristics of point of information

A request for information

- ✔ Can interrupt a speaker who has the floor
- ✔ Doesn't need to be seconded
- ✔ Isn't debatable
- ✔ Can't be amended
- ✔ Requires no vote be taken
- ✔ Can't be reconsidered

Other Requests and Inquiries

The last incidental motions in the list make it possible to handle, in an orderly manner, just about anything that may be requested. Two specific situations, which are covered in Robert's Rules and which I discuss briefly in the sections that follow, are

- ✔ Request to Withdraw a Motion
- ✔ Request to Read Papers

Any other requests, such as a request to address the membership when no other business is pending, are generally best handled informally by general consent. But the members should always be allowed the final say on whether to grant any request at all.

What was I thinking? Request to withdraw a motion

There may come a time when you make a motion that turns out to be just a bad idea; you don't really want it to be considered, but that motion has been stated by the chair and now technically belongs to the group. In situations like this, a special request is available only to you as the maker of the motion. You can request that the motion be withdrawn (or changed).

Using the request to withdraw a motion

You take advantage of this privilege simply by getting the recognition of the chair and making your request by saying, "Mr. Chairman, I request permission to withdraw my motion."

The chair can put the question if he receives a second, or he can just announce that you have made the request and ask for general consent.

Additional information

If the request to withdraw your motion is granted, the parliamentary situation is no different than if the motion hadn't been made in the first place, so your motion can be made again at the same meeting.

Just let me read this: Request to read papers

As a means of protecting a group from any member who wants to read a lengthy item in connection with debate on a motion, it's out of order to "read papers" if anybody objects, unless the permission of the group is obtained.

Robert's Rules recognizes that sometimes a quick excerpt of some factual material may be pertinent and acceptable, so reading papers isn't expressly forbidden. But it must be done with the consent of the members.

Using the request to read papers

If you think that the members need to have some information that would require you to read something, state that you "have something you'd like to read if no one objects." You should tell the group what the material is and how long it is, too.

If someone objects, the chair asks the members, "Ms. Smart would like to read [state the item]. What is the pleasure of the assembly?"

If the members agree to listen, read your material. If they don't agree, don't try to force it. It's just not worth the price of their goodwill.

Additional information

This rule can't be used to limit the ability to have material that is before the group for adoption read during consideration. Reading from papers generally refers to reading material with the purpose of bolstering a position in debate. If the question is on the adoption of a report or resolution, you should expect to have the report or resolution read aloud so you'll know exactly what it is you're voting on.

Six key characteristics of requests and inquiries

A request or inquiry

- Can interrupt a speaker who has the floor if immediate attention is required

- Must be seconded (but a motion to grant someone else's request doesn't need to be seconded).

- Isn't debatable

- Can't be amended

- Requires a majority vote

- Can be reconsidered except for an affirmative vote on a request to withdraw a motion

Chapter 12

Haven't We Talked About This Already? Motions Which Bring a Question Again Before the Assembly

● ●

In This Chapter

▶ Revisiting and changing previously made decisions

▶ Removing motions from the hands of committees

▶ Taking motions off the back burner

● ●

*N*o matter what your group's final vote is on a motion, sometimes you have second thoughts. In some cases, you want to revisit a decision made during a current meeting, and other times you want (or need) to take a second look at something decided several months ago.

But although your group needs to be able to change or reverse its decisions, you don't want to make the process too easy. After all, everyone would get very frustrated if one or two votes one way or the other kept your group forever voting and revoting, going back and forth so that nothing ever really got settled.

Luckily, Robert's Rules has a set of motions designed to let you revisit decisions without letting those revisits getting out of hand. Throughout this chapter, I discuss the *Motions Which Bring a Question Again Before the Assembly* (that's a mouthful!) and how to use them to reexamine decisions in an efficient and orderly way.

Been There, Done That!

Among all the rules in Robert's Rules, few are more important than those that prevent somebody from incessantly requiring your group to vote over and over on essentially the same motion.

Imagine how little you'd ever get done if, right after you spend an hour discussing your organization's budget and vote to adopt it, Ms. Maxie Jawbone (who tried to second guess the Finance Committee on every third line item) makes a motion that the budget be opened back up for discussion and requires you to take your time going over every second line item this time around.

Or suppose you've just voted to refer a motion to reroof the clubhouse to committee to get bids and report recommendations back in two months. After all is settled, a member remembers that his cousin is a roofer, and the member wants to make a motion to just let his cousin go ahead and fix the roof next weekend (being as he needs the work and is available). If members could get away with making motions that require you to rehash a decision you just made, you'd never get anything done.

These examples illustrate the need for a couple of basic principles of parliamentary law aimed to keep the minority from controlling things by wearing down the majority. These principles are

- ✔ After you've disposed of a motion (Motion A), it's not in order to entertain another motion (Motion B) that proposes essentially the same question as the one already decided (Motion A) unless you're using one of the procedures I discuss in this chapter.

- ✔ Changing something that's already been decided shouldn't be as easy as making the decision in the first place. Depending on the situation, Robert's Rules places restrictions on who can ask that a decision be revoted on in the same meeting, and the parliamentary authority requires a higher vote, a notice, or maybe both a higher vote *and* a notice for motions revisited in later meetings.

Whatever the situation, most of the time when you decide something, you've done all the talking you need to do and you're ready to move on. But that's not always the case.

Later in a meeting, new information can come up that affects a decision your group has already made. Or something may change over time, and old procedures just no longer work.

Robert's Rules gives you a way to revisit the questions and change your collective mind. General Robert was an engineer, and he wisely provided a means for your group to dig itself out of a hole without getting too muddy in the process. Whatever the situation, the right tool is found in the *Motions Which Bring a Question Again Before the Assembly*. These motions are

- Reconsider

- Rescind or Amend Something Previously Adopted

- Discharge a Committee

- Take from the Table

Table 12-1 provides a short rundown of situations in which you use these motions.

Table 12-1 When to Use the Motions Which Bring a Question Again Before the Assembly

If You Want to . . .	Then Use . . .
Revote on something you voted on in this meeting	Reconsider
Repeal (or strike out) a motion that has been adopted	Rescind Something Previously Adopted
Make a change to (or amend) a motion that has been adopted	Amend Something Previously Adopted
Take a referred motion out of the hands of a committee	Discharge a Committee
Revote on something you voted on in this meeting	Reconsider
Resume considering a motion you laid on the table	Take from the Table

I discuss each of these motions in detail in the following sections of this chapter.

Wait, I'm Having Second Thoughts: Reconsider

You've probably been in a meeting in which a vote was taken and a motion was disposed of, but even though you voted the way of the majority, that little voice inside started nagging at you. Maybe the decision was made without enough information, or perhaps it just wasn't well thought-out. It's possible that the decision was just made in too much of a hurry. Whatever the reason, you realize that maybe it would be a good idea for the group to go back and take a second look at that motion.

If you voted on the prevailing side in a case like this, you can ask the group to revisit the same motion in the same meeting by making the motion to *Reconsider.* If the majority agrees to discuss the original motion some more, then it adopts the motion to reconsider. At the appropriate time, the chair can open the floor for debate on the original motion as if it had not been voted on at all.

Understanding "reconsider" as a parliamentary term

All of the motions in the class of motions which bring a question again before the assembly assist your group in revisiting previously considered motions. For this reason, you may find that members may talk about reconsidering a motion when they really want to rescind or amend something previously adopted. Or they may just want to renew a motion that failed in an earlier meeting. Using the word "reconsider" in a generic sense in a parliamentary situation can cause problems.

The motion to reconsider is a distinct parliamentary motion! When you use the word "reconsider" in a parliamentary situation, it refers only to this specific motion.

The motion to reconsider poses the question, "Shall we give further consideration to a motion already voted on?" The motion is subject to some unique limitations:

- ✔ It must be made on the same day (or on the next day if the session is more than one day) as the meeting in which the motion to be reconsidered was decided.

- ✔ It must be made by a person who voted on the prevailing side of the motion to be reconsidered.

The motion to reconsider is *not* the same as the motion that is to be reconsidered. The former is the parliamentary motion that's the subject of this section. The latter is the motion that is the object of the motion to reconsider.

Using the motion to reconsider

Suppose your business networking group voted earlier in your meeting to bestow its coveted Silver Tongue Award on Farley Motormouth, the local radio announcer known as the Voice of the Hometown Niners, your city's minor-league baseball team. What an honor! You were among the rather large majority who voted in favor of giving the award to Motormouth.

Then, during a short recess in the meeting, Charlie Frumpdiddle hands you the evening paper, and there on the front page is a photo of ol' Farley being hauled out of the baseball stadium in handcuffs. He's accused of saying something nice about the Swamp City Puddle Jumpers, the archrival of the Hometown Niners.

That does it. You like Farley, and he may be a fine guy, but if he says something nice about those no-good Puddle Jumpers from across the county line, he's not gonna get that award if you have anything to say about it.

So, when the meeting reconvenes after the recess and the president starts to recognize the next speaker on whatever business is pending, you take the first opportunity available to stand up and get recognized by the chair. You say, "Mr. President, I voted with the prevailing side for the motion to give the Silver Tongue Award to Farley Motormouth, and I move to reconsider the vote taken earlier this evening." Of course, your friend Charlie Frumpdiddle hardly misses a beat when he calls out, "Second!"

Notice that you voted on the prevailing side. In this case, if you had voted against the motion, you wouldn't be allowed to make a motion to reconsider. That's a rule that keeps the losers from just using the motion in a dilatory manner to wear down the majority.

Knowing the rules, the chair says, "The motion to reconsider the vote on awarding Farley Motormouth the Silver Tongue Award has been made and seconded. Discussion on the motion to reconsider isn't in order at this time, but the motion to reconsider can be called up when no other business is pending." So, he doesn't ask the members to vote on whether to reconsider just yet. Instead, he proceeds with the pending business. Later, when nothing else is pending, you or someone else can *call up* the motion to reconsider.

Waiting for the right time to reconsider

Because of the nature of the motion to reconsider, it's not always appropriate to consider it at the same time it is made. In other words, reconsider isn't a privileged motion (flip back to Chapter 10 for more information on privileged motions). It's important that the members know that someone has had second thoughts, even though the time may not be right for a discussion. As a result, you can make the motion anytime, but you can't actually talk about reconsidering except when no immediately pending motion is on the floor.

Calling up the motion to reconsider

Your motion to reconsider is *called up* by any member at any appropriate time (and doesn't need to be seconded) by saying, "Mr. Chairman, I call up the motion to reconsider the vote on bestowing the Silver Tongue Award on Farley Motormouth."

Even though anyone can call up your motion to reconsider, you're entitled to have the reconsideration called up at whatever time you think best. Robert's Rules gives you that privilege.

Whenever the motion to reconsider is called up, however, that's when you have the chance to speak about Farley's indiscretion and why you made the motion to reconsider. But you need to be prepared for the possibility that other members may want to leave things as they are and therefore may argue against reconsideration.

Even so, the thing to recognize here is that when you're discussing reconsideration, you're not discussing whether to give the Silver Tongue Award to Farley. You're just discussing whether to vote again on the motion to make the award.

A special form of reconsider: Reconsider and Enter on the Minutes

Suppose a motion is made in a meeting in which the group in attendance is not at all representative of the usual attendance. Maybe you're near the end of the meeting and several members have left. You still have a quorum, but the usual minority is now in the majority. Your favorite malcontent, Hugo Chump, moves to direct the treasurer to transfer the group's funds to his investment brokerage company. You, along with the few good members who know better, are appalled, but you don't have the votes to stop Hugo's motion. What do you do?

By using the motion to *Reconsider and Enter on the Minutes,* you can prevent Hugo's motion (if it's adopted) from being put into effect until the more representative membership is again present to make a final decision.

As with the basic motion to reconsider, you have to have voted on the prevailing side to make the motion to reconsider and enter on the minutes, so you may have to hold your nose and cast your vote in favor of Hugo's motion. And you still need a second. But after you make this motion, the action to transfer the money is on hold, and the other members have a chance to be informed of the issue so they can arrange to attend the next meeting. At that meeting, you can call up the motion to reconsider and hopefully undo Hugo's little shenanigan.

In a few departures from the usual rules for reconsider, the motion to reconsider and enter on the minutes

- ✔ Can only be moved on the same day that the motion to be reconsidered was voted upon

- ✔ Outranks the regular motion to reconsider

- ✔ Can be applied only to motions finally disposed of, such as motions that are adopted, that fail, or that are postponed indefinitely (see Chapter 9)

- ✔ Can't be applied to a motion if the object of the motion would be harmed by the delay of a day (for example, a motion to hire a limousine to pick up the guest speaker at the airport tomorrow morning)

- ✔ Can't be moved at the last meeting of a session if the next business meeting will not be held within a *quarterly time interval* (see Appendix A)

- ✔ Can't be called up on the day the motion's made, unless it's made on the last day of a session and called up at a later meeting on that same day

More considerations on the motion to reconsider

Here are a few more details you need to know to properly use the motion to *reconsider:*

✔ **Applicability to motions originally adopted by unanimous consent:** If the motion you want to reconsider was adopted by unanimous consent, then anybody can move to reconsider it because of a presumption that all the members were on the prevailing side.

✔ **Suspension of action authorized by a motion to be reconsidered:** As long as a motion to reconsider is made, even if it hasn't been called up and acted on, it suspends any authority to carry out the action ordered by the motion that is to be reconsidered.

✔ **Rules for debate on a motion being reconsidered:** Debate on a motion being reconsidered is subject to the following rules:

• If reconsideration of a motion is taken up on the same day, members who used all their debate time when the original motion was considered can't debate without permission of the group. (But because they can debate on the motion to reconsider, they will probably have had their say anyway!)

• If reconsideration of a motion is taken up on the next day, a member's right to debate is not affected by his participation in debate on the previous day.

✔ **Using the motion to reconsider in committees:** A motion to reconsider, when used in a committee

• Isn't subject to the usual time limitations. It can be made at any time, even several days or weeks later. And a motion can be reconsidered as often as the committee chooses.

• Can be moved by any committee member, who didn't vote on the losing side.

• Requires a two-thirds vote to adopt unless all the members who voted on the prevailing side are present or were notified that the motion to reconsider would be made.

Six key characteristics of the motion to reconsider

The motion to reconsider

✔ Can interrupt a speaker who has the floor before he begins to speak (It is, however, in order to make a motion to reconsider when other business is pending, but dealing with the motion can't interrupt pending business — that part of the process must wait until nothing else is pending.)

   ✔ Must be seconded

   ✔ Is debatable if the motion being reconsidered is debatable

   ✔ Can't be amended

   ✔ Requires a majority vote

   ✔ Can't be reconsidered

Should We Really Have Done That? Rescind or Amend Something Previously Adopted

Nothing is forever, and in the world of clubs and organizations, that's especially true. Last year's good idea can turn into this year's problem. But thanks to General Robert's wisdom and foresight, you always have a way out!

Using the motion to *Rescind* or to *Amend Something Previously Adopted,* you can undo, or change, any decision made by your group in the past.

   ✔ The motion to *Rescind* (or repeal or annul) is used to cancel a motion altogether.

   ✔ The motion to *Amend Something Previously Adopted* is used to make a change to a motion either by making a simple change or two, or by substituting something else in its place.

Using the motion to rescind or to amend something previously adopted

Motions to rescind or to amend something previously adopted are more common than you may think. More often than not, they're used to make policy changes. After all, policy is adopted by motion and vote, so if you want to change the policy or vacate it, then you need to do so by motion and vote. When using the motions to rescind or amend, keep in mind

   ✔ The vote required, which is determined by whether there has been previous notice of the motion

   ✔ Whether any proposed amendments are within the scope of your notice

Vote requirements

Three possible variations of vote requirements allow you to rescind or to amend something previously adopted:

- ✔ **Two-thirds vote without previous notice:** Suppose your organization adopts a budget proposed by the Finance Committee, which provided for an increase in the salary of your executive director. Then, later, when new business is being considered, Ernest Pennypincher proposes to roll back all spending to last year's budget amounts. Because this motion would have the effect of rescinding the budget just adopted, it requires a two-thirds vote.

- ✔ **Majority vote with previous notice:** But what if Ernie, instead of making the motion during this meeting, just gives notice that he will make the motion at the next meeting? Well, when the motion comes up at that later meeting, it can be adopted by a majority vote.

  The switch from a two-thirds to a majority vote may make a big difference because it could be easier to get a majority vote than to get a two-thirds vote. The equalizer is the requirement for notice. Because both sides of an issue have the chance to rally their troops and campaign for the result they want, the factor of previous notice reduces the requirement for a two-thirds vote.

- ✔ **Majority of the entire membership:** In a situation in which there's no notice, a motion to rescind or to amend something previously adopted can be adopted if it receives the affirmative vote of a majority of the entire membership.

  You may be thinking that receiving this type of vote is an impossible requirement anyway, so what good is this last option really? After all, you've probably never even had a majority of the entire membership attend a single meeting at the same time anyway. But consider the option's application in a small board. Suppose that you have a board of 15 members, and 13 are present at your meeting. A two-thirds vote requires 9 votes, but a majority of the entire membership is only 8. So, sometimes it's easier to achieve a majority of the entire membership than it is to get a two-thirds vote.

Scope of notice

Suppose that your group decides to raise the amount of annual dues (which, in this example, isn't fixed in your bylaws, but rather is decided from time to time by the membership). To keep from having to meet a two-thirds vote requirement, you gave previous notice at the last meeting (or in the call to the meeting) that this meeting would see a motion to raise the dues to $50 per year (up from $35).

When you gave the notice to make a motion to raise dues to $50, your notice covered any increase you might actually wind up with up to $50. Any number over $35 up to $50 is said to be within the *scope of the notice* and can be adopted by a *majority vote* because notice was given to raise dues to $50. But raising the dues any higher than $50 (or lowering them below $35) doesn't qualify as being within the scope of notice. So you need a two-thirds vote to change the dues to some amount less than $35 or greater than $50.

Some rules carry stricter requirements for amending or rescinding. According to Robert's Rules, amending bylaws or special rules of order requires previous notice *and* a two-thirds vote. This require-ment is based on the premise that rules like bylaws and special rules of order must, by definition, be very stable from session to session. Members are entitled to notice of any proposed change and to have rules that can't be changed in the face of opposition from a minority greater than one-third.

Knowing what motions you can't rescind or amend

Some motions can't be amended or rescinded. They are

- ✔ **Motions subject to being called up for reconsideration.** Using rescind or amend is unnecessary if you can simply reconsider a vote.

- ✔ **Motions that have already been carried out and that cannot be undone.** If you voted to repaint the church, it's too late to rescind the motion after the church has been repainted.

- ✔ **Motions to accept resignations or actions electing or expelling a person from membership or office** (if the member is present or has been notified). After a resignation has been accepted or a membership terminated by expulsion, the resign-ing or expelled person can only be reinstated by following the procedures for admitting them to membership or for election to office. Rescinding an election requires either a provision in the bylaws or the following of specific procedures for removal from office, which I cover in Chapter 18.

Six key characteristics of the motion to rescind or to amend something previously adopted

A motion to rescind or to amend something previously adopted:

- ✔ Can't interrupt a speaker who has the floor
- ✔ Must be seconded
- ✔ Is debatable
- ✔ Can be amended
- ✔ Requires a two-thirds vote without notice, a majority vote with notice, or a majority of the entire membership with no notice
- ✔ Can be reconsidered if it fails

Okay, We'll Take It from Here: Discharge a Committee

After your group refers a matter a committee, the matter is no longer in the hands of the group but rather is under the committee's control. According to Robert's Rules, it's not in order for your group to act on business that's currently in the hands of a committee.

But sometimes the group needs to take charge again, and the motion to *Discharge a Committee* is the way to bring the motion back to the assembly for further action.

Using the motion to discharge a committee

The motion to discharge a committee is used in two general situations:

- ✔ When the committee to which a motion has been referred has failed to report as instructed or in a timely manner
- ✔ When the matter referred to the committee needs immediate action by the entire group

In both situations, the motion to discharge a committee requires a two-thirds vote. (According to Robert's Rules, this motion is generally considered to be a form of the motion to rescind or to amend something previously adopted. See the section "Should We Really Have Done That? Rescind or Amend Something Previously Adopted," earlier in this chapter.)

In a situation where it's possible to reconsider a vote referring a matter to a committee, it's more efficient to use reconsideration and simply reverse the motion to commit because reversal can be achieved by majority vote. (For more information on the motion to reconsider, flip to the section "Wait, I'm Having Second Thoughts: Reconsider," earlier in this chapter.)

Depending on whether you're dealing with a special committee or a standing committee (see Chapter 16), you make the motion to discharge a committee by using the following forms:

- **Special committee:** "Madam Chairman, I move the special committee to plan a spring picnic be discharged."

- **Standing committee:** "Madam Chairman, I move that the Meeting Arrangements Committee be discharged from further consideration of the proposed conference in July."

In placing the motion before your group, your presiding officer takes a rising vote because the motion requires a two-thirds vote for adoption. If the motion passes and the committee is discharged, the chair immediately places the motion that had been referred to the committee on the floor by saying, "There being two-thirds in the affirmative, the committee is discharged. The question is on the motion to have a club picnic this spring. The committee reports it has secured the clubhouse at Lakewood Acres park for June 7. All those in favor rise. . . ."

After a special committee makes its final report (discharge is automatic in this case — no motion is required) or is discharged by motion by your group, the committee ceases to exist. The matter it was handling is then immediately in the hands of your group unless the motion to discharge the committee established a particular time to take up the committee's report and recommendations.

Six key characteristics of the motion to discharge a committee

A motion to discharge a committee

- Can't interrupt a speaker who has the floor
- Must be seconded
- Is debatable
- Can be amended

✔ Requires a two-thirds vote without notice, a majority vote with notice, or a majority of the entire membership with no notice (Exception: A committee can be discharged by a majority vote without notice if the committee has failed to report by the time required in its instructions, or whenever the assembly is considering its partial report.)

✔ Can be reconsidered if it fails

What's That We Left on the Table? Take from the Table

In Chapter 9, I discuss the motion to *Lay on the Table,* the highest-ranking subsidiary motion. This motion is used to temporarily set aside a pending main motion, permitting something else to be addressed or done.

In most cases, the "something else" carries a sense of urgency, such as the need to allow your guest speaker to address your group at a particular time without compromising her schedule. However, whatever the reason for placing something on the table, after the more urgent matter has been attended to, it's in order to take the motion from the table and resume consideration of it at the point where you left off. But taking the motion from the table requires a motion and a second; otherwise the chair may properly advance to the next item of business.

If no motion to *Take from the Table* is made, or if the chair doesn't assume the motion and obtain unanimous consent to resume where you left off, you can still move to take from the table any item that lies on the table. The only requirement is that you make the motion by the end of the next regular business session of your group (unless you meet less frequently than quarterly, in which case you must make the motion before your current meeting adjourns).

Using the motion to take from the table

Suppose you're in a meeting of your professional association, which is considering a resolution to take a position in support of increasing statutory continuing education requirements being considered by your state legislature. Your group's debate has been heated and has gone on longer than you anticipated, and your guest speaker is running on a tight schedule. You aren't finished with the debate on the motion, but you needed to let your speaker make her presentation. So, you adopt the motion to lay on the table the question on the resolution.

Making the motion

The speaker concludes her presentation, and the president announces the next item of business on the agenda. If you're ready to get back to work on that continuing education resolution, rise and say, "Mr. Chairman, I rise to move to take from the table the resolution on continuing professional education."

It is in order, and remains in order, to move to take from the table as long as you haven't yet moved on to a new class of business, such as going from "unfinished business" into "new business." But if you wait too long and have moved on from the class of business that gave rise to the motion, you can take the resolution from the table only at the appropriate time in the next business meeting, or by moving to *Suspend the Rules and Take from the Table* (see Chapter 11 for information on this incidental motion) to take something out of its proper order.

Obtaining recognition

Because this motion to take from the table enables the assembly to resume consideration of an undecided question, and because time limits on its use are in place, whoever rises to offer the motion is entitled to preference in recognition by the chair.

That being the case, you can make the motion to take from the table even if another speaker has the floor. You simply seek recognition at any time up until the chair states the question on another item of business.

The presiding officer should give you preference in recognition for the purpose of making this motion because it's generally desirable to finish dealing with a motion that hasn't been disposed of before going on to something else. But after consideration of another motion has begun (by being stated by the chair), you must wait for the next lull in the proceedings before you can move to take from the table.

Even though a motion that's laid on the table dies if it's not taken from the table by the next regular business meeting, it can be brought up again by just renewing the motion. Therefore, if you can't get back to a motion that lies on the table via the motion to take from the table, it's not usually a big deal except when time is critical.

When you can't take from the table

It's generally in order to move to take a motion from the table just about any time motions in the same class are in order. But if a series of motions needs to be handled, the motion to take from the table can't be made. This situation may occur

- ✔ When you've voted to suspend the rules to allow the introduction of another main motion

- ✔ When a motion has just been laid on the table expressly to allow consideration of another motion

- ✔ When your group has rescinded a previous motion to allow a conflicting motion to be made and considered

- ✔ When a main motion has been voted down because a member said that if it was voted down, he'd offer a particular motion to handle an issue in a better or more acceptable way

Six key characteristics of the motion to take from the table

A motion to take from the table

- ✔ Can't interrupt a speaker who has the floor
- ✔ Must be seconded
- ✔ Isn't debatable
- ✔ Can't be amended
- ✔ Requires a majority vote
- ✔ Can't be reconsidered

Part III
Getting Involved in Leadership

The 5th Wave   By Rich Tennant

"I told you not to miss so many
'Angry Villager Meetings'."

In this part . . .

The surest way to build a successful organization is first to understand the officers' roles and duties and then to put the right people into office. It's also important that each member be willing to take his or her turn in service to the organization. But the willingness to serve is only half the job. When you accept a leadership position, you have to know your duties and perform them with dedication to the goals of the organization.

The first two chapters in this part discuss the procedures for nominations, elections, and appointments to leadership positions. In the next two chapters, I make recommendations on how to choose the right leaders and how to work together. The next chapter contains the fundamentals of communicating your leadership activities to the members so they're not just sitting around wondering what you've done between meetings. And finally, in this part, I tell you how to get rid of the deadheads and arrogant, self-important do-nothings (if you're unlucky enough to have elected one or more of them in the first place).

Chapter 13

Who's Going to Do the Work? Following Nomination Procedures

***

In This Chapter

▶ Understanding why nominations are necessary

▶ Using different nomination methods in different situations

***

*G*etting the right leaders for your organization isn't always easy. One of the biggest problems in this area is that the person who's great at getting elected isn't necessarily the best person for the job.

Your membership has to live with its mistakes, even if that means operating under poor leaders. The best way to avoid this type of mistake, however, is to have a system for selecting leadership that puts the right people at the front of the line. In Robert's Rules, *nominations* are the tools for setting up that system. The types of nominations in Robert's Rules are

- ✓ Nominations by the chair
- ✓ Nominations from the floor
- ✓ Nominations by a committee
- ✓ Nominations by ballot
- ✓ Nominations by mail
- ✓ Nominations by petition

I go over nominations in detail throughout this chapter, and I help you determine which types to use in certain meeting situations.

I list the six nomination methods in the order Robert's Rules provides for them to be voted on if all six were proposed in a motion to prescribe a method for nominations. Even though I've never run into such a situation, I wanted to cover that arcane point of order just in case you're on a big money TV quiz show and the question comes up.

Nominations by the Chair

This method is used whenever the membership wants to rely on the presiding officer to recommend candidates but also wants to reserve to itself (or its designee — such as the board of directors) the approval of the nominee. This method is applicable when

- Appointing members to committees, if specified in the motion creating the committee, or if prescribed in the bylaws
- Electing a presiding officer in a mass meeting

A member wishing to use this type of nomination method includes it in the motion to establish the committee. For example, "Mr. Chairman, I move that a committee of five be appointed to study and recommend on the contract, the members of the committee to be elected from nominations made by the chair."

An example of a bylaw prescribing the method might read: "The president shall appoint the members of all the standing committees (except the Nominating Committee) subject to the approval of the board of directors."

Nominations from the Floor

Sometimes called *open nominations,* this method is probably the most familiar. It's used in the vast majority of situations where members elect their officers at a meeting. Even if a Nominating Committee is in place, under Robert's Rules, nominations from the floor are in order at some point before the election is pending.

Opening the floor for nominations

Your group's rules and customs determine the time at which floor nominations are accepted. Sometimes nominations aren't taken until the election is pending, and sometimes they're taken at other times, such as at a meeting before the election meeting.

Unless the bylaws contain a specific rule about nominations, the privilege to deal with floor nomination procedures is reserved to the assembly. The assembly may tailor its nomination procedures to any particular situation it may encounter by using the procedures for handling incidental *motions related to nominations,* which I cover in Chapter 11. The assembly's privilege to determine its nomination procedure is important, and you need to keep that privilege in mind when a question comes up about whether nominations could or should be made.

Depending on your organization's bylaws, special rules of order, or the rules you decide on during any pending election, nominations from the floor may be taken for each office just before the election for that office, or they may be taken for all offices before any elections take place. In either case, the default order for taking nominations is the order in which offices are listed in your bylaws.

To open nominations from the floor, the chair declares, "Nominations are now in order for the office of Top Banana. Are there nominations for Top Banana?"

Handling nominations from the floor

After each nomination, the chair repeats the name as having been nominated. For example, he may say, "Cletus Potzbius has been nominated. Are there further nominations?"

The process of making floor nominations is subject to the following rules:

- ✔ **Recognition by the chair is not required to make a nomination.** A member may call out a nomination while remaining seated. However, in larger organizations, calling nominations from your seat is usually impractical. In such cases, members may adopt a more formal nomination process either by rule or by the adoption of an incidental motion for that particular meeting or election.

- ✔ **Nominations don't have to be seconded, but it's not out of order for members to second a nomination to signal their endorsement.**

- ✔ **A member shouldn't offer more than one nomination to a position if there are several seats for the same office — such as for nominees to a board or a committee — until all other members have had the opportunity to make nominations.** However, if a member does make more nominations before others have had their chance, his additional nominations aren't out of order unless someone objects to his actions.

✔ **If the bylaws don't prohibit it, a person can be nominated for more than one office and can even serve in more than one office if elected.** However, if the bylaws do prohibit, then either the nominee or the electors must choose one office among multiple nominations. I discuss the options for handling this situation in Chapter 14, where I cover the election process.

✔ **Nominations are taken for successive offices in the order they're listed in the bylaws.**

Closing nominations

According to Robert's Rules, motions to close nominations are usually unnecessary because the nomination process simply continues until no one wishes to make further nominations. When the nominations stop, the chair just declares nominations closed.

But before he makes such a declaration, he's obligated to be sure no more nominations are forthcoming. This obligation may be the source of another misunderstanding that many people have about closing nominations: A presiding officer must call for nominations three times before declaring them closed. To set the record straight, *no such rule exists,* but the practice isn't completely unreasonable because it establishes a good way to make sure that no further nominations are forthcoming.

Hey, don't slam the door on nominations!

One of the serious misunderstandings I often encounter about closing nominations is the notion that they can be closed in such a manner as to prevent any further opportunity for making additional nominations.

More often than I'd like to hear about, loyal supporters of a particular candidate attempt to close nominations as a strategy to keep opposition candidates off a ballot.

Even if they're successful at slamming the door on other nominees (by commanding a two-thirds vote to close and overruling the chair that the motion is out of order), these supporters can't keep a write-in vote from being entered on a ballot, so they don't accomplish much but to create acrimony. (Chapter 14 contains more information about write-in votes.)

In any event, closing nominations is out of order when anyone remains wishing to nominate. And even when properly closed (by a two-thirds vote after no one wishes to make additional nominations), a majority vote is all it takes to reopen nominations.

Suppressing nominations is not only out of order as long as anyone wants to add to the list, but it also wastes a lot of time and is a futile strategy.

Still, some presiding officers think there's some magic to uttering the call three times, and in their partisan haste to effect a closure of nominations for political reasons, they babble out the phrase three times and declare nominations closed all in one breath. When you hear that happening, you can be sure that the presiding officer either doesn't know the rules or is using his position to thwart the nomination process.

From a practical standpoint, it serves no purpose to attempt to declare nominations closed if members want to continue making nominations, because, after all, nominations don't elect! So why would any self-respecting presiding officer give up his appearance of impartiality by trying to suppress nominations? Perhaps he just wants to make points with a large faction. But by pushing to close nominations, he reveals that he's unable to discharge his duties with impartiality, which is a serious breach of duty.

According to Robert's Rules, a motion to close nominations is out of order *as long as any member wishes to make a nomination.*

Nominations by a Committee

In even the smallest local organization, the use of a Nominating Committee to assemble a list of willing and qualified candidates for office can greatly benefit members when the time comes to select their leaders.

If the committee does its job well, the membership can enjoy some basic assurance that the candidates nominated have at least expressed interest in the job, have agreed to serve, and are qualified for the offices for which they're nominated.

Selecting the committee

The more broad-based the selection of the Nominating Committee, the more confidence the membership will have in its recommendations. For that reason, it's most advisable for the committee to be elected by the general membership or the executive board, rather than be appointed by the president or chair.

In fact, Robert's Rules specifically advises against allowing a sitting president to have any influence over the Nominating Committee by recommending bylaw provisions to prohibit him from being the appointing power or from serving ex-officio as one of the committee's members.

Working on the committee

A Nominating Committee's service is most useful if its job is to report a single nominee for each office or position to be filled. That way, it can focus on identifying, in its considered judgment, the best available candidate to serve in a particular position.

Sometimes, the bylaws require a Nominating Committee to nominate more than one candidate per office, probably because somebody thought there should always be a contest for elections. But a Nominating Committee can defeat the intent of such a bylaw by nominating its preferred candidate along with a surefire loser. So, Robert's Rules calls such bylaw requirements unsound, and I agree!

If your organization uses a Nominating Committee, pay attention to this section. The committee's duty is of paramount importance because its decisions can truly have the most far-reaching effects of any decision made by a board, committee, or officer.

Learning about your rules

Like any other committee, the Nominating Committee is subject to all the procedural rules that apply to committees. (I discuss committees in detail in Chapter 16).

Depending on your organization's rules, the authority that created the Nominating Committee may have appointed your chairman, or you may have to elect your own chairman. If your chairman hasn't been selected at the time the committee is appointed, then your first order of business is to elect your chairman. The chairman is responsible for conducting business according to proper form; she should make it her immediate personal goal to become informed of the full duties of a committee chairman, to ensure the committee can discharge its duty without ever giving any appearance of impartiality or impropriety.

A Nominating Committee should conduct all deliberations in in-person meetings. To afford itself maximum accord, all members should be present for all deliberations. It isn't unusual for the committee to have several meetings before reporting to the membership, so your first meeting should be called as soon as possible after the committee's appointment.

Although it's possible to conduct some committee business outside of meetings and correspond by e-mail, your Nominating Committee shouldn't be a "committee of correspondence." The subject of your discussions will be people and their fitness for certain jobs — take my advice and keep that out of e-mail! The committee must maintain its integrity and hold the trust of the membership, two things that may be in jeopardy if the content of your discussions falls into the wrong hands.

Nominating Committee meetings may certainly be casual, but they should always be conducted in such a way that no member is denied full expression in the presence of the others.

Getting down to business

The first stage of a Nominating Committee's work is carried out as a series of steps to

1. **Identify potential candidates.**

2. **Identify the best candidates.**

3. **Agree on a nominee and *then* determine his willingness to serve.**

The immediate need at the first meeting is to assemble a preliminary working list of names for consideration. However, persons who are being considered for nomination should *not* be contacted until they're the first choice for nomination.

If the committee is nominating to fill several seats on a board, it should prioritize its choices and contact them in order of preference until the number of accepting nominees is the same as the number of the seats to be filled.

The committee should refrain from making any inquiry of any candidate or prospective candidate until the committee is in agreement that the candidate will be placed on the ballot if they accept the nomination. Courtesy inquiries are neither necessary nor appropriate; if the committee would almost certainly not recommend an individual for service, then inquiring about the person's willingness to serve is of no useful purpose.

Considering incumbents

The Nominating Committee's duty to the membership is to recommend the candidates who are believed to be the best for the organization. For this reason, no requirement says that incumbents must be nominated. Maturity, experience, leadership ability, good judgment, commitment to the organization, attitude toward service, ability to work with others, and personal dependability are important qualities for candidates. Unfortunately, not all incumbents will have demonstrated a capacity to serve the organization.

The same is true for members who have served in other leadership positions or been active in committees. The Nominating Committee has no obligation to nominate anyone because they're simply willing to serve or because they have made a good first impression. In fact, you can probably look to your own experience to know that appearances can be deceiving, and impressive candidates have the potential to be big disappointments.

The committee's obligation is to nominate those who are best suited to serve your organization. Period.

Contacting your first choices for nomination

After an initial list of acceptable candidates has been assembled, committee members should make the initial contacts as soon as possible. The inquiry should be short and simple: "If nominated for the office of Exhausted High Steamblower, would you accept?"

A candidate who hasn't served before may have questions or concerns about what service involves. Your bylaws establish your meeting schedule and the duties of the different officers and directors. Information about the frequency and location of meetings will be important to the candidate and should be disclosed. Also be prepared to discuss the job requirements frankly with your nominee.

Finalizing the list

At the second meeting of your committee, review each name and corresponding inquiry response. The initial list will be shortened as you remove from consideration those who declined or even those who agreed to serve but whose answers may have raised doubts about their fitness (for example, "Well, yes, if you can't get somebody else!" or "Sure thing! I'd like to let you folks know how to really run an organization!").

At each meeting, additional names may be considered for the final list, and new information or developments may be considered on names previously added or removed.

During the committee's deliberations, members should keep *all* discussions confidential. Although advice or information may be sought from current leadership, care should be taken to avoid premature announcements or publication of your working list.

Seeking insight and advice from current and past leaders

If you're following Robert's Rules, then your president should not be on your Nominating Committee and should actually be *excluded* from serving. However, this exclusion doesn't mean that the committee is prohibited from consulting with the president for his or her advice or opinion.

The president is in a unique position to know and understand who has the qualities of leadership necessary for a particular office and, in turn, may have valuable information that the committee finds useful. Similarly, other officers, committee leaders, and members of executive management may have information about prospective candidates or the duties of the office that can be useful to the committee. The Nominating Committee can make effective use of this information if it chooses, but the committee must avoid sharing information on the current status of particular candidates.

The Nominating Committee is free to consult with any member or officer for information or advice, but it's under no obligation to do so. Committee deliberations should take place only in executive session, because such discussions require the same environment for candid discussion as personnel-related matters.

Getting answers to questions about procedure

Answers to questions about your organization's procedures relating to the Nominating Committee's work should be obtained from your president (or executive staff, if you have one). But situations exist where information may be tainted by an incumbent eager to influence your report. To avoid this situation, I recommend the careful preparation of an extract of all bylaws and other written rules adopted by your organization in any way related to the work of the Nominating Committee. Such a document can then be furnished to the members of the Nominating Committee, eliminating the need for them to be too dependent on the current officers for information on the procedures for carrying out their task.

Reporting your nominations

When the time to report draws near, the Nominating Committee should arrange a final meeting and prepare its final report. The list of nominees should be prepared, reviewed, and finalized as the recommendation of the committee. Coordinate with your president or staff to be sure the report is submitted in time for the preparation of a ballot or other publication if your rules require it.

The report should be simple, listing the nominee or nominees for each office in the order the offices are listed in the bylaws: "The Nominating Committee reports its nominees as follows: For president, Portulaca Grapevine; for vice-president, Hermione Frump. . . ."

Wisdom dictates that your committee report should not be disclosed or circulated until it's officially presented, or perhaps shortly in advance of the election meeting. Circumstances can change and so may your final recommendation. However, the time to release your report is more often than not established by custom or by rule.

Handling the committee report

In many cases, it's assumed that the nominees recommended by the Nominating Committee will be elected. Nevertheless, the chair is mistaken if he entertains a motion to accept the committee report; by doing so, he ignores the rights of members to make nominations from the floor. Even if such a nomination is ultimately futile or is made in pointed protest, it's still in order. For that reason, the question is never on the adoption of a Nominating Committee report — it's always on the election of the officer.

Even in the presence of a Nominating Committee report, nominations from the floor should be taken for offices in the order the offices are listed in your bylaws. And depending on the rule or custom of your organization, nominations from the floor can be taken in two ways:

- ✔ Take all nominations for all offices and then proceed to the elections.
- ✔ Take nominations for an office, conduct the election for that office, and then proceed to nominations for the next office.

Nominations by Ballot

This method of nominations is not as complex as it is different. It's based on the principle of allowing *all* voters to make nominations for all offices by completing a nominating ballot.

The ballots are tallied very much like an election ballot (see Chapter 14), and the report becomes the list of nominees for each office. This method gives voters an idea of the group's preferences without holding an actual election.

The election balloting then proceeds on a separate ballot, with each voter casting a vote for the nominee of his choice. Although it may seem that the nomination ballot should just be adopted as the election ballot, doing so is improper because it's no different than holding a write-in election without any nominees; the likelihood of such an election producing a winner on the first ballot is so small that it could hide under the period at the end of this sentence.

The nominating ballot system has the advantage of eliminating some of the time spent on nominations from the floor in addition to giving information about the preferences of the other members.

Compromising on the dark horse

The practice of limiting voting to the top two nominees on a nominating ballot (or of holding a run-off between the top two vote-getters when neither has a majority) is *not* proper under Robert's Rules.

Even though these options seem like good ideas, the rule states that you continue to vote (*re-ballot*) until someone receives a majority of the votes cast. Sometimes re-balloting takes a lot of time, but unless the candidates consistently drawing the low votes withdraw from the contest, they have every right to be listed on the ballot.

The advantage to this voting rule is that, more often than you may think, Mr. Listbottom may just be the ideal compromise candidate that the two hopelessly deadlocked factions can agree on. When people start to realize they aren't going to win but they still don't want to vote for their candidate's archrival, they begin to see the benefit of voting for that third name on the ballot that's consistently drawing some pretty good numbers.

As these stubborn voters warm up to the dark horse candidate, they begin to realize that by switching to this candidate, they may be able to hold together an organization in danger of splitting if the members are forced to choose between two sharply contrasted candidates.

So, the next time you're tempted to call for a run-off, consider compromising on the dark horse instead of barreling towards deadlock. You may be really glad you did!

Nominations by Mail

Taking nominations by mail is the same as taking nominations by ballot, except that the former is handled through the mail. Kinda obvious, isn't it? Security measures are taken to protect the privacy of the nominating ballot; each member is instructed to fold his or her ballot inside a signed envelope and mail it back in an outer envelope. When the nominating ballot is received, the signed inner envelope containing the ballot is logged in against a list of voting members, and the ballot is deposited in a receptacle for tallying like an election ballot.

All other procedures for taking mail nominations remain the same as for taking a nominating ballot in a meeting. The added advantage of mail nominations is that a more widespread base of nominees can be obtained. If voting is also to be conducted by mail, then the bylaws must permit it. See Chapter 8 for more information on voting by mail.

Nominations by Petition

Some organizations add nominees to the ballot only if the name is submitted on a petition signed by some minimum number of members. Nomination by petition is another method of nominations by mail; provisions must be made for it in the bylaws, and standard forms must be provided to candidates and electors upon request.

Chapter 14

Holding Elections and Making Appointments

*O*ne of the real challenges for many organizations is to make the right decisions when it comes to electing officers and directors and staffing committees. Making mistakes is easy when you don't know the proper procedures or the rationale behind them. For example, take the myth that when nobody wins on the first ballot, you automatically drop the candidates who received the lowest votes and hold a run-off for the office. The truth is that taking that route instead of following the correct procedure compromises both the election and the group.

This chapter covers the default procedures for elections and appointments as well as the other options available for making choices in selecting leaders, as outlined by Robert's Rules. If you want to make the best group decisions when selecting your leadership team, take a close look at this chapter and make some comparisons with your current procedures. Any changes you need to make should be pretty clear.

This chapter may look a little bit like a rehash of the material in Chapter 8, but it actually goes beyond the basic discussion of voting methods I cover there. The information presented in this chapter further develops the information from Chapter 8, especially as it applies to holding elections and making appointments. In this chapter, I tie the voting basics to the process of arriving at your decisions about who will serve your group in leadership positions.

Conducting Elections Like a Maestro

It's my experience that the election process itself is the easiest part of deciding who handles a particular job in the organization. By the time you get to the actual election, things are mostly (as they say) "all over but the crying." The choices are pretty well narrowed down through the nomination process, and the campaigns, if any, are finished. Now's the time to see if the members have the wisdom to put the right people to work.

An election is really nothing more than the handling of an assumed motion, with the question being on whom to elect to fill a position. Like any incidental main motion, an election can be decided by voice vote or by ballot. And you may even make your decisions by plurality or by order of preference instead of by a majority (see Chapter 8 for a full description of the different methods of voting and determining a result).

The point of all these details is that your group has decisions to make about elections before you actually hold an election. And, if you want to save yourself a lot of angst around election time, you'll decide on these methods ahead of time and make necessary provisions for them in your bylaws.

Electing by ballot

I can't say for sure, but I suspect that most organizations use the method of electing officers and directors by ballot. Ballot voting (see Chapter 8 for details) is by far the surest way to allow for the free expression of the will of the membership. The decision of who you trust to do the work is certainly important enough to justify the extra effort required to assure each member a right of secrecy and the integrity of the count and the result.

When holding ballot elections, you have two procedural options:

- ✔ Nominations for all offices conclude before any balloting begins.
- ✔ Nominations for each office are followed by the election for that office.

Each of these two options is unique and has its advantages and disadvantages.

Closing nominations for all offices before balloting

Nominations are closed (see Chapter 13) for all offices, and balloting for all offices can take place on the same ballot. The advantages of closing all nominations before any voting takes place are twofold:

✔ It saves time.

✔ It permits polling outside the meeting.

When the meeting is large and time is a real factor in counting ballots, this method works best if you hold your elections early in the meeting. Doing so allows you the best chance of completing any re-balloting required in the case of a tie between candidates.

One of the disadvantages of this method is that unless voters plan ahead and nominate a member for more than one office before balloting begins (which is certainly permissible), the voters will miss the opportunity to elect a candidate to an office voted on later if he loses an office voted on earlier. So, when using this procedure, members should be instructed that a person can be nominated for more than one office and can be *elected* to more than one office, in which case he can either choose which office he accepts or serve in more than one position if not prohibited. If your group does elect a nominee to more than one office and he can't accept or doesn't choose to accept both positions, you need to conduct another election for the office left empty.

Closing floor nominations for each office before balloting for that office

The main advantage of this procedure is that it allows members to consider the election results of one office before proceeding to the election of another office.

To use this procedure, you take nominations from the floor for one office, and when no further nominations are forthcoming, you proceed to the balloting for that office. Your tellers then count the ballots and report the count, and the chair announces the results. Then, you do it all again for the next office.

The disadvantage to closing nominations for one office at a time is that it requires more time for the election process, making it probably best limited to smaller groups.

No matter which procedure you use, the order in which you take up each election is the order in which the offices are listed in your bylaws.

When your bylaws provide that elections shall be by ballot, waiving that requirement is never permissible, even if only one person is nominated or running for the office. A rule requiring ballots is a rule protecting the right of an individual to vote in secret, which is considered a *basic right of the individual member*.

Write-in votes

Voting by ballot adds another dimension to an election; it enables a member to vote for a candidate not formally nominated by writing a name on the ballot and marking the name to indicate that it's the voter's choice. This is called a *write-in vote,* and write-in votes are always counted. A write-in vote is a legal vote unless it's unintelligible or cast for an unidentifiable or ineligible person or for a fictitious character, in which case it's counted as an illegal vote. (Flip to Chapter 8 for the birds-eye lowdown on how to count both *legal* and *illegal votes.*)

Electing by voice vote

If your bylaws don't require you to conduct an election by ballot, and if candidates are unopposed or there's no major contest for an office, then an election by voice vote (or *viva voce*) may save you some valuable time.

The procedure for a voice vote election is fairly simple. After nominations are closed, the vote is taken on each nominee in the order in which they were nominated.

For example, suppose the nominees for the office of treasurer are Mr. Spender, Ms. Froogle, and Mr. Dazzler. The chair begins by saying, "If there are no more nominations for the office of treasurer, we will close nominations and proceed to elect a treasurer. Are there further nominations? [pause for additional nominations] Hearing no further nominations, nominations for the office of treasurer are closed."

The chair continues, "The nominees for treasurer are Mr. Spender, Ms. Froogle, and Mr. Dazzler. All those in favor of electing Mr. Spender to the office of treasurer say 'Aye.' Opposed, 'No.' The noes have it, and Mr. Spender is not elected."

The election's not over yet — you have two more candidates to consider.

The chair proceeds to the vote on the candidate nominated second. He says, "All those in favor of electing Ms. Froogle to the office of treasurer say 'Aye.' Opposed, 'No.' The ayes have it, and Ms. Froogle is elected to the office of treasurer."

Now that the assembly has elected the treasurer, the question on the election of Mr. Dazzler has become moot.

The only real problem with the voice vote method is that if the members don't understand exactly how it works, the ones whose preferred candidate doesn't get voted on are likely to think something is amiss.

Because this form of voting favors one candidate over another based on the order of nomination, you should avoid using it except in mass meetings or when there's no serious contest for the office and a ballot is not required.

Depending on the group and your members' familiarity with the process, your presiding officer can avoid misunderstandings by explaining to the assembly exactly how the voice vote works. In doing so, Madam President may explain, "If you want to be sure someone down the list has a chance at being elected, you should vote *against* those higher up on the list. Your failure to cast a negative vote for candidates who get voted on before yours can actually help the fortunes of the candidates nominated before yours."

If a candidate for office is unopposed and a ballot isn't required by your bylaws, your presiding officer should simply declare the candidate elected.

Electing by roll call

If your assembly's members are accountable to a constituency, your rules may require you conduct your elections by roll-call vote. You follow the same procedures as I outline for elections by ballot (in the earlier section "Electing by ballot") as far as arriving at the point of the election is concerned. But instead of casting your vote by ballot, each member announces his or her vote when the secretary calls that person's name. The secretary should repeat the vote after recording it to ensure accuracy. I cover roll-call voting in Chapter 8.

Determining who wins

Elections are decided by majority vote unless your bylaws provide differently.

Viva voce elections

As far as elections by voice vote are concerned, a majority elects anyway because all you can discern with a voice vote is win-or-lose, and you stop when you have a winner. Tie votes are unlikely in elections viva voce, and if you do encounter a tie, you solve the problem by division of the assembly (see Chapter 11) or even by switching to a counted vote or a ballot vote.

Ballot elections

When it comes to ballot elections, your election is not complete until a position is filled, and a position is never filled until a candidate receives the threshold number of votes required for election. In most cases, the threshold is a majority of the votes cast. If you have only two candidates and the vote is a tie, you repeat the balloting until one candidate receives a majority.

Follow the same practice even if more than two candidates are on a ballot for one position. If no one receives a majority, you vote again.

Balloting must continue until a candidate receives a majority. It's never proper to drop the candidates receiving the lowest vote totals from a ballot unless they withdraw voluntarily. That means run-offs are just plain out of order. The requirement for election by ballot is a majority, and a candidate has no obligation to withdraw just because he polls low numbers. Your members may wind up voting for Mr. Low as the compromise candidate.

Counting the ballots

In Chapter 8, I cover in detail how ballots are counted and how voting results are determined. But there are a couple of points about counting ballots in elections that I want to mention here:

- ✔ When you have several seats to fill on a board or a committee, a voter doesn't have to vote for more than one person for the office for the ballot to count. However, a blank ballot doesn't count at all.

- ✔ When you're tallying up the votes, if more candidates than the required number of positions to be filled receive a majority, then the winners are determined by ranking the total votes received. If some but not all seats are filled on a ballot, then the candidates who receive a majority are elected, and you re-ballot to fill the remaining positions.

Mail ballots

Mail ballots (which must be authorized in your bylaws) can be a great way to elect leaders of organizations that have a large membership spread over a wide area. But they have one major drawback: When no candidate receives a majority, the price of re-balloting can really bust the budget! Take a look in Chapter 8 for details about conducting a vote by mail.

To make sure that you don't have to re-ballot when holding an election by mail, authorize in your bylaws that mail ballot elections can be decided by plurality or preferential voting. (I cover both of these methods in Chapter 8.)

Dealing with incomplete elections

Despite the best of plans, sometimes your group just can't finish its order of business in a given meeting or session. If you run out of time before you've elected all the positions you plan to fill, don't worry. It's not the end of the world — just the end of the meeting! And meetings being what they are, you can be sure there will be another one. With that in mind, if you expect that you're not going to finish your work, you should provide for an adjourned meeting in which to conclude your election. (I tell you how to do this in Chapter 10.) However, if your next regular meeting is scheduled within a quarterly time period (see Appendix A) and you're able to wait, you can also finish your election at the next regular meeting.

If you're wondering who your officers are either after an election or during an incomplete election, keep the following points in mind:

✔ Elections are final immediately upon their conclusion unless the elected person isn't present and hasn't consented to serve; or declines to serve when notified of his election, whether present at the time of election or not.

✔ An election can't be reconsidered after it's finalized.

✔ The newly elected officer assumes office immediately unless the bylaws state a specific time for the commencement of the term of office.

✔ If the bylaws require an installation ceremony, failure to conduct the ceremony doesn't affect the time at which the term commences, nor does it prohibit the candidate from assuming the office.

Making Committee Appointments

In Chapter 16, I cover committees and the considerations necessary to staff them properly. Those considerations relate to the nature of the committee, its task, the size of committee necessary to handle the task, and the members' abilities and temperaments. In this section, I branch out to explain procedures for committee selection. (You may find it helpful to read this section in conjunction with Chapter 16.)

Exploring the methods of appointing committees

The two most common methods of selecting committee members are:

> ✔ Appointment by motion
>
> ✔ Appointment by the chair

Appointment by motion

This method is pretty self-explanatory; the suggested appointees are simply named in a motion.

In many cases, the motion is the same as the motion establishing the committee. For example, a member may say, "Mr. Chairman, I move that we refer the pending motion to contract out the landscaping of our main entrance to a committee of three members to seek bids and to review and recommend to the membership at our regular meeting in two months, and that the members of the committee be Hector Knuckles, Shirley Buckles, and Luther Chuckles."

You can instead make the appointment in a second motion that follows the committee's establishment. In this case, a member may say, "Mr. Chairman, I move that Hector Knuckles, Shirley Buckles, and Luther Chuckles be appointed as the Landscape Proposal Bid Review Committee just established."

Members may wish to add other names for consideration for appointment to a special committee with a fixed number of members; those names are taken as nominations, and the motion is treated in the same way that nominations and an election would be held. (Flip to Chapter 13 for details on handling nominations from the floor.) Alternatively, a motion to reconsider the motion establishing the committee (see Chapter 12) can be adopted and the number of members to serve on the committee can be changed.

The motion to appoint specific members to the committee may also name a chairman for the committee. If a chairman is not determined in this manner, then a separate motion can appoint the chairman, or the motion can authorize the committee members to select their chairman from among themselves. If no chairman is named or no provision made for the committee to elect its chairman, then the first person named to the committee is the chairman.

Direct appointment by the chair

Many organizations allow the chair or president to appoint committees. In fact, a group's bylaws may make the appointment of all committees an express responsibility of the president. In those cases, members don't have any power over the appointment of committee members; they only can hope that the president heeds their recommendations.

If the bylaws don't provide that the president shall appoint all special and standing committees, then there are two ways to charge the presiding officer with the task. One way is to add the task to the motion creating the committee, such as "I move to create a committee of five members to be appointed by the president, to gather information about a new place to hold our meetings and to report back to us next month." This method delegates any authority to select the committee members directly to the president.

The other way to give the president the authority to appoint members to a committee is to make a separate motion following the adoption of the motion establishing the committee. The member taking this approach says, "Mr. Chairman, I move that the members of the Meeting Location Committee just established be appointed by the chair."

Finding more ways to appoint committee members

When it's time to appoint members to committees, you have four methods to choose from, in addition to the ones described in the previous section. Although these methods aren't used nearly as often as the others, nevertheless they are available and sometimes are established in bylaws or special rules of order as a particular method to use for certain committees. These methods are

- ✔ Ballot election
- ✔ Open nominations
- ✔ Nominations by the chair
- ✔ Appointment by definition in bylaws

Ballot election

Ballot election is the procedure most often used to staff important standing committees having great power and authority. Whenever a group wants members to select the appointees and wants to afford members the benefit of the secret ballot, ballot election is the way to go. I cover the procedure in the section entitled "Election by ballot," earlier in this chapter.

Open nominations

Selecting members of a committee by open nominations is a procedure by which nominations are taken from the floor (see Chapter 13) for potential committee members. This method reserves the control over appointment to the membership but doesn't carry the requirement of a secret ballot.

If the number of members nominated is no greater than the number of committee members to be appointed, then the nominees can be declared appointed. Otherwise, the chairman calls for a voice vote on each nominee in the order nominated until the required number is elected. You can find more information on this kind of voting in the section "Electing by voice vote," earlier in this chapter.

Nominations by the chair

Using this procedure, you can take advantage of the chair's knowledge of the strengths and capabilities of members as they relate to the requirements of service on the committee, but you ultimately reserve the final decision for your group.

The chair offers her nominees and puts the question as follows: "The chair nominates Hoss Traynor as chairman, and Ben Dare and Don Daat as members. Shall these members comprise the committee?"

You can propose a veto of any member nominated by moving to strike out one or more of those named. Your chair should handle such a motion as a subsidiary motion to amend (see Chapter 9). But when appointing committees by nominations from the chair, you can't offer a replacement. Instead, your motion to strike out is voted on by the membership. If it passes, the chair offers other nominees. If it fails, the question is again on whether to approve the chair's nominees as members of the committee.

Appointment by definition in the bylaws

Some committees are appointed as directed under specific provisions of bylaws. (I cover bylaws in Chapter 2.)

An Executive Committee, for example, must be specifically authorized in the bylaws and is usually defined by the express enumeration of officers who will comprise the committee. Consider a bylaw that reads, "An Executive Committee, consisting of the president, the vice-president, the secretary, and the treasurer, shall have all the authority of the board between its meetings."

Another example is a standing committee appointed under the bylaws by a combination of several of the methods listed in this section. The bylaw for such a committee may read, "The Finance Committee membership shall consist of the treasurer, the chairman of the Audit Committee, the chairman of the Budget Committee, the executive director, two members appointed by the president, and three members elected by the membership at the annual meeting."

Chapter 15

Running the Show: Officers and Directors

. . . .

. . . .

*Y*our organization can't reach its full potential without the right leadership. Nothing can help an organization achieve its purpose like the right people in the right jobs. And nothing can cause it to fail like the person who is interested only in having a title.

Choosing your leaders can be a challenge, and if you want to see the right results, then you need to keep one key thing in mind: The ability to get elected is not the ability to do the job. I've seen organizations with the best bylaws, the finest members, and the most noble of purposes become totally ineffective because they wind up with a president who thinks his job is to control the members or directors who think they own the club.

A leader's job is to fulfill the duties of office, acting for the good of the group. But in order to fulfill your duties, you have to know what they are. This chapter gives you information on the various offices in any organization and lays out the standard responsibilities for each officer.

Perfecting Presidential Presence

Serving as president (or grand factotum, or whatever title is given to your presiding/chief executive officer) gives you the unparalleled opportunity to make a difference in your group's work.

Staffing your organization

A common misconception is that officers have to be members of the organization. That's really not the case unless you establish membership qualifications for officers in your bylaws.

In reality, a membership is free to elect whomever it chooses to serve in its offices. Adopting limiting qualifications diminishes this freedom. I'm not saying you shouldn't limit who can be an officer, but when you consider the option, keep these two things in mind:

✔ Sometimes a nonmember is better for the job.

✔ If the ultimate decision rests with the members anyway, why limit your choices?

Examples of nonmembers serving as officers include

✔ **Secretary:** Often, a board elects a staff member to this office.

✔ **Treasurer:** How many times has a member's spouse who is a service-minded accountant been roped into doing this job? Plenty, I assure you.

✔ **Directors:** It's not unusual to see boards made up of interested and well-connected members of the community who are not members of the organization.

✔ **President:** Look at the United States Senate — its presiding officer is the vice-president of the United States, not an elected senator. Your group may choose a professional presiding officer to serve as presiding officer at all your meetings, and you may want to staff a paid manager to handle operations between meetings.

Whether or not you put membership qualifications on officers is up to your membership. Although there's nothing wrong with setting limits, what's important to know is that no rule says that your officers must be selected only from within your membership.

However, before you ever think about buckling down and implementing your bold ideas for the new millennium, you need to make yourself familiar with the basics.

Preparing to lead

I list ten tips for presiding officers in Chapter 20, but your success as president depends on your willingness to absorb a lot in a short time. Here are the things you need to do before you call your first meeting to order:

> ✔ **Get a *current* copy of your group's adopted parliamentary authority.** If that authority is Robert's Rules, then be careful not to buy one of the many knock-offs of the title or an early edition that has long since been superseded by authorized revisions. The current edition of *Robert's Rules of Order Newly*

Revised is the only book containing the name "Robert's Rules" in its title that is recognized as authoritative by the Robert's Rules Association, the National Association of Parliamentarians, and the American Institute of Parliamentarians.

✔ **Read and understand your organization's charter, bylaws, special rules of order, and standing rules.** You've probably already read these documents at least once if you're a member of the organization, but read them again as if it were the first time. Pay attention to any of your rules that seem to be in conflict with the way things have been done lately, and set a course to do things according to the rules under your leadership. Members have a right to have things done by the book, and these documents are your book! (See Chapter 2 for more information on bylaws and the like.)

✔ **Read Parts I and II of this book.** The first two parts of *Robert's Rules For Dummies* contain the fundamental knowledge necessary to fulfill your duties as a presiding officer in meetings. Pay special attention to the rules for recognition of members and assignment of the floor as well as other principles of debate (see Chapter 7), and get a firm handle on ranking motions in Chapters 9 and 10. When you're finished reading through this book, *familiarize yourself with the corresponding sections of your adopted parliamentary authority.* You'll find expanded information there. Your adopted parliamentary authority is binding on your group, and it's your duty to know how to find and apply the rules as your parliamentary situation may require.

Presiding with pizazz

Although the information in Chapters 5 and 7 covers much of the details related to presiding in meetings, I outline some of the more basic principles you need to master in the lists that follow.

During meetings of your organization, you have the duty to

✔ Determine if a quorum is present and call the meeting to order (see Chapter 4).

✔ Bring business before the meeting according to your order of business (see Chapter 5).

✔ Recognize members who seek and are entitled to the floor (see Chapter 7).

✔ Put all legitimate motions before the group (see Chapter 7).

✔ Enforce the rules of debate, and grant all members who wish to speak in debate the opportunity to do so subject to rules and limits of debate (see Chapter 7).

✔ Conduct the votes on all questions, and determine and announce the results (see Chapter 8).

✔ Rule improper motions out of order (see Chapter 7).

✔ Decide questions of order, or ask the members to decide when you're in doubt (see Chapter 11).

✔ Respond to parliamentary inquiries or points of information (see Chapter 11).

✔ Conclude the meeting by declaring it adjourned when voted by the members, when the appointed hour for adjournment arrives (see Chapter 10), or when there is an emergency and safety demands it.

Along with polishing up your presiding skills and techniques, you can adopt a few practices to ensure the quality of your meetings. The tips that follow are recommendations for producing effective meetings that run smoothly.

✔ **Keep your rules handy.** You never know when you'll have to stop and check on a rule from your bylaws or rules of order. Always have a copy of your bylaws, special rules of order, and parliamentary authority with you at every meeting.

✔ **Plan your meeting.** You know from everyday life that it's easier to go from one place to the next if you plan well and know how to get there. So, make your meeting journey simpler by using a working agenda. I cover this subject in detail in Chapter 5 and give you a sample in Appendix B — and I hope you use it!

✔ **Insist on following fundamental procedures.** Remain in control of the floor. For example, don't let members disrupt the meeting by calling out motions without being properly recognized. Except in limited situations, members have to be recognized before making a motion. Know which motions can interrupt a speaker, which ones are debatable, and which ones are amendable. Help members frame their motions correctly, and even if they make the wrong motion but it's clear what they want to do, announce the motion as the one they're really trying to make. I'm not recommending you be a bossy control freak. In fact, a key to successful presiding is knowing when it's appropriate to relax formalities (as long as it's not at the expense of member rights).

✔ **Make sure the members know what they're voting on.** Before you take a vote, repeat the motion in understandable terms. For example, you may say, "The question is on adoption of the motion to purchase a new computer for our staff secretary at a cost not to exceed $700. [pause] Are you ready for the question? [pause] All those in favor say 'Aye,'" and so on.

✔ **Avoid the temptation to say, "You've heard the motion. All those in favor say 'aye.'"** Much of the time, the members *haven't* heard the motion, and confusion will inevitably erupt if not before the vote, then right afterward. Save the time wasted by confusion and outbursts, and be clear about the exact wording of the question that the next vote decides.

Maintaining magnanimity

If there was ever a key to success as a presiding officer, *maintaining the appearance of impartiality* is it. Members may know you have an agenda for the organization. In fact, you were probably elected because you have some vision and ability. But when you're presiding over the meeting, leave it to your members to do all the debating; step back and let things take care of themselves. You'll sink your ship of state quite quickly if you attempt to throttle members unjustly or take advantage of their ignorance of proper form or procedure.

Some of the best presiding officers I have known have also been some of the most opinionated. But they knew how to lead by participating in working committees and helping move their program by selling members on it, not forcing it on them. A reputation for giving full sway to the minority when debating contested issues is what gave these leaders the respect of all the members.

Conversely, the worst presiding officers seem to have as their hallmark the propensity to keep members who disagree with them from speaking at meetings. These leaders (in name only) almost gleefully rule a motion they disagree with out of order based on any hair-splitting technicality they can get away with.

The presiding officer who helps the assembly arrive at its true deliberative will is the winner on all counts.

Rounding out the job

As your group's president, you're more than likely also the chief administrative officer. That means you'll have to sign things, like countersigning checks and attesting to resolutions published as extracts of the minutes (such as those furnished to banks when opening or changing info on accounts). If your group buys or sells any real estate or enters into any contracts, your signature is the seal of the organization.

Your bylaws may also assign other duties to the president. You may be considered a member of all your standing committees, and you'll probably have some responsibility to make committee appointments.

Choosing a presiding officer

According to Robert's Rules, a presiding officer should be chosen primarily for his or her ability to preside.

That's one of those rules that honestly should be taught in the first grade, along with 2 + 2 = 4. The rule is so fundamentally true that it'd be great not to have to wait so long to discover it.

Most presiding officers get their training by ordeal. They get elected because they know how to get elected. Understanding the organization, the bylaws, and the rules for presiding are rarely important until they have one of those meetings that motivates them to call a parliamentarian and take a private lesson in procedure before the next meeting.

You'll probably never change the world by making it your personal policy to support presiding officers on the basis of the ability to preside impartially, knowledgeably, and skillfully over debate on a controversial subject. But by doing so, you may make a big difference in your own organization.

You'll never be better off in a meeting than when you have a presiding officer who takes the time to learn how to do his job right. The best presiding officer obtains the skills and techniques required to assist the assembly in arriving at its will efficiently, orderly, and with goodwill between all sides of controversial issues.

One thing to remember is that you serve the members, not the other way around. I get a good bit of mail from members telling me about how their president orders people around and keeps people from exercising their rights. I tell them about the procedures in Robert's Rules that allow them to adopt motions without worrying about whether the chairman likes it, remove a chairman from the chair during a meeting, or get rid of him altogether. It usually comes as a big surprise to the chairman to have the last page of Robert's Rules (where the procedure for removing a presiding officer from the chair is found) thrust in front of his face. The unsuccessful chairman likely wouldn't have wound up in such an embarrassing situation if he'd read some of the other pages first.

Playing (Not-so) Second Fiddles

There's only one first chair violin in an orchestra, but it takes the entire ensemble to fill the hall with music. Similarly, although the presidency is a key leadership position in any organization, a successful organization is one that has a good leadership team working in concert. Other officers, especially those in key administrative positions such as the ones listed in this section, have responsibilities that are just as important as those of the president, and which may take as much or more time to do well.

If you accept an election or appointment to serve as an officer, you can't go wrong if you spend as much time as the best president would in studying your bylaws and rules of order. Knowing your job and your organization's structure and rules is the first step to a successful term of service.

Waiting in the wings: Vice-president

The one function of a vice-president as provided in Robert's Rules is to serve in the absence of the president and to automatically succeed to the office of president in case of that officer's death or resignation. In fact, members can't elect a new president to fill a vacancy in that office unless the bylaws expressly call for it. Thanks to the automatic succession rule, you never really have a vacancy in the presidency. Your vacancy immediately becomes one in the office of vice-president.

You may have several vice-presidents in your organization. Sometimes, these officers have specific responsibilities, overseeing certain aspects of the organizations committees or programs. Unless the bylaws provide otherwise, succession to the presidency is in order of vice-presidents, with the last vice-president's position being the one vacated as he moves up the food chain.

Your bylaws may dictate other specific duties for a vice-president and often will authorize the board or the president to assign certain duties. For this reason, it's a good idea to know just what your bylaws say about the office of vice-president before accepting the position!

Keeping jots and tittles: Secretary

The secretary is one of the two officers your organization absolutely can't do without. It takes a presiding officer and a recording clerk to conduct a meeting and have a proper record of it, and the secretary is the recording clerk for the assembly.

If any office is more important to the smooth functioning of your group, I don't know what it is. The work of the secretary is absolutely essential, and it takes a special person to do it correctly and do it well. Not because the work's difficult, but because it's so important. Dependability, organization, and the ability to refrain from editorializing are the key attributes of a successful secretary.

Under Robert's Rules, a secretary's job description includes the following duties:

- ✔ **Take minutes at all meetings and submit them for approval to the membership at the following meeting.** Minutes are the record of the proceedings in your meetings, and become official when approved (see Chapter 17).

- ✔ **Serve as custodian of your organization's records (except those specifically assigned to other officers), including minutes; reports of officers, boards, and committees; and official correspondence.** The secretary also certifies copies of these documents when necessary.

- ✔ **Make sure the official bylaws, special rules of order, standing rules, and current minute book are available for reference at all meetings.**

- ✔ **Make the organization's records available to members in accordance with your rules.**

- ✔ **Keep the official membership roll.** Sometimes this duty is specifically assigned to the treasurer or a staff member because the roll is often updated frequently based on dues payments or lapses.

- ✔ **Ensure that officers, committee members, and delegates are notified when elected or appointed, and are given credentials and any necessary papers.**

- ✔ **Issue the notice (or call) of meetings, and serve as a correspondence secretary unless a separate position is established for that function.**

- ✔ **Prepare the order of business for the presiding officer, showing everything known to be up for consideration at the meeting.**

- ✔ **Preside over the election of a temporary chairman for a meeting if the president and vice-president are absent.**

If you're the secretary, don't wear yourself out trying to write (into the minutes) everything everybody says in meetings. In fact, it's actually improper to do that. Chapter 17 contains detailed information about what should and shouldn't be included in your minutes, but it boils down to this: Minutes are the record of what is *done* in the meeting, not what is *said*.

Balancing the books: Treasurer

You've got a big job on your hands if you're the treasurer. Before you accept this position, find out exactly what it entails. No matter the size of the organization or the number of figures to the left of the decimal on your group's bank balance, your basic job description includes the following:

- ✔ **Serve as custodian of the funds of the organization, keeping careful records of all receipts and making no disbursements without the authority of the assembly.**

- ✔ **Prepare financial statements, and report to the board and members.**

- ✔ **Take responsibility for any and all reports required by taxing authorities.**

That may look like a short list, but each one of the three items can carry a pretty significant workload. Fortunately, the bigger the job, the more likely there are to be sufficient resources to do a little outsourcing. In other words, if the membership is small and the budget isn't very big, you probably won't be faced with more transactions than you can handle. But if you're dealing with a large membership and tracking dues and a major budget, you'll probably have some professional help. In any event, when it comes to taking care of somebody else's money, you definitely need to know what's involved before you agree to take over the position.

Robert's Rules suggests that any officers who handle an organization's money should be bonded at the expense of the group in an amount large enough to protect it from loss. The decision to obtain a fidelity bond is one for your membership to decide, and the choice depends on the group's actual finances.

 Small organizations don't necessarily have inconsequential finances as far as the Internal Revenue Service (IRS) is concerned. You're mistaken if you think your group is automatically a nonprofit or tax-exempt organization because it isn't organized as a business. The point? If you're the officer responsible for taking care of your group's money, don't assume anything. Before you sign any checks, ask a professional if your organization is required to file any kind of tax returns, and get the answer in writing. Whatever the professional says, be smart and take the advice.

Tackling Other Tasks

Besides the offices of president, vice-president, secretary, and treasurer, Robert's Rules lists a handful of other offices often established in different types of organizations based on need. The name of each office suggests the general duties, and for the most part, you define the specifics in your bylaws depending on the needs of your group.

Managing the business: Directors

Your *directors* (also known as *trustees, managers,* or *governors*) are those people seated on your executive board. The directors' duties depend on the authority of the board, which is established in the bylaws.

Keeping the peace: Sergeant-at-arms

A *sergeant-at-arms* (also known as *warden,* or *warrant officer*) usually has the duty of acting on the orders of the chair to preserve order. Other duties related to the security of the floor may be assigned depending on the needs of the organization. Some organizations establish deputies or assistants who serve under the sergeant-at-arms and who may also be referred to by the same title.

Guarding the gate: Doorkeeper

If your organization closes its meeting hall to nonmembers or verifies membership credentials for admission, you may have a *doorkeeper* (also known as a *guard,* or *tiler*). This officer often is responsible for closing the hall.

When is an officer not an officer?

Robert's Rules uses the term *officer* generically. Any set of duties assigned to an appointed or elected individual is generally understood to be an *office,* and the person elected or appointed is an *officer.*

But it's not uncommon to see the term *officer* used to define a specific subset of officers as defined in Robert's Rules. For example, bylaws may refer to *Officers and Directors,* while Robert's Rules lists *directors* among *other officers.*

But the terminology needn't be confusing if you simply stick to the context of the respective document. A director is, in the common sense of the word, an officer. But then, your bylaws may define the president, the vice-president, the secretary, and the treasurer as officers. To thicken things up, add the consideration that if those officers are on the board of directors, then they're directors, too!

So when the bylaws say something about "The officers shall . . .," the context will tell you whether it means to include the directors. And if it isn't clear, let your membership handle the interpretation.

Take it from somebody with experience: Try not to get too hung up in that kind of terminology wrangling. If anything in your bylaws is too ambiguous for you to know exactly what it means, interpret it or clarify it by amending it, and move on!

Continuing the saga: Historian

Your group may maintain a written historical record (other than official minutes and reports) of the activities and accomplishments of your organization during a term. If that's the case, you probably have an official *historian*. Some historians simply prepare a journal, which the members adopt for entry into an official history journal. Other historians may work with a standing committee and publish a yearbook.

Shelving the tomes: Librarian

If your organization maintains a collection of books, publications, films, or other cataloged media resources, the officer in charge of taking care of this property and making access available to your membership is your *librarian*.

Stowing the scepter: Curator

Some organizations possess valuable items and objects of important symbolic or historical significance. Custody of this property is vested in a *curator,* whose duty is the preservation of these items.

Speaking words of wisdom: Chaplain

The *chaplain* is responsible for leading your group in its opening prayers or invocations and closing benedictions at any meetings and functions where they may be included. Some organizations, especially those of a fraternal, religious, or charitable nature, may require the chaplain to be available for personal counsel to members, and perhaps to recommend on benevolent disbursements.

Managing the staff: Executive director

An executive director (also known as an *executive secretary* or *chief executive officer*) is usually a full-time, salaried employee of a large organization that manages and administers the day-to-day business operations of the organization. Depending on the organization, this officer usually serves under contract and is selected either by the board or by the membership.

The executive director almost always serves under the direction of the board or executive committee, and she usually has the authority to hire and fire staff members and set their salaries. The specific duties of this officer, her method of selection, and the term of service should be specified in your bylaws.

Advising on procedure: Parliamentarian

While many organizations either elect or authorize their president to appoint a parliamentarian from among their members, this function may also be handled by a professional who can render advice and opinions without having an interest in the outcome (other than that it be an orderly process, of course). It's really rare that smaller organizations should even need a parliamentarian. But even so, consulting a credentialed parliamentarian for help is wise when you have serious questions about member rights and procedures, or when you decide to make substantial changes to your bylaws.

In any case, the parliamentarian's role in a meeting is to advise your presiding officer on matters of parliamentary procedure. He doesn't make rulings but rather is a consultant only. Rulings are the sole responsibility of the chair.

If you want to get the most out of your parliamentarian, involve him in the planning and preparation of your meetings. In fact, most of the work of a professional parliamentarian is actually done outside the meeting.

Because it's critical for your presiding officer to have complete confidence in the parliamentarian, it's a good idea for your group to authorize your president to appoint a parliamentarian of his choice.

Your group may choose not to hire a professional parliamentarian, but rather to elect a member to the position. The member parliamentarian has a big decision to make when accepting an appointment to the position. Because of the complete impartiality required, he's duty-bound to forego completely his right to vote on any question at any time, unless the vote is by ballot (and he can therefore vote anonymously).

Chapter 16

Gearing Up for the Real Action: Committees

*I*n all but the smallest of organizations, committees are the organizational units in which the real work gets done. I seldom run
into someone who really likes three-hour board meetings, but I find
plenty of dedicated members who don't mind devoting considerable
time to their respective committees, focusing on specific projects
or goals they find especially interesting.

I wrote this chapter with an eye toward helping you and your
group understand the value of using committees to achieve group
objectives. And the best thing about committees is that they help
you reach your goals without spending tremendous amounts of
time in regular meetings, going over the minute details of every
idea that every member may offer.

In this chapter, I cover the technical aspects of committees as subordinate groups that each have a limited focus on a particular subject
or aspect of your organization's operation. I cover different types of
committees and the ways in which members may be appointed to
committee posts. Finally, I give you some tips about how to effectively work on committees.

Defining the Ordinary Committee

According to Robert's Rules, *ordinary committees* are regular committees you establish either in your bylaws or as-needed to consider various items of business and operational matters outside of the organization's regular meetings.

The term *ordinary* distinguishes the two usual types of committees from the *committee of the whole* and the *quasi-committee of the whole,* both of which I discuss in greater depth in Chapter 3. These non-ordinary committees are created when an entire assembly decides to relax its rules to consider some item of business; the assembly changes itself into a committee of all the members of the organization who are present.

The two types of ordinary committees used most of the time are described in the sections that follow:

- ✔ **Standing committees** are committees that have perpetual existence in your organization.

- ✔ **Special committees** are committees established for a specific purpose (sometimes called *ad hoc* or *select committees*), and they cease to exist after the task assigned to them is completed and the committee makes its final report.

Standing committees

Usually, standing committees are established in your bylaws to serve a permanent and continuing function for the organization. Your membership can create additional standing committees if authorized by the bylaws.

Some of the more common examples of standing committees are

- ✔ **Nominating Committee:** Generally established to recommend candidates for the offices of the organization. Members of this committee should generally be elected by the membership, and the president should not be an ex-officio member.

- ✔ **Auditing Committee:** Even an organization with limited funds should appoint members to review the treasurer's financial records for accuracy, with an eye on whether the funds are disbursed as authorized by the members. This committee, often appointed by the chair or the executive board, generally reports at the annual meeting. The treasurer should not be a member of this committee because it's the treasurer's records that are reviewed.

✔ **Membership Committee:** Although not as common as the committees appearing earlier in this list, many organizations provide for a committee to consider and recommend on membership recruitment and retention, or even on the admission of prospective members. Members of the Membership Committee are commonly appointed by the chair or the executive board.

✔ **Finance and Budget Committee:** Its necessity depends on the needs of the organization, but a Finance and Budget Committee does what its name suggests. This committee is expected to consider the financial resources and obligations of the organization, establish a budget, and recommend on financial matters for the benefit of the executive board and the membership.

The list of an organization's standing committees depends largely on the group and its needs. Neighborhood associations may have standing committees on Beautification, Security, Zoning, and Deed Restriction Enforcement; professional associations may have a Legislative Affairs Committee. The variations are endless. Anytime an organization faces a continuing need to focus on some particular subject matter, the membership can benefit from establishing a standing committee to deal with that issue.

Automatically referring business to a standing committee

In some cases, bylaws (see Chapter 2) may provide that certain types of motions or items of business are referred automatically to a particular standing committee (or to the board). The motions or items in question may not be considered at all by the membership until the assigned committee has reviewed and reported on them.

Problems with a rule such as this may arise if it's used to keep legitimate business from coming before the assembly. Take care when you're writing bylaws for your group — make sure that automatic referral doesn't necessarily preclude consideration of a motion that hasn't been *approved* by a committee (or a board) first.

You may like the idea of bylaws that can keep troublemakers from wasting the group's time. But if a faction of so-called troublemakers gains control, then the same rule that protected the rest of the group may have the opposite effect and put the rogues in almost total control of your organization. They have the ability to turn the automatic referral rule against you, blocking *your* motions from being considered. Let this be fair warning. It's usually best to make sure your entire membership has the final say on any motion made.

So, if you decide to require all motions to first go before a committee, don't box yourself in by requiring that committee's approval. All you really need is their report and recommendation; let the membership have the right to make the final decision.

Special committees

Special committees are formed by motion and vote anytime your group needs to delegate a task or carry out some function not covered by the existing standing committees. These special committees exist only as long as it takes for them to complete their work and report back to the members.

To create a special committee, a member may say, "Madam President, I move that a special committee of six members to be appointed by the president be created to research the possibility of our organization's purchase of the vacant property next to our meeting hall." Another example of a motion to create a special committee is, "Mr. Chairman, I move that the motion to buy a sailboat for our president be referred to a committee to investigate the costs involved and report back to the membership next month."

A committee of special standing

A *standing committee* is defined as one established in your bylaws and having perpetual existence. A standing committee of an organization reports to the membership. So what do you call a committee that's established in your bylaws, has perpetual existence, but instead of reporting to the membership, reports to the *executive board?*

The only committee mentioned in Robert's Rules that meets all these conditions is the *Executive Committee.*

The reason behind establishing an Executive Committee is to grant to a small but trusted group of officers the authority to make any critical decisions (usually reserved exclusively to the board) in between board meetings. It's not uncommon to give an Executive Committee almost all the power of the board yet make the committee's decisions subject to the board's ultimate approval.

Because an executive board can't delegate its authority to a subordinate body without the approval of the general membership, an Executive Committee can't be created or appointed unless it is expressly authorized in your bylaws.

Hence, as a permanent committee established in the bylaws by the membership, but one that is completely subordinate to the board, the executive committee — given the parliamentary definitions — is neither *special* nor *standing*. But that just makes it a committee of very special standing. If you use one, use it wisely, because it gives a small number of people a considerable amount of power.

The first example creates a special committee by making a main motion (see Chapter 6). The second example uses a subsidiary motion (see Chapter 9) to commit or refer and creates a special committee to look into the details of enacting a motion on the floor. In both examples, the committee ceases to exist after it completes its task and reports back to the group. After the report, the committee has no function.

Taking Stock of Committee Appointment Methods

When the time comes to get specific about who's going to serve on a committee, Robert's Rules gives you six different methods for deciding exactly who you want to do what. Each method is particularly well suited to a different situation (but is by no means exclusive to that situation). I list the appointment methods, brief descriptions, and their customary uses here. You can find a more detailed discussion of all these methods in Chapter 14.

- **Appointment by motion:** This method is most often used for appointing special committees. Using this method, you either name the prospective committee members in the motion that establishes the committee, or you name them in a separate motion after you adopt the motion to create the committee.

- **Appointment by the chair:** This method is also commonly used for appointing special committees, but it can also be used in the appointment of standing committees. To use this method, you can either specify appointment by the chair as part of your motion creating the committee, or you can use a separate motion to appoint using this method. Appointment by the chair is also commonly established in bylaws (see Chapter 2) to prescribe that a group's president appoints standing committees listed in the bylaws.

- **Ballot election:** Generally used to appoint members to important standing committees, this method is used when a group wants to select the committee members with the benefits of a secret ballot.

- **Open nominations:** This method is used any time the members want to elect members to a committee but don't require a secret ballot. Using this method, nominations (see Chapter 13) are taken from the floor, and election is usually by voice vote. See Chapter 14 for details on the election process.

✔ **Nominations by the chair:** When you want to take advantage of the chair's knowledge of individual members' capabilities, you can use this method. The chair offers his nominees and the membership votes on each usually by voice vote. See Chapter 14 for the specifics.

✔ **Appointment by definition in the bylaws:** Some committees are established with the bylaws (see Chapter 2) prescribing details as to who serves. For example, a bylaw defining a Finance Committee may read, "The Finance Committee membership shall consist of the treasurer, the chairman of the Audit Committee, the chairman of the Budget Committee, the executive director, two members appointed by the president, and three members elected by the membership at the annual meeting."

Considerations in Appointing Members to Committees

A committee is only as good as the members you appoint to it. Appointing committee members involves two steps. The first step is deciding which of the six methods for appointing members is appropriate for your specific situation. The second step is considering the committee's task, the size necessary to handle that task, and members' abilities and temperaments. For information on the first step, back up to the previous section or to Chapter 14. For information on the second step and how it applies to committees with specific functions, read on.

Making appointments for the right reasons

Committees are formed for the purpose of getting things done, and it's never a good idea to saddle the willing and able with a fellow member who never participates except by standing for recognition at the end of the job.

If you're operating under the notion that any good is served by making committee appointments either as patronage to pay off political favors in your organization or to *honor* an appointee, distance yourself and your organization from that kind of thinking as quickly as possible! I've seen committees crippled by the inability to achieve a quorum because members were appointed for those reasons.

Appointing special committees for investigations or deliberations

Special committees intended to handle investigations or deliberations should be large and include anyone likely to have a lot to say about the matter referred to it. (Following this general guideline will save you a lot of time in your regular meetings.) The goal of a committee like this is to arrive at a report that best reflects the will of the entire organization. Therefore, nothing's accomplished if the committee is one-sided and all factions aren't included in the committee discussions. Limiting participation to one side or the other will probably just assure an acrimonious debate when the committee reports its recommendations.

For example, consider a special committee to revise bylaws. If you exclude those members who always have a lot to say about how things should be done just because they're always oppositional, then you only postpone the inevitable; any work you do in your committee may just become a lost motion. But by including these opinionated members in the committee work, you're more likely to wind up with most of what you want, and you may also have their support when the time comes for the rest of the members to vote on the revision. If you argue and compromise in the committee, then you have a better chance of successfully passing an acceptable revision.

Picking the right mix for committees carrying out a specific task

Some committees produce better results when they include representatives of all factions. On the other hand, a special committee tasked with carrying out an order of the membership should be limited to those in favor of the task and should have no more members than are necessary to get the job done. Robert's Rules advises that if a member of the committee isn't in agreement with the goals, he should ask to be relieved from the appointment.

Selecting ideal members for standing committees

Appointments to standing committees should be made with all due consideration of the abilities of the prospective members and their willingness to actively serve. These committees should be of sufficient size to handle the volume of work reasonably anticipated to come before them during their term.

Working on a Committee

Successful organizations contain effective committees comprised of dedicated members who give generously of their time. However, dedicated members with time to give aren't a dime a dozen, so as a good leader, you must make committee service meaningful for members and see that committee tasks are completed. Just as importantly, it is incumbent on committee members to participate, and everyone must pull their own weight and accept an individual share of the work.

Presiding over a committee

Successful committees are ones that get to work quickly. Your first duty as chairman is to call a meeting of the committee. If you fail to do so quickly, you run the risk of losing members whose schedules may be overloaded if they have to do too much at the last minute.

To get a committee up and running in a timely fashion, Robert's Rules permits any two members to call a meeting of the committee if the chairman fails in his duty. So, if you're the chairman, set the tone for success by establishing a time and place for the first meeting of your committee, and call the meeting to order on time.

As far as notice and quorum are concerned (see Chapter 4), your committee meetings are subject to the same general rules as any other meeting. And just like in boards or small assemblies, you can attend a committee meeting by teleconferencing or videoconferencing if (and only if) the bylaws specifically authorize it.

 For all but very large committees (where size demands the same degree of formality as any regular assembly), committees can conduct their business meetings using considerably relaxed rules of procedure. I discuss those procedures in detail in Chapter 3.

Participating as a committee member

Earlier in the chapter, under the section entitled "Making appointments for the right reasons," I make the point that committee membership means work, and wisdom dictates that appointees be those who are willing to do what it takes to get the job done.

Unless your only goal is to line up with the glory hounds for recognition when your committee makes its final report, you'll make the word "Participate!" your watchword. Make it your business to

✔ **Take an active interest in your committee's work.** You don't have to be one of those eager beavers that wear everybody out with overkill in the enthusiasm department, but you should avoid being a bench warmer, too.

✔ **Think creatively about the task at hand and offer suggestions for effective ways to achieve the objectives of the committee.** Offer your committee the benefit of your experience. Don't be a complaining naysayer. Instead, help find ways to solve problems and make things work.

✔ **Do your share without waiting to be asked.** No matter what the tasks necessary to achieve the committee's goals and purpose, take some of the load. Committee work is hands-on and usually involves some grunt work. Don't be too good for that. In fact, the higher you think your station is, the more valuable others will see your willingness to roll up your sleeves and wield the proverbial shovel.

✔ **Show up for all meetings and be on time.** Everybody is busy. Your time is no more valuable than any other member's time. If you don't have time to serve on a committee, don't accept appointment. If you accept appointment, set an example by being a loyal, working member of the team.

Adjourning committee meetings

Unless your committee is holding its final meeting before making a final report to the assembly, you can simply adjourn with or without setting a time for the next meeting. You may have established a regular meeting schedule or the time for the next meeting, but if you haven't done either, then your committee meets again on the call of the chair.

You can't use the motion to adjourn if yours is a special committee and you're in your final meeting, having concluded your work. Instead, use the motion to rise and assign one of the members or the chairman to present the report to the appointing group. The motion to rise signifies that your committee has completed its task. The more seasoned you become with all this meeting stuff, the more you will come to learn that rising is much more fun than simply adjourning!

Chapter 17

Reporting to Your Organization

● ●

In This Chapter

▶ Taking accurate minutes

▶ Following good form on your treasurer's report

▶ Knowing what makes a good committee report

▶ Acting on report recommendations

● ●

*R*obert's Rules contains a basic premise that I don't think has ever been reduced to words until now: When all is said and done, there's still the paperwork!

It's true! The only way you can really let your members know what's going on in the day-to-day operations of your organization is by preparing and presenting reports at meetings. Newsletters may generally inform members about this or that, but the official reports of officers, the board, and committees are critical to your operation as an organization. After all, your reports recommend action and furnish the necessary information on which sound decisions are based.

Paperwork is a necessary evil, and everybody hates it, at least to a certain extent (although not many people complain when it comes to having to endorse their paychecks and make out deposit slips).

Neither do many folks complain when they get the exact information they need to make good decisions, without having to wade through a lot of superfluous information.

In this chapter, I share the information necessary for proper and informative reporting to the membership, including details about form and content of the minutes, treasurer's reports, and reports of officers, boards, and committees. I also provide tips on how to advance the recommendations contained in those reports, including the proper methods for taking action on such recommendations.

You'll still have to deal with paperwork after reading this chapter, but if you make good use of the information here, you may get away with less of it, and what paperwork you do have may be more concise and better organized.

Using Minutes to Report on Meeting Events

The first lesson I learned about minutes was that they should include what was *done* in the meeting, not what was *said*. That rule doesn't seem to get the widespread coverage it deserves. Considering how meticulously some secretaries try to record every word spoken, I can't help but wonder if they wouldn't prefer to write short, concise minutes that leave no doubt about the final results on all the motions. Recording all the he-said/she-said chatter that occurs in a meeting is a time-consuming and frustratingly tedious task, but unfortunately that's what constitutes the minute books of I-don't-know-how-many organizations I encounter. So, when I hear or read minutes prepared by folks who don't know that, I do my best to tell them about the "include what's done, not what's said" rule because it's sure to be some of the best news they've ever heard!

Composing your meeting's minutes

To help save you time and unnecessary work, Robert's Rules spells out exactly what needs to go into your minutes.

The first paragraph should include

- ✔ The kind of meeting (as in regular, special, annual, adjourned regular, adjourned special, and so forth)

- ✔ The name of the organization

- ✔ The date, time, and location of the meeting (don't list the location if it is always the same)

- ✔ A statement confirming that your organization's regular presiding officer and secretary are present (or the names of the persons substituting for them)

- ✔ A mention of whether the previous meeting's minutes were read and approved (and the date of that meeting if it wasn't a regular meeting)

Corrections to minutes are noted in the minutes being corrected; they're not detailed in the minutes of the meeting at which the corrections are adopted. (The minutes of the meeting containing corrections should merely state that minutes were corrected.)

Good form for the body of the minutes requires you to separate into paragraphs each subject item and the names of the members who made any motions. The body portion of the minutes should include

- ✔ All main motions (except those that are withdrawn). Main motions are defined in Chapter 6.

- ✔ Motions bringing a question again before the body (except for those that are withdrawn). These motions are listed in Chapter 12.

- ✔ The final wording of the motions, either as adopted or as disposed of. If it's appropriate to include mention of debate or amendment, these items can be noted parenthetically.

- ✔ The disposition of the motion — including any adhering amendments — if it's only temporarily disposed of.

- ✔ Secondary motions (see Chapters 9 through 12) not lost or withdrawn, where necessary for clarity (example motions include recess, fix time to which to adjourn, suspend the rules, postpone to a particular time, ballot vote ordered, and so on). Allude to the adoption of secondary motions by saying, "A ballot vote having been ordered, the tellers. . . ."

- ✔ Notices of motions.

- ✔ All points of order and appeals (see Chapter 11) and their subsequent dispositions, with reasons given by the chair for the ruling. (Rulings often establish precedent, so a careful record here is important.)

The last paragraph of your report should include the hour of adjournment. And that's it! Well, except for the following additional notes you should keep in mind when finalizing your report:

- ✔ The name of the person who seconds a motion isn't entered in minutes unless ordered by the membership.

- ✔ When a count has been ordered or a vote is taken by ballot, the number of votes on each side is reported in the minutes.

- ✔ If the vote is a roll-call vote, then the names and votes are recorded, including the names of those who declare "Present" or "Abstain" or who otherwise announce their abstention in some way. If members don't respond, you may simply enter enough names to reflect that a quorum was present.

- ✔ The proceedings of a committee of the whole aren't included in the minutes, but the fact that the move into committee occurred and the report of the committee are included.

✔ When a question is considered informally, the same information should be recorded as in regular rules. Informality is only permitted in debate.

✔ The full text of any report is included in the minutes if it is so ordered.

✔ Record the name of any guest speaker and the subject of his or her presentation, but make no summary of his or her remarks.

Signing the minutes

Minutes are to be signed by the secretary and, if customary, may also be signed by the president. Minutes are your group's legal record of its proceedings, and the secretary's signature establishes evidence of the original document's authenticity.

Avoid using the term *Respectfully Submitted* — it's now considered passé.

Approving the minutes

The minutes of one meeting are normally approved at the next regular meeting, following the call to order and opening ceremonies. I cover meeting procedure in detail in Chapter 5.

If the meeting is an adjourned meeting (see Chapter 3), you approve the minutes of your previous meeting (the meeting that established the adjourned meeting) before taking up business where you left off in that meeting. Also, the minutes of the adjourned meeting should be approved at the next adjourned or regular meeting.

When you hold a special meeting, the only business in order is the urgent business for which the meeting was called — the business that can't wait until the next regular meeting. For that reason, the minutes of your regular meetings aren't brought up for approval at a special meeting (unless the approval of minutes is the urgent reason you called the special meeting). The minutes of a special meeting are approved at the next regular meeting.

Minutes drafted ahead of time aren't the official minutes *until the members approve them.* Because changes may be made in the minutes before they're approved, it's good practice for the secretary to note somewhere on the distribution copy that it's a "draft for approval."

When minutes are approved, the secretary annotates the original file copy with any corrections in the margin, writes "Approved" on the minutes, and adds his initials and the date to the record.

Publishing the minutes

If your organization publishes its minutes (meaning that your minutes are actually "made public" as opposed to simply being distributed to members), then you need to include everything I list in the sections above, plus a list of the speakers on each side of every question and a short summary of each speech.

Sounds like one onerous task for the secretary, but fortunately, Robert's Rules stipulates that if you're going to go any further and really publish your minutes *in full,* then you need to have an assistant secretary and a stenographic reporter. Robert's Rules also reminds the chairman that clearly identifying all speakers is essential to an accurate report. When you're reading one of those monstrous transcripts, it's no fun to go back and try to remember who said what. Also note that publishing in full means that you include all the reports that were given at the meeting, too.

Your organization may be one that likes to capture every jot and tittle of the proceedings by having a stenographer who then transcribes things. If this is the case, please consider making an extract for unpublished minutes that contains just the essential items of business. Keep these unpublished minutes handy in your record book, and call them *minutes* or *parliamentary minutes* to distinguish them from that fat (published) book that nobody ever reads again anyway unless the meeting was especially heated.

First Things First: The Treasurer's Report

The treasurer generally reports basic financial information at every regular meeting. Today's accounting-made-easy software allows a treasurer to print out a report that shows receipts, disbursements, and cash balances pretty easily. But for organizations with simple and uncomplicated finances (maybe they just have a cash fund or a checking account), all that's really necessary is a simple, single-page report that shows the opening balance, the itemized receipts and disbursements, and the closing balance. In fact, that's the basic information most members want and need to make decisions.

You can find a sample treasurer's report in Appendix B; detail beyond what's represented there is usually just a waste of the members' time. The treasurer's job mostly involves working behind the scenes taking care of the funds. The Audit Committee has the task of examining financial records in detail at sufficient intervals; the committee's goal is to alleviate any concerns members may have about the details of the fund management. So, if any member requires more detail than appears in the treasurer's report, then that member should make arrangements to meet with the treasurer outside of the meeting to go over more detailed records.

After it's presented to the membership, the treasurer's report is simply filed for audit, and no other action is necessary. The time for formal action on your financial reports is when you receive your Audit Committee's report on the treasurer's annual report. (More information on meeting agendas and the order of business is available in Chapter 5.)

No matter what the official procedure is for filing a treasurer's report after presentation, every meeting has its own Millie Motionmaker who loves to move to accept the treasurer's report. If you know Millie, please remind her (and your chairman) that the proper way for the chair to handle the treasurer's report after it's presented is to say, "Thank you. The treasurer's report will be filed for audit. The next item of business is. . . ."

Next Up: Reports of Other Officers

Other than the treasurer's report and the secretary's report, which usually only contains the draft of minutes for approval but may include a report of correspondence received, other officers don't usually make regular reports.

Officers other than the treasurer and secretary may have information from time to time that needs to come before the assembly, and motions may arise out of the presentation of such information. An officer's need to make a report is usually of sufficient importance to justify priority placement in the order of business. (Robert's Rules endorses this practice, in case you were wondering.)

When an officer makes a report that contains recommendations for action, a member other than the reporting officer should make any motion tied to the report.

For example, the president receives an offer of ten tickets to the Lake Wassamatta Submarine Races for the organization to raffle. After the president makes his report recommending that the organization accept the offer, you agree with him and say, "Mr. President, I move that we accept the offer of the tickets and that you be authorized to appoint a Raffle Committee to make arrangements for a raffle and report back to us its plan at next month's meeting."

 Don't just move to accept the report or adopt the recommendations. Your motion in the example above is precise and to the point; you make it very clear exactly what the members are being asked to decide.

Wrapping Up Reporting: Reports of Boards and Committees

In well-run organizations, the executive board (if there is one) and committees are loaded up with work between meetings of the assembly. These subordinate bodies need to keep the general membership informed of their activities and recommendations, and they do so by furnishing reports to the body to which they're accountable.

 Reports should certainly be made when there's business to report or recommendations to make, but not just for the sake of giving a report. Boards and committees don't have to furnish reports if they haven't done anything since their previous report. There's no rule in Robert's Rules that requires your committees or boards to automatically add to the profits of the paper mills just because you're having another meeting.

Hearing from the executive board

Your executive board is charged with much of the management of your organization that's necessary between membership meetings. The board commonly reports its accomplishments at the end of its term (at your big election meeting, whenever that is). But if you hold membership meetings more frequently than annually, your board may also report to the membership at other times when important matters require membership attention or when the membership has requested a report on a particular matter.

The executive board should select the person or persons to draft the report, but the president or secretary may be assigned this duty by custom or rule. The board considers the draft for adoption, amends it at its pleasure, and the report is then presented to the membership.

Handling committee reports

The nature of any committee makes it a subordinate body to the group or person under whose authority it is appointed or elected. Therefore, the committee's ultimate product is a report back to that authority. Its report must contain its findings, the results of its actions in carrying out the task assigned to it, its recommendations, or all of these things.

Writing the committee report

The committee's report should always be submitted in writing, unless it's so brief that its entire substance and content can be easily entered in the minutes from an oral report. Generally, committees like to elaborate on their work, so reports are often too lengthy to report orally. But committees can give oral reports occasionally, especially when a motion has been referred for a recommendation and the only report is, for example, a recommendation on how to dispose of the motion. No need for a written report there!

When creating your written committee report:

- ✔ **Do identify it as the report of the committee and not of the committee chairman, even if the chairman presents the report.**

- ✔ **Do write in the third person.**

- ✔ **Do identify the committee.** For example, "The committee appointed to report on the advisability of purchasing the vacant lot next door reports that . . ." or "The Legislative Affairs Committee reports that. . . ."

- ✔ **Do ensure that the report is signed by all the committee members who concur, or by the chairman alone if authorized by the committee.** In that case, he should include the word "chairman" next to his name as a means of certifying that the entire committee adopted the report.

- ✔ **Don't address or date it.** After all, the report's recipient is the group to whom it is presented, and the date of the meeting in which it's presented is already reflected in the minutes.

- ✔ **Don't include the words "Respectfully submitted" before the signatures.** This closing is no longer customary and is actually considered superfluous (if not altogether passé).

Covering recommendations for action in committee reports

Most committee reports contain some sort of recommendation, especially when motions and amendments are referred to a committee.

In those cases, the committee is usually called upon to report its recommendations on the motion's disposition. It may recommend amendments to the main motion or that a pending amendment be defeated. Reports with recommendations of this kind really just return the motion to the hands of the members.

After the committee makes its recommendations on a motion referred to it, the chair should restate the motion in its original form (as it went to the committee); if the committee's recommendation is to be advanced, either the committee or another member makes the appropriate motion and the discussion begins again.

Some special committees simply report the results of an investigation or their findings on some matter. (Flip to Chapter 16 for a rundown on special committees.) Their reports may require no action at all because the information they provide adds to discussions on some question or issue of concern or interest to the members. When no action is required, the chair responds to the committee report by saying, "Thank you. The report needs no action and will be placed on file" or "Thank you. The next item of business is. . . ."

Organizations sometimes handle reports from Nominating Committees improperly. Moving to adopt the report of a Nominating Committee as a means of electing the slate proposed is never in order. After a Nominating Committee presents its report, the chair proceeds directly to take nominations from the floor and continues doing so until no further nominations are forthcoming. You can find the complete procedural guidelines for this committee in Chapter 13.

Knowing What to Do with Reports and Recommendations

Consider yourself a prisoner of your words. When the time comes to present a report to your organization, be sure you use terms correctly and in the proper context — you don't want to do or say something you wish you hadn't! To avoid a lot of unnecessary trouble and confusion, keep the following things in mind:

- ✔ **Reports are *received* when they're presented.** Motions to *receive* reports after they're read make no sense because the report has already been received. The only time a motion to receive a report makes sense, or is even in order, is when you want a report to be presented at some time other than when reports are in order according to your agenda.

✔ *Adopting* (or *accepting*) a report is problematic. The odds are good that you don't want to adopt the whole report. If anything, you probably want to adopt only *some* of the motions or resolutions recommended in the report. The only time it really makes sense to *adopt* a report is when you want to endorse the entire contents of a report that was prepared for adoption as the report of the group. For example, a board's report to the assembly is usually drafted by one of the members for consideration by the board as the report it will make to the assembly. Only when the board *adopts* the report does it become the actual report of the board.

Adopting (or accepting) recommendations rather than taking up the recommended questions (or motions or resolutions) can create considerable confusion. If a committee recommends a resolution's adoption, then you don't want to consider a motion to adopt the recommendation — the question instead is directly on the adoption of the resolution. Think about the trouble you run into if you need to amend the resolution: Just how do you amend a resolution if the motion is to adopt the recommendation?

Recognizing Members' Rights to Consult the Records

Over the years, the minutes, treasurer's financial reports, and other reports of officers, boards, and committees become an important archive for your group. All these reports constitute your organization's records and generally should be accessible to the members. If your group is incorporated, members may even have a legal right to inspect any of these records (and more) at any reasonable time.

Robert's Rules recognizes, however, that an assembly's records are not open to inspection to the extent that members wanting to view records can excessively pester the secretary or other custodian.

A few basic rules apply to the availability of some records:

✔ **Assembly minutes are only available to members of that assembly, unless the group has authorized them to be viewed by nonmembers.** This rule applies to boards, too, and means that you're not automatically entitled to view your board's minutes if you're not on the board. However, if the assembly superior to the board orders the minutes to be made available to the members, then the board must follow orders.

✔ **You don't necessarily have unlimited access to membership information.** You *probably* have the right under rule or law to view or copy basic member contact information on your organization's membership list, at least for personal use in making contact with other members. But a membership list is proprietary information to the group, and your right to the list is not a right to furnish the list to others outside the group.

✔ **Your organization's records belong only to the organization, which can and should devise policies concerning the permitted use and access to the records.** Consulting with an attorney is the best way to know whether any of your records are subject to public inspection or to inspection by the members regardless of internal policy.

When it comes to the minutes, financial reports, and reports of boards and committees, you have to balance the rights of members with the rights of the organization as a whole. You can save a lot of worry and trouble by putting in place a standing rule to establish a privacy policy regarding the availability of your records to members and to the public.

Chapter 18

We Gotta Get Rid of this Guy! Disciplining and Removing Officers or Members

- -

In This Chapter

▶ Knowing when and how to remove someone from office

▶ Using proper methods to charge and try members for offenses

▶ Learning how to expel disorderly members from meetings

- -

*P*eople behave themselves most of the time, but sometimes members and officers alike get the urge to create problems or make a scene in meetings. However infrequent they may be, you need to know how to deal with problem situations when they occur.

And not all problems crop up in meetings. Even outside the meeting milieu, a member may conduct himself in a manner inconsistent with the standards your group requires of those who wish to maintain an association with your organization. This chapter gives you information on how to deal with situations that shouldn't occur, but unfortunately do.

Dealing with a Dictator

Has your presiding officer donned the crown of King Kong? Does he refuse to allow your proper motion to come before the membership because of his obvious effort to maintain and protect his own personal agenda or faction? If so, he's violating his duty to the assembly to maintain an impartial bearing in the chair.

Not to worry. You can exercise some options that may just cause him the utmost darned astonishment.

Putting a question from your place

Suppose that the presiding officer is blocking your motion by refusing to let it come before the membership for consideration. Your first line of defense in this sort of passive-aggressive attack on your rights is to raise a *point of order* (see Chapter 11) and to *appeal* any ruling that's wrong or self-serving. If the chair refuses to entertain your appeal, then you get to have some fun and put the question from your place.

Putting the question from your place means you can simply ignore the chair's recalcitrance and announce to the members that the chair's unwillingness to put the question on your appeal entitles you to place before them the motion you originally wanted to make.

Go for it! The rules are on your side. By this time, King Kong has probably lost some serious brownie points and may be close to having his name changed to Gorilla B. Gone.

In order to put the question from your place, you need to know your political situation. You can't get far if you aren't confident that the majority is on your side. And if *you* are actually the problem and are just being a pill, then challenging the presiding officer can't help you.

Removing the presiding officer from the chair

If King Kong continues to abuse the rights of the members, then you have another weapon in your arsenal. You can move to suspend the rules and remove him from the chair (for the current meeting at least) with a two-thirds vote. (For information on the incidental motion to suspend the rules, see Chapter 11.) After your gruesome gorilla is out of the way, elect a temporary chairman and contemplate the more permanent solution of busting the big ape down to little monkey.

Removing an officer . . . permanently!

A good number of my consultations address situations in which a president decides that the membership exists to serve his personal agenda, and sorry is the poor soul who dares to suggest an alternative approach to anything.

Before you and your fellow members just give up and abandon your treasury to the control of King Kong and his minions, you may want to consider the alternative action: Remove the mighty monkey from office.

Removing someone from office isn't necessarily easy, but if your bylaws include a provision that the members can remove an officer, then you can do it without much ado as long as you get a two-thirds vote on the proposal. (You can actually accomplish the removal with a majority vote if you've given notice, or if you have the votes of a majority of the entire membership.) Removing an officer is just a particular use of the motion to rescind or amend something previously adopted (see Chapter 12), and with this action, you are, in effect, amending your original election and electing someone else.

You may encounter a couple of stumbling blocks in your quest to make your meetings once again safe for democracy. If your bylaws say nothing about members removing officers, then you can only follow the procedure I outline in this section if the bylaws provide that the officer's term of office is a certain length of time "*or* until his successors are elected and assume office." If you don't see that *or* in your bylaws but find an *and* in its place, then you're out of luck. If that's the case, then to bring down King Kong, you can only subject him to charges of dereliction of duty and hold a trial. I cover the steps for this procedure in the section "Holding a trial," later in this chapter.

The officer removal process is the same even if you're not particularly motivated by the desire to defeat a despot. You can attempt to remove an officer for any good reason (it has to be good if you expect to reach removal through a trial), such as when Mr. Meanswell gets elected but has only attended one meeting in the past year since his election. In fact, if your bylaws provide for removal, or if your term-of-office clause has that little *or,* then you can rescind the election of any officer at any time for any reason. Not that you'd want to, but it's good to know you can!

Disciplining Members Who Shame Your Group's Name

Your bylaws may include sections on discipline and list offenses and remedies along with a procedure for dealing with them. But even if your bylaws don't address these issues specifically, you're not obligated to allow a person to continue as a member if they behave in a way that could injure the work or good name of your organization.

In cases in which undesirable behavior occurs outside a meeting, in which the facts and circumstances aren't clearly witnessed by the entire membership, a formal process for preferring charges and permitting the accused an opportunity of defense is essential.

Trials and disciplinary proceedings are probably quite rare in most small deliberative assemblies. In the groups where such things may be more common, such as professional or trade associations, specialized procedures are usually defined in bylaws or special rules of order. However, every group needs to have a basic procedure for handling members who disregard group standards, and Robert's Rules provides you with one.

Checking out the facts first

Suppose that someone in the group discovers a problem that may cast a shadow on Mr. Prollydiddit's reputation in connection with the organization. The first thing to do is appoint a committee of people whose integrity is irreproachable and give them the task of investigating the allegations before any formal charges are mentioned. The details of the allegations should, in all cases, be excluded from the formal motion to appoint such a committee. It's sufficient to move, "That a committee of [some number] be [appointed/elected] to investigate certain allegations, which if determined to be true, would cast doubt on the wisdom of retaining Mr. Prollydiddit as a member of our organization."

Under no circumstances is it ever in order for an *individual* to offer a resolution directly charging a member with an offense — that can only be done by a committee, and then only after a preliminary investigation determines that sufficient cause exists. And even then, it's never appropriate to offer a resolution that *reveals the nature of the offense or suggests that certain allegations are true.* The group has nothing to gain and everything to lose by making the rush to judgment that these kinds of motions suggest.

Considering the rights of all

Robert's Rules requires that any disciplinary proceedings brought against a member for offenses outside a meeting be brought and considered in executive session. Allowing this kind of business to be made public and discussed outside of the organization is a mistake. The rights of your group and of the accused depend on this principle of privacy, and violation of the secrecy of executive session is generally considered grounds for expulsion.

Your group has the right to insist that members meet certain standards for membership. When your group decides that a member must be held accountable for unacceptable behavior, it's in the interest of both your group and the accused member to proceed carefully and fairly before making any decisions that could unfairly or wrongfully expel or otherwise penalize a member.

The appointed committee's job is limited to conducting a basic investigation of any allegations that underlie the proceedings. The committee may not compel anyone to come forward and give information, but it should make a concerted effort to gather facts. Any confidential information it obtains may not be used in any trial that it may recommend. But it may be useful in making its final determination.

When the committee arrives at its conclusion, it reports its recommendation to the membership, either by offering a resolution formally charging the member with a specific offense, or by declaring the allegations unfounded.

Depending upon the committee's findings, it may be a good idea to engage the subject of the investigation in a private and frank discussion and hear his spin on the spam. At this stage, a trial may still be avoidable. The accused may see the wisdom in resignation if he's likely to be removed from membership when formal charges are brought and a trial conducted. Conversely, he may bring the truth to shine on his innocence and show his accusers to be in error or improperly motivated.

Reporting findings of cause

The foundation for a trial is established with the adoption of the investigating committee's report that the allegations have merit and that facts exist to substantiate formal charges. The assembly must then make some specific decisions about the following items, which, ideally, should be the subject of the committee's recommendations and should appear in a series of resolutions. These decisions determine

- ✔ The date and location of the trial, affording reasonable time for managers to prepare to present the case and for the accused to prepare for his defense.

- ✔ Whether the trial will be conducted by the entire membership or by a committee.

- ✔ The *charges* (being the offense) and the *specifications* (being the actions of the accused that give rise to the offense). *Charges* should cite the violated standards that give rise to penalties.

- ✔ Selection of the *managers,* members who will present the case against the accused.

- ✔ The *citation* of the member requiring him to appear and show cause why the penalty being sought should not be assessed based on the charges and specifications. The citation should include the details of the penalty, charges, and specifications.

Holding a trial

The trial for a disciplinary matter of a deliberative assembly has many parallels to trials with which you may be more familiar. However, this type of trial is a *private* proceeding in the nature of a *formal hearing,* and its result is but a *judgment of your assembly* on the fitness of the accused to remain as a member of the organization.

At all times in the disciplinary process, all proper precautions should be taken to provide the accused with proceedings that are irreproachable in their fairness.

Basic considerations for fairness in the trial include the following:

- ✔ The accused is still afforded the right to defense counsel, and the defense counsel may be an attorney. But any defense attorney must be a member of the organization, unless the trial panel (or assembly, if the trial is being conducted by the membership) agrees that a nonmember attorney may be admitted.

- ✔ The accused may call witnesses in his defense.

- ✔ Nonmembers may be called as witnesses, but their presence may not be permitted in the trial except when they're giving their testimony.

Opening the trial

The trial begins when the chair opens the meeting and addresses preliminary matters.

1. **The chairman calls the meeting to order and gives immediate notice that the meeting is in executive session, which means the proceedings are secret and may not be disclosed to nonmembers under penalty of expulsion.**

2. **The secretary reads all of the resolutions adopted in the preliminary proceedings and verifies the service of the citation on the accused.**

3. **The chair announces the names of the managers (members who present the case against the accused) and inquires of the accused whether he is represented by counsel.**

4. **Charges and specifications are read, to which the accused enters his pleas of guilty or not guilty to each charge and then to each specification. If a guilty plea is entered, a trial is unnecessary and the penalty hearing may then be held.**

Trying the case

In each of the following steps, the managers present first, followed by the defense.

1. **Opening statements**

2. **Witness testimony**

3. **Witness rebuttal**

4. **Closing arguments**

During the trial, cross-examination is permitted, and witnesses may be subject to recall. No persons other than the managers or the defense may have the floor during these stages of the trial.

Deciding the verdict

Generally speaking, the rest of the trial is downhill. The managers and the defense counsel remain and participate in the discussion; only the accused must leave the room during the deliberations.

At the outset of deliberations, the chair states the question on the guilt of the accused as follows: "The question before you now is 'Is Mr. Prollydiddit guilty of the charges and specifications as follows, [read each charge and specification]?"

Discussion and voting is handled like it would be for any main motion, but a ballot vote *must* be taken if any member demands it. Flip back to Chapter 7 for the lowdown on debating motions and Chapter 8 for the bottom line on voting.

In some instances, in light of facts brought in the trial, the assembly determines that the accused is guilty of a lesser charge than the one originally proffered. It's permissible to adopt a finding of guilt to the lesser charges, but those lesser charges must be consistent with, and within the scope of, the charges with which the accused was noticed and tried.

If the accused is found not guilty of the original charges, then he's exonerated. If he's found guilty, then the assembly or panel moves into deliberations to determine and fix the penalty.

The accused is immediately notified after the deliberations are complete and the results are determined.

When the trial panel is not the assembly itself but rather an appointed committee, the panel's decision is framed as a recommendation to the assembly, which must act on the recommendations. In this case, the assembly must consider the recommendation in executive session, and the accused should be given the opportunity to rebut the findings of the committee. After his rebuttal, he must remove himself from the room pending the final decisions of the assembly.

Maintaining Order in Meetings

You can find problem people in all walks of life, and they're in no short supply at meetings. Everyone comes across a sore loser or a member who likes attention so much that he's willing to create a scene over any little thing. People who behave this way are everywhere, and you may have little choice but to put up with them if they're your customers, co-workers, or neighbors. But you don't have to tolerate them in meetings.

Although you can take action when Joe Flack tunes up for a tirade, you shouldn't really have to if your presiding officer takes advantage of this section's techniques for taking care of problem people.

Understanding rights of the group

When you're in a meeting, the right to say who can be present is completely within the control of your group. This right doesn't mean that you can arbitrarily exclude a member who has a right to be there, nor does it mean that you can fail to comply with provisions of a public meetings' law.

But your assembly has the absolute right to eject a member if he becomes of sufficient annoyance that the proceedings of the meeting can't continue peacefully. Same thing goes for a nonmember in a meeting of a public body, subject, of course, to provisions of your local laws regarding ejecting disruptive attendees.

Understanding what's expected of individuals

As a member of an assembly, you have a duty in your meetings to respect the position of the presiding officer. You're expected to generally obey his orders, but you have the right to appeal from any decision in a polite and proper way.

Your presiding officer has a corresponding duty to refrain from shouting down a member or otherwise being drawn into a fracas. The chair who allows a ranting member to fizzle out usually has the most success in bringing an assembly back to order. It's generally best for the presiding officer to remain calm and deliberate and ultimately let questions of discipline be decided by the membership.

Managing misbehaving members

Minor breaches of order, such as wandering beyond the bounds of the question under consideration, interrupting a speaker who has the floor, or speaking without recognition, can usually be handled by simply reminding the member of the proper way to do things. The presiding officer may say, "The member will please confine his remarks to the subject under discussion," or "The member will please address his remarks to the chair."

However, sometimes in the thick of things, ol' Joe Flack goes beyond the bounds of propriety and questions the motives of another speaker or commits some other breach of decorum (see Chapter 7). When that happens, the group can turn to a nice, polite little procedure called *calling a member to order*.

Calling the member to order

When Joe Flack goes off (as he's prone to do sometimes) and starts talking about this or that, or maybe he launches into some diatribe, the chair first warns Joe that he needs to confine his remarks to the motion under consideration. But if Joe ignores this warning, then the chair may say, "The member will come to order and be seated." This approach is the nicest way to tell Joe to shut up and sit down. Hopefully, he gets the message.

If the chair doesn't act quickly enough, or if a member believes the chair needs to call Mr. Flack to order, then the member may, without first being recognized, call out, "Mr. Chairman, I call the member to order." The chair proceeds to handle the situation as described earlier in this section. However, if Joe has been properly assigned the floor and the chair isn't convinced that the complaining member's point is well-taken, he may ask the group if Joe should be allowed to continue speaking. A voice vote can decide that question.

"Naming" the offender

If Joe doesn't take the hint and continues on his errant path, then the chair may direct the secretary to note the breach in the minutes. The chair can then take direct official action against the member by *naming* him and saying something like, "Mr. Flack, the chair has asked you thrice now to refrain from personal attacks on members, yet you persist in refusing to obey the orders of the chair and continue in your conduct in a manner wholly unacceptable to the chair and the assembly."

If Joe doesn't sit down and shut up, it may be time to demand an apology or even ask him to leave. But the chair shouldn't attempt to take such action by himself. The membership gets to decide Joe's fate now.

If you're lucky, when things get this far, Joe apologizes and sits down, and the chairman accepts his apology and continues with the meeting. But Joe has a way about him that may mean you need to take things to the limit and turn to the membership.

Penalizing the offender

At the point the chair has reached the end of his rope in his dealings with Joe Flack, his last option is to ask the group what to do about Joe. Should he be censured? Should he be removed from the meeting until he apologizes? Should he be expelled from membership?

If the situation has gone this far, the chair may say, "Members, the chair is at wits' end. I regret to put the question now before you, but find I must prepare you to speak to the question of whether Mr. Flack shall be removed from the meeting. Before we consider the question, however, I ask Mr. Flack, 'Sir, do you wish to make a statement to the membership before I place the question on your removal?'"

Your chair should give Joe a final opportunity to comply or at least speak in his own defense. But if Joe doesn't straighten out fast, any of the remedies mentioned above are possible. The hard truth is that if Joe can't behave in a meeting, you don't even have to allow him to continue his membership. But terminating his membership requires a two-thirds vote, unlike other remedies that require only a majority vote. In any case, any member can demand that a vote on this kind of decision be taken by ballot.

Removing nonmembers from the meeting

You have the right to conduct your meeting without the presence of nonmembers, and to that end, the chair has the authority (on his own initiative) to require nonmembers to leave the meeting. He should be ready to use this authority in the event that the peanut gallery (or any individual peanut) becomes rambunctious. Just to make sure that the chair doesn't act in opposition to the will of the assembly, however, any member may appeal the chair's order for nonmembers to leave, and the question then becomes one for the members to decide.

After a removal has been ordered, whether it's removal of a member or a nonmember, the chair may exercise whatever reasonable means necessary to execute the removal. If those removed don't leave of their own accord, he may appoint a committee to escort them from the meeting, or, if necessary, the chair may summon peace officers to remove the offenders and restore peace to the assembly.

Part IV
The Part of Tens

In this part . . .

*P*eople say, "What you don't know won't hurt you," but if somebody had given me all the information in the following chapters, I would probably have avoided a lot of blunders and saved myself some embarrassment in my early ventures into parliamentary procedure.

But I don't just cover myths and the mistakes in this part. The list of ideas for special rules for your group can come in handy whether you're starting a new organization or trying to streamline an existing one.

Parliamentarians seem to like lists. And just so you know, the lists in this part were assembled with the help of several of my colleagues who gave me the benefit of their own experiences. (I thank them directly in my acknowledgements, and I hope you read that part of the book, too. You may need a good parliamentarian one of these days, and if I'm not available, one of them may be!)

Chapter 19

Ten (Or So) Meeting Procedure Myths

*I*n my experience, I find that most members and presiding officers really do have an interest in doing things according to Robert's Rules. The real trouble is that more often than not, they've never really *read* Robert's Rules or even a book like this about Robert's Rules.

The trouble is, when you haven't *read* the rules, but instead just operate based on what you've *heard* are the rules, you unknowingly help to create or strengthen a procedure myth. Unfortunately, Robert's Rules are often misinterpreted, and a lot of common meeting procedure myths are floating around out there.

It's time to dispel the myths and reveal why some things really should be done a certain way. If your goal is to have good meetings and avoid wasting time, you'll be glad you read about these ten (or so) myths, and you'll see how things actually should be done according to Robert's Rules.

Robert's Rules Are Just a Guide: You Don't Have to Follow Them

BZZZZZT!! Sorry, but no cigar for you! (This one has to be the mother of all myths — it's completely baseless!) If your bylaws provide that Robert's Rules is your parliamentary authority, then the rules are binding on your group.

Most of the time, people who say this just don't know the truth, or just don't think about it. Only rarely are they trying to manipulate the organization or take advantage of the members' lack of familiarity with the rules.

I can't argue that Robert's Rules doesn't contain a lot of guidance. It does! With all its *should* rules, it offers members and leaders alike plenty of advice and solid recommendations based on common sense and logic. But as helpful as it is as a guide, when you've adopted it, Robert's Rules is the definitive authority for decisions on parliamentary procedure, and it's as enforceable as you care to make it.

If you adopt a parliamentary authority, its rules are binding on the organization insofar as they don't conflict with the bylaws or special rules of order adopted by the organization.

Only One Motion Can Be on the Floor at a Time

Robert's Rules establishes that it's a *fundamental principle of parliamentary law* that only "one question can be considered at a time." I'm not arguing. You can only *consider* one question at a time. The myth arises because the actual rule is often misstated: Several pending motions can actually be on the floor at one time when you include any *secondary motions* that may be made during the handling of a main motion.

These motions can be made while another motion is pending, subject only to their particular rules of applicability and precedence. They're added to the stack of pending motions as they're made, and they're voted on (or considered) one at a time, from highest ranking back down to the lowest ranking, in their proper order. Flip back to Chapters 9 through 11 for a more in-depth discussion of secondary motions.

For example, a motion is made to hire a management company to handle your condo association's business dealings and physical building maintenance. A member then moves to amend the motion in some way. While the amendment is being discussed, someone moves to refer the motion with the amendment to a committee to report back next month. While the motion to refer is being discussed, someone moves to limit the debate on the motion to commit to ten more minutes and then take a vote.

Your parliamentary situation is that you have four motions pending, or *on the floor,* at one time. But you can only *consider* one question at a time. In this case, you take up the question whether to limit debate and decide it before you get back to the motion to commit. You consider the question whether to commit; then, if it fails, you go back to consideration of the amendment. After you decide the question on the amendment, you're again able to consider the original main motion.

Many *pending motions* can stack up during the course of a discussion, but only one *question* can be considered at a time.

The Presiding Officer Can Only Vote to Break a Tie

This popular myth, and its variation that the chair *must* vote to break a tie, are more common than ants at a picnic. And it's simply not so!

Robert's Rules says that the presiding officer (if a member) votes with the other members when a vote is by ballot; but for other forms of voting, the chair's duty to maintain the appearance of impartiality while presiding requires him to refrain from voting, except when his vote will affect the result. (Chapter 8 contains more information on voting procedures.)

The myth comes about because of two misconceptions. The first is based on the misunderstanding that a tie vote is not decisive. On the contrary, whenever a majority vote is required to adopt a motion, a tie vote *is* decisive; a motion that fails to achieve the majority vote necessary to adopt it *fails*.

If the vote is tied, the presiding officer doesn't need to vote unless he wants the motion to be adopted. He can then vote in the affirmative, and the motion passes.

The presiding officer does not get to cast a second vote. If you're voting by ballot and the result of a ballot is a tie, the motion fails. If an election ballot ties, however, everybody just votes again.

If the vote isn't tied but the affirmatives outnumber the opposition by one vote, the chair doesn't need to vote unless he wishes the motion to fail. He can then cast a vote in the negative, creating a tie and causing the motion to fail.

The second misconception contributing to this myth comes from the failure to consider that that the chair's vote can also affect the outcome when the threshold for adoption is anything other than a majority. For example, if a motion requires a two-thirds vote to pass, the chair's vote can make a difference if it causes the motion to reach (or not reach) the two-thirds threshold. In either case, the chair can vote if he wants to affect the result.

The chair should vote along with other members whenever the vote is by ballot; otherwise, he should vote only when he wants to use his vote to affect the result.

The Parliamentarian Makes Rulings to Decide Procedural Questions

Some presiding officers like to pass the buck when it comes to handling points of order and parliamentary inquiries. They say things like, "The parliamentarian just ruled that . . ." or "The parliamentarian says you can't (or can) do so-and-so."

But a presiding officer who knows her stuff stands in control of the meeting. She assumes the responsibility incumbent upon her after consulting with and paying heed to the parliamentarian's opinions on matters of procedure.

The parliamentarian's job is to advise the presiding officer and give his opinion when asked. But the sole responsibility for ruling on a point of order or answering a parliamentary inquiry lies with the chair.

A Motion That's Adopted without Being Seconded Is Void

The purpose of the requirement for a motion to be seconded is to avoid wasting your group's time on a motion that no one other than the person who makes the motion wants to discuss.

If the members debate an unseconded motion, vote on an unseconded motion without debating it, or adopt it by unanimous consent, the motion is adopted, being presumed to have a second because members discussed it or acted upon it.

A point of order that a motion is not in order for lack of a second must be made before any discussion or vote takes place on the motion.

Abstentions Count As Yes or No Votes

One of the most frequent questions asked of parliamentarians is "How do we count abstentions?" The answer is simple: You don't. Abstentions are *not* votes. They're instances of members choosing not to vote.

The confusion probably comes from the fact that voters who abstain typically do, by their abstention, influence the outcome of a vote. For example, if the requirement for adoption is a majority vote, then abstentions have the effect of a vote for the prevailing side. By not voting, members have helped the winner.

On the other hand, if the vote required for adoption is the affirmative vote of the majority of the members present, then an abstention has the same effect as a negative vote.

But in any case, abstentions are never counted toward one side or the other even if the fact that a member doesn't vote has a direct effect on the outcome.

A member has a duty to vote, but he can't be compelled to vote, because he also has the right to remain neutral on a particular question. Therefore, requiring a motion to be decided based on the number of members present is usually not a good idea; this arrangement denies a member his right to be neutral on the question. (I discuss abstentions and vote-counting procedures in Chapter 8.)

The Chair Should Always Ask for Unfinished Business

You're not alone if you or your fellow members think that *unfinished business* is that part of the agenda where you rehash old ideas that never went anywhere. Those who have knowledge of the term but have never considered its true definition under Robert's Rules perpetuate the myth.

Unfinished business is business brought over from an earlier meeting. It consists of motions not finally disposed of, perhaps postponed from the prior meeting, or pending when the meeting adjourned. A class of business, its items are determined based on what happened at the prior meeting. Unfinished business is not the place for members to bring up old ideas that never took off.

The presiding officer and the secretary aren't doing their jobs if neither knows whether the group has any unfinished business. If the presiding officer does know, then he should announce the first item in the class as soon as the meeting reaches the point in the order of business when unfinished business is addressed.

The Chair Must Call for Nominations from the Floor Three Times

This myth seems to have a life of its own, like some kind of urban legend. It rivals the myth that all a member has to do to stop debate is to holler "Question!" from his chair. (I discuss that mistake in Chapter 21.)

Perhaps this myth has its foundations in a reasonable policy that some judicious presiding officer once adopted to be sure that nominations were not closed as long as there was a member who wished to make a nomination from the floor. He may have thought, "If I call for nominations once, hear none, and declare nominations closed, somebody is sure to say, 'Hey, wait, you can't just close nominations like that!' If I try again and call for nominations a second time, then those who didn't hear me the first time are likely to react the same way. So, I'll just ask three times before I say 'Hearing none, the chair declares nominations are closed.'"

All this is very reasonable, and it's certainly not a bad policy. But it isn't a rule.

The motion to close nominations is never in order as long as anyone wishes to make a nomination. In fact, the motion is rarely even necessary. The chair, upon determining there are no further nominations forthcoming from the members, simply declares nominations closed.

If an Election Winner Doesn't Serve, the Second-place Candidate Takes Over

This myth is one of those misconceptions that sounds so reasonable until you give it some thought. The second-place candidate is either the loser of a two-candidate race or one of several people rejected by the members in favor of someone else. In the first situation, he was rejected outright; in the second situation, no one knows how the members would have voted had the original winner not been on the ballot. You can't assume that the second-place candidate would have been the winner if all the members who voted for the actual winner had voted for someone else.

Sorry, but if the winner declines the office after being elected, you have what Robert's Rules calls an *incomplete election* (see Chapter 14). To resolve the incomplete election, you need to reopen nominations and have another try at it.

If the winner fails to serve out his term of office, you're left with a vacancy, and you need to follow the rules in your bylaws for filling the vacancy. Depending on the particular office and your bylaws, you may have to hold another election, or your executive board may be able to appoint someone to fill the vacancy. If your bylaws say nothing about filling vacancies, you hold another election for the office.

Except when your bylaws provide expressly for filling a vacancy *in the office of president,* if your president dies or resigns, the vacancy actually occurs in the office of vice-president, who automatically becomes the president. You then fill the vacancy in the office of vice-president.

If the winner of an election declines to serve, the election is incomplete. Vote again! Otherwise, vacancies in an office are filled either according to the bylaws or rules of order, or by the electing authority if no applicable rules are in place.

Officers Must Be Members of the Organization

If your organization follows this policy, it's not because of anything in Robert's Rules. The only way you can properly put a limitation on whom to elect is by establishing that qualification in the bylaws. If you don't have this kind of limitation, however, Robert's Rules recognizes the complete autonomy of a membership body to select anyone it wants to serve as an officer.

Frequently, organizations rely on nonmember officers. A treasurer may be an accountant who is not a member but who is willing to give his service. Similarly, a secretary (or even the president/CEO) may be an employee of the organization but not a member.

If your group wants to limit its own power to decide who serves by adopting a bylaw requiring officers to be members, that's fine. But Robert's Rules sees this action as a limitation on the right of the membership itself to make the final decision on whom it wishes to elect to serve.

The membership can elect whomever it wants unless the bylaws establish qualifications for the office.

Ex-officio Members Can't Vote

Now that's just plain silly. Of course they can vote! They're members, aren't they? *Ex-officio* simply refers to how they came to be a member: They hold membership *by virtue of* some *office.* Members can always vote, no matter how they come to be a member, unless there's some concrete rule specific to your group that restricts the voting rights of a particular class of members.

Motions Don't Take Effect Until Minutes Are Approved

If this statement was true, you could never even have approved minutes, because minutes of one meeting wouldn't be officially approved until the minutes of the meeting where they were approved get approved, and those minutes wouldn't be approved until the next meeting (and so on)! You'd have a never-ending wait for approved minutes.

The way it really works is that motions are in effect upon adoption, unless the motion provides for some other effective date. The fact that minutes aren't yet approved has nothing to do with whether a motion is in effect. Approving minutes only approves the record of the adoption of the motion, not the motion itself.

Chapter 20

Ten Tips for Presiding Officers

*W*hether you're presiding over a meeting of 2,500 members or a small board or committee meeting, your job is the same when it comes to the goal of successfully managing a meeting. And to ensure that you manage successfully, here are some tips to help you establish yourself as a knowledgeable, well-organized, and helpful leader.

Know Your Rules

One of the best ways to establish your credibility as a leader is to know your rules. If you don't know your rules, your members will know it, and you'll come to a sudden understanding of how it probably feels to be a deer staring into oncoming headlights. (I know of what I speak. I was there once — caught unprepared, not staring into oncoming headlights. And I don't ever intend to be in that position again.)

No feeling is quite as bad as standing in front of a room full of people who know more about your job than you do. For what it's worth, General Robert was in that position once, too. After his experience, he wrote a book on the rules!

To avoid being caught unprepared, make sure you're well read on your group's charter, bylaws, special rules of order, and parliamentary authority. No one other than a person who has held your office before you (and your parliamentarian) should know as much about these rules as you do.

Plan Your Meetings

Nothing benefits you and your group as much as being prepared for your meetings. Planning your meeting in as much detail as possible assures the best chance of completing the agenda within the time available (or at least knowing if you'll need to hold an adjourned meeting to finish your business). The process of planning your meeting so that you can cover everything you need to cover is much easier if you follow the tips outlined below:

✔ **Make it everybody's business to know the agenda.** Use the minutes from the last meeting as your primary planning and management tool. Distribute the minutes and reports in advance of the meeting. The more everyone knows, the better you can budget your time.

✔ **Call on your officers and committee chairmen to submit their reports early.**

✔ **Call on members to advise the presiding officer of motions they know they intend to introduce.**

✔ **Read the reports so that you know what motions the committees will make, or what motions will be necessary to adopt recommendations.**

Start Your Meetings On Time

People have busy schedules. Your time is valuable, but it's no more valuable than that of the members who have arrived on time and are ready to start at the appointed hour.

I've been to too many meetings where the presiding officer allows a few minutes past the scheduled time to accommodate members who are late. In my opinion, that's a big mistake. An effective presiding officer accommodates the members who arrive on time and insists that the habitual latecomers adjust to everyone else instead of everyone adjusting to them.

Nothing you do commands the respect you must have as the chair as much as starting your meeting on time. Your members know you mean business, and that's fine, because that's what you're all there for.

Use Unanimous Consent

I discuss the concept of *unanimous consent* (when the chair declares a motion to have passed without taking a vote and instead asking simply if there's objection) in Chapter 8. And in several places throughout this book, I mention its use in handling particular motions.

Unanimous consent is a remarkable tool for handling any motion for which it's clear and obvious that the assembly's will is to pass the motion.

The most recognizable situations where unanimous consent is used are in the approval of minutes and when adjourning a meeting. But unanimous consent is just as useful even if the question is on a bylaw amendment, as long as no opposition is apparent. Members rarely object to unanimous consent when they know that opposition is so minimal that it won't affect the outcome.

If you ask for unanimous consent and a member objects, you simply take the vote. Otherwise, it's a great timesaver, and members really do respect presiding officers who know how to save them time.

Use Committees

Encourage new proposals to be brought through your organization's committees. Members often have good ideas, but those ideas sometimes need some work before they're ready for a vote. Teaching your members how to take their ideas to committees can have great benefits for you and your organization. But members need to have confidence in their committees' willingness to help and assist them with their ideas. Take a look at Chapter 16 for more discussion about how to create effective committees.

Let members know that they can save time in general meetings by perfecting their ideas in committees. Saving time increases your own stock as a leader. Committees will be respected for making solid recommendations, helping to get motions easily decided one way or the other.

If your committees are set up well, everybody who's really interested tackles the discussion in the committee meetings, and the rest of the members know that the committee's recommendations are based on sound reason. But good committees go to waste without a strong leader to make efficient use of them — that's you.

Preside with Impartiality

Nobody expects you to actually *be* impartial. You were probably elected or appointed because you have an overall agenda and a program you hope to advance. But when you're presiding in your meeting, you must put your personal agenda aside and help the members make their decisions. You can't lose if you do this, because ultimately, the decision belongs to the majority anyway. You're far better off being known as a leader who ensures that the minority has a full opportunity to present their case than as one who uses your power to thwart their efforts to be heard.

As I explain in more detail in Chapter 7, the presiding officer must leave any personal or political agendas to those members on the floor who support the same program. As presiding officer, you really only control the floor (and you're expected to follow clear and definite rules about how the floor's assigned). Everything else is really in the members' hands. It's *always* in your best interest to be known as a leader who helps the minority to make its case — and to do so no matter how you personally feel about their position.

To preside with impartiality:

- ✔ **Don't enter into debate.** When a member concludes his speech, don't rebut him, or argue with him, or explain why he's wrong. Say "Thank you," and recognize someone on the other side of the issue.

- ✔ **Don't gavel through motions.** What clearer indication could there be that you don't have any respect for the opposition?

- ✔ **Don't vote (except by ballot) unless your vote will affect the result.**

- ✔ **Don't refuse to recognize someone just because you don't want him to be heard.** Instead, take extra care to assist all members in their efforts to be heard.

The surest road to your success as a presiding officer is to take the position that the members control the decision, and you're there to help them do just that.

Never Give Up the Chair

Although at first this tip may appear to be an elaboration on my previous tip to maintain the appearance of impartiality, it's a little more than that.

No matter how strongly you feel about an issue, your job is to preside. True enough, Robert's Rules provides that if you can't preside impartially because you feel too strongly about an issue, you must step down and let someone else preside until the vote is taken. But I caution you to always consider whether giving up the chair is really wise. And, also consider that the person who takes the chair may not gracefully return the position to you! That can get mighty uncomfortable. Take my advice: Don't give up the chair.

Don't Share Your Lectern

Put simply, never share your lectern with other speakers. Instead, provide a separate and distinct station for other officers and committee chairmen to use when giving their reports.

During a business meeting, your duty requires that you're always in control of the floor, and you can't be in control of the floor if you can't use your station to address the assembly without moving somebody else out of the way.

When officers and committee members make their reports, motions may arise and questions may come up. By having two lecterns, you can manage the discussion from the chair and the reporting member can remain available to respond to questions as the chair may request.

Members always address their remarks and comments to the chair, and the chair recognizes members to speak and ask questions. It's your job and your station. Make the place from which you preside yours exclusively.

Keep Your Cool

Sometimes presiding over a meeting just isn't easy. When disorder erupts, no amount of hammering a wooden mallet on a sounding block is going to do anything but aggravate an already bad situation.

When Benjamin Bombastic decides to ignore the rules and fly off into seventeen different disorderly rants, you should calmly rap the gavel once and ask the member to come to order. If he ignores your request, the most effective thing you can do is stand firmly at your station. Don't allow yourself to become engaged personally with the member. Instead, calmly entreat him to come to order.

It has been my experience that those extremely difficult situations — when an entire assembly erupts in disorderly demonstration — often come about as a reaction to perceptions that the chair is being partial to one side or the other. Whatever the reason, sometimes its just best to wait until the inevitable silence finally falls, and then ask for unanimous consent to a recess so that tempers may ease. If you make mistakes that give rise to disorder, meet with those members in a position to assist you in reestablishing the respect due to the chair so that the meeting either can continue or adjourn.

Use a Parliamentarian

In the world of Robert's Rules, you don't have to go it alone. No matter what size your organization may be, when you have problems or questions, you can seek out the services of a professional parliamentarian. Resources are available online to answer questions, and local units of parliamentarians exist all over the country.

Small local organizations sometimes engage parliamentarians to assist with particular problems or with bylaw amendments and revisions, but it doesn't take an extremely large budget to have a professional parliamentarian serve regularly at your meetings. With a little planning, you can afford the assistance more than you probably realize, especially when you break down the real cost per attending member and the benefits of the assistance.

The parliamentarian's job is to make you look good in the chair. Much of your parliamentarian's work is done outside the meeting, helping you prepare for your meeting and know your rules. But when it comes time for the meeting, nothing beats the confidence you feel if you have a parliamentarian there to advise and assist you.

Chapter 21

Ten Motion Mistakes to Avoid

In This Chapter

▶ Using the proper terms when making motions

▶ Understanding the purposes of common parliamentary motions

*R*obert's Rules are rules designed to facilitate the transaction of business by your group, not to hinder it. Nitpicking on minor technicalities is against the rules. Robert's Rules warns that calling attention to purely technical errors when no one's rights are being violated is a mistake.

If you're going to be effective in meetings, you need to know the right — and wrong — ways to use parliamentary motions.

The list in this chapter is far from being exhaustive. Details for using all the basic motions are found in Part II of this book. The purpose of this list is to clue you in to the more frequent and obvious places where some members reveal their ignorance by trying to prove that they know so much.

Speaking without Recognition

First, and most importantly, just shouting out a motion is a mistake. Indeed, it's a mistake to make just about any motion without first being recognized by the chair.

You've probably heard folks shout out motions at meetings. The world would be a calmer place if they would only learn a little meeting etiquette and refrain from calling out their motions (except for points of order) until they have the recognition of the chair. Don't make the mistake of being one of those rude people. Rise and address the chair ("Mr. President" or "Madam Chairman"), and seek recognition in proper form. You don't always get the first shot, but you're entitled to preference in recognition way ahead of all those others who just shout out their motions. Take a look at Chapter 7 for more information on getting the floor in meetings.

Moving to "Table!"

In just about every meeting I've attended lately, when anything controversial comes to the floor, somebody calls from their place, "I move to table!" In addition to the offense of speaking without recognition, the member is misusing one motion in an attempt to accomplish the object of a completely different motion.

You and I know that the offending member is opposed to the pending main motion and wants to kill it. But (if you've read Chapter 9) you also know that a member doesn't kill a motion by moving to table it — at least not if the group follows Robert's Rules. The motion to table is actually the motion to *Lay on the Table,* and you use it to set a pending motion aside temporarily in order to take up something else more pressing or urgent. If you want to *kill* a main motion, you move to *Postpone Indefinitely.*

In situations like this, I generally advise the chair to ignore a motion to table unless it's made after a speaker is recognized. If the speaker has properly obtained recognition, then the chair can attempt to discern whether the speaker's intent is to lay a pending motion on the table or to kill the main motion. If it's the latter, I suggest the chair put the question as the motion to postpone indefinitely, which is how you decide whether to kill a motion under Robert's Rules. Find more information about motions to lay on the table and postpone indefinitely in Chapter 9.

Calling the Question

When members get tired of hearing the same arguments go back and forth on a pending motion, they get impatient. Inevitably somebody calls out, "Question!" or "I call the question!" Like the call to table (jump back to the previous section), the member adds to his misuse by not seeking recognition of the chair before speaking.

Sometimes the fact that no one else wishes to speak is obvious, and the chair can simply say, "If there's no one else who wishes to speak, then, without objection, we'll vote on the motion." But your presiding officer may prefer to take the opportunity to tell the members that *calling the question* actually requires a formal motion from a member after being recognized by the chair. See Chapter 9 for the complete details on this motion (*Previous Question*).

A presiding officer needs to help members understand that it's his job to offer the members the opportunity to vote when it's clear that no one else wishes to speak; calling out "Question" without first obtaining the floor is just plain rude.

Tabling It until Next Month

This attempt at a motion is yet another misuse of the word *table*. What the member who makes this proposal really wants to do is to *Postpone to a Certain Time,* not *Lay on the Table.*

About now, you may be thinking, "Why all this emphasis on the correct words if you know what the member is trying to accomplish?" The reason has a lot to do with the order of precedence of these motions and the rules covering whether the motion is debatable, amendable, and so forth.

A motion to lay on the table outranks the motion to postpone to a certain time. Lay on the table is neither debatable nor amendable (a motion's either going to be laid on the table or it's not). Postpone to a certain time is both amendable as to time and debatable as to whether to postpone. All these factors influence the decision to be made, and one of the chair's many duties is to make sure the question sought by the member is the one put before the members.

"Reconsidering" a Vote

The motion to *Reconsider* is often a problem not because of the complexity of the motion itself, but because the word *reconsider* finds broad use outside its parliamentary context. Under Robert's Rules, however, *reconsider* is a specific parliamentary motion with a specific and limited application.

Frequently, someone moves to reconsider a vote that was taken at a prior meeting. However, the correct motion in this case is either *Rescind* or *Amend Something Previously Adopted,* or simply renewing a motion that failed in an earlier meeting. The choice depends only on whether the motion you're trying (incorrectly) to reconsider passed or failed, respectively.

The problem is compounded when a presiding officer allows a motion to reconsider a vote from a prior meeting and applies the rule that only a person who voted on the prevailing side is entitled to offer the motion. On the contrary, any member can move to rescind or amend something previously adopted, or renew a motion that failed (in a prior meeting) at a new meeting.

When it comes to parliamentary usage, *reconsider* is something you can do *only with respect to a decision made in the current meeting* (or on the next day, if the session lasts more than one day). See Chapter 12 for discussions of all these motions.

Requesting a Point of Information

The big problem with this motion is that some people think it means they can get the floor to *give* information. Sorry, wrong number! When the chair doesn't know any better, misuse of this motion is often a sneaky way for a member to inject himself into the debate even after he has exhausted his right to speak.

A *Point of Information* is made to enable the member to *request* information, not to give him an opportunity to speak again!

Offering Friendly Amendments

Most everybody has encountered a well-intended member who offers, "I want to make a friendly amendment." As if! General Robert never even used the term *friendly amendment*. It finally showed up in the current edition of Robert's Rules only to explain that it's not what everybody thinks it is.

The term is often used as a means of asking permission of the motion's original maker to add the amendment. Ol' Schmedley doesn't want people to think that he doesn't like Ernestine's idea. He's just trying to help! But the fact is, when a motion is on the floor, the maker of the motion no longer owns it. Whether or not Ernestine accepts Schmedley's amendment is of no consequence. Any motion to amend a main motion depends upon the acceptance of the assembly, not the person who made the original motion.

If Schmedley offers his friendly amendment before the chair states Ernestine's motion and Ernestine accepts Schmedley's change, the chair states the motion as changed and there's no need for the members to vote on the so-called friendly amendment. It's part of Ernestine's motion from the start.

Offering a friendly amendment is really patronizing. The best thing to do is to simply get recognition of the chair, move your amendment, and tell the membership why you're offering the amendment. Believe me, Ernestine's feelings won't be hurt. She'll probably be pleased that you cared enough to help perfect her idea. Amendments are covered in detail in Chapter 9.

Making Motions to Accept or Receive Reports

The belief that you need to do something official with a report presented to your group is pretty widespread. But, except in some specific situations, which I list below, motions to *accept* or *receive* reports after they're presented shouldn't be entertained. Instead, the chair should simply thank the reporting member and go on to the next item of business. If anything besides "Thank you" needs to be said, stick to something like, "The report requires no action. The next item of business is. . . ." A written report can be acknowledged by the chair simply saying, "The report will be placed on file."

Sometimes, a report contains recommendations or suggests the need for the group to take some specific action. In those cases, the presiding officer states the question *on the motion that arises* from the report, not on whether to adopt the recommendations contained in the report, and not on whether to receive, adopt, or accept the report.

The only situations in which it's proper to accept or adopt a report are when a particular body wishes to make a report its own, as in the following situations:

✔ When a board or committee wants to adopt a draft of its own report, which is prepared by members of the board or committee for the purpose of reporting to the general membership.

✔ When the assembly wishes to endorse every word of a report, such as with:

- An auditor's annual report of the financial records of the treasurer. Endorsement relieves the treasurer of further liability except in the case of fraud.

- A Convention Credentials Committee report. Endorsement establishes the membership of the convention.

- A Convention Standing Rules Committee report. Endorsement adopts the convention standing rules.

- A Convention Program Committee report. Endorsement adopts the convention agenda.

Two situations when adopting or accepting a report is never proper are in the case of a Nominations Committee report, which is always followed by nominations from the floor, and a treasurer's report, which is always simply filed for audit.

Reports are received when they're presented. A motion to receive them after the fact is superfluous.

Dispensing with the Minutes

You don't want to dispense with the minutes; you want to *dispense with the reading of the minutes.* For now, at least!

In parliamentary terms, you make the correct version of this motion in order to enable your group to handle the approval of the minutes at a later time, out of the regular order of things. It absolutely does *not* equate to approval of the minutes.

I've attended many meetings where moving to dispense with the minutes has become quite the custom. For example, *Approval of Minutes* is on the agenda. Fonquetta J. Figaro famously does her duty and offers, "Madam President, I move we dispense with the minutes." Madam President dutifully responds with, "If there is no objection, we will dispense with *the reading of* the minutes. [pausing in case someone objects] Hearing none, the reading of the minutes is dispensed with. The next item of business is. . . ."

Do you think the minutes are approved? Maybe Fonquetta does, and maybe Madam President does. But unless the question is on the *approval* of the minutes, they haven't been approved. Instead, they've just been formally ignored.

Minutes must be approved in order to become the official record of the assembly's action. Dispense with their reading if you must, but ask for corrections and approve them at some point in order to have a complete and official record of your meetings.

Wasting Breath on "I So Move"

Oh, come on now, Hildegarde! What is your motion? State it! When the presiding officer says, "The chair will entertain a motion to take a recess," say, "I move we take a recess for ten minutes." If you just say, "I so move," then you haven't actually made a motion. You've only confused half the members and bumbfuzzled the rest. Whatever possessed you to think that it's okay to make a motion that doesn't propose any action?

Think of it like this: The chair says, "Ms. Portulaca moves 'so.' All those in favor of 'so' will say 'aye.' Opposed, 'no.' The ayes have it, and we will 'so.'" Obviously, this doesn't make any sense because you need to know what "so" stands for, but this is what happens when you say, "I so move."

When you make a motion, propose your action as exactly and specifically as you can. Leave no doubt as to what it is you're asking the membership to agree to.

Part V

Appendixes

In this part . . .

In Louisiana, we have a long tradition of always giving a little something extra, or, as we call it, *lagniappe*. This part is offered in that tradition. (Regardless of what they call it at Dummies headquarters, this part is lagniappe, and lagniappe by any other name is, well, never an appendix. Check out the Introduction for tips on how to tell the difference!)

To help you sort out meanings when you run into the jargon and lingo of Robert's Rules, I compiled a glossary of parliamentary terms and include it in this part. I also gathered examples of minutes, bylaws, agendas, committee reports, teller's reports, and report reports and included them in their own lagniappe chapter (er, appendix), complete with links to a Web site where you can download goodies for your own use.

People say, "A picture is worth a thousand words." Well, this part contains a few thousand words to help you really get the picture!

Appendix A

Glossary of Parliamentary Terms

. . . .

absentee voting: Voting by (postal or electronic) mail, fax, or proxy by persons not in attendance at a meeting; not permissible unless authorized in bylaws.

abstention: The result of abstaining from casting a vote. An abstention counts neither when considering the number of votes for or against nor in determining the total number of votes cast.

accept: To adopt, as in "accept a proposal." Due to the technical definition, it's usually unwise to vote to accept a report except in specific and certain circumstances.

acclamation: An election by unanimous consent.

ad hoc: Lat. "for this purpose only." Used with committee. See *special committee.*

adhering motions: Pending subsidiary motions that must be decided before the main question can be decided and, as a result, remain pending along with the main motion when a motion is referred or postponed or laid on the table.

adjourn: To close a meeting.

adjourn sine die: To close the final meeting of a session with no further meetings of the same group. See *sine die.*

adjourned meeting: A meeting that continues a session working through a single order of business.

adjournment: 1) The closing of a meeting, as in "Everyone left after adjournment." 2) An adjourned meeting, as in "Tonight's meeting is an adjournment of last week's meeting where we ran out of time."

adopt: To accept or agree to.

agenda: A list of the items of business to come before a meeting. See *order of business.*

alternates: Substitute delegates who serve if the regular delegate is unable to serve.

amend: (v.) To change; (n.) Name of a subsidiary motion that proposes to change a main motion before it's finally adopted.

amendment: A proposed change. Offered as a motion to amend.

annual meeting: As provided in a group's bylaws, a meeting held once a year at which a group elects new officers and hears annual reports of officers, the board, and standing committees. An assembly that holds regular monthly or quarterly meetings may designate one of the regular meetings as the annual meeting.

assembly: A deliberative body. The membership present at a meeting.

ballot: A slip of paper on which a voter's preference is written. A ballot is always understood to be a secret ballot unless specifically qualified otherwise, as with a signed ballot.

board: A management and policymaking deliberative assembly that is either subordinate to a larger assembly or autonomous and established by law or charter.

bylaws: An organization's rules about itself and of such importance that no change should be possible without previous notice and a two-thirds vote. In Robert's Rules, the term refers collectively to the constitution and bylaws if a society has both documents.

call (or notice) of a meeting: Written notice of the time and location of a meeting, which is sent to all members entitled to vote. Must include specific items to be considered if the meeting is a "special meeting."

call up the motion to reconsider: The motion to reconsider can be in order even if it's not in order to consider it at the time it's made. In such a case, the motion is made and works like a notice, and the actual decision of whether to reconsider is made later, when a member calls up the motion to reconsider. If it's in order at that time, the vote on whether to reconsider is taken up.

censure: Official expression of disapproval.

chair: The presiding officer, or the station of the presiding officer in a meeting. The reference of the presiding officer to himself, as in "The chair rules the motion out of order."

chairman: A gender-neutral term that refers to a group's presiding officer or the presiding officer of a committee.

charter: A group's articles of incorporation. Also, a document issued by a superior organization authorizing or establishing a subordinate or constituent unit or society.

close nominations: To formally end the nomination process and proceed to the election. This action is not in order as long as anyone wishes to make nominations.

close the polls: To conclude the acceptance of ballots and proceed to the count and determination of the result.

commit: To send, or refer, a motion to a committee.

committee: A group of persons (or one person) assigned to a particular task by, or under the authority of, a deliberative assembly.

committee of the whole: The entire assembly acting as a committee and chaired by another member who is not the presiding officer of the assembly; operates under rules for committees instead of regular assemblies. Affords considerable informality in discussion for a particular subject.

consent agenda (consent calendar): A list of noncontroversial items of business that can be adopted all at once, saving the time that would be consumed if each item were voted on separately. The list can also contain special preference items to be considered in order at the appropriate time.

consideration by paragraph: See *seriatim.*

constituent society: A quasi-independent organization subordinate to (or otherwise operating under the authority of) a superior organization. Also known as a constituent unit.

constitution: An organizational document once more widely used than is common today. A constitution is different from bylaws only in that the constitution contains articles that rarely change and amending it requires a higher voting threshold than for bylaws. Robert's Rules uses the term bylaws to refer to both constitutions and bylaws.

convention standing rules: Rules of order and policy that are adopted by a convention of delegates and apply to the conduct of business during a complete session.

cumulative voting: A form of voting used when filling positions on boards or committees or when appointing delegates. The process allows a voter one vote for each seat to be filled and permits the voter to cast all the votes in any combination for any number of the choices.

dark horse: A candidate for office who is the first choice of few, but who may have wide support as a second choice; a compromise candidate.

debate: Formal discussions of the pros and cons of motions.

decorum in debate: Being nice; keeping debate on the merits of the question and not venturing into questions on the motives of members. Also refers to following the rules for debate.

delegates: Elected or appointed representatives from constituent units chosen for a single session of a larger assembly that's convened to act in the name of the entire society.

deliberative assembly: A group convened to discuss and debate action to be taken in the name of the group; operates under the rules of parliamentary procedure.

dilatory: Intending to thwart the will of the assembly by misusing parliamentary motions.

division of a question: An incidental motion that results in voting on parts of a motion separately.

division of the assembly: A rising vote required on demand of a single member who doubts the result of a voice vote.

executive board: A body subordinate to a society that is empowered to act in a management or administrative nature in the name of the society between regular meetings of the membership. See *board.*

executive committee: A committee (that must be expressly authorized in bylaws) appointed to act for, or in the name of, an executive board.

executive session: A session during which only members and invitees are permitted to attend, and in which all discussion is to be held in confidence by those in attendance.

ex-officio: Lat. "by virtue of office."

ex-officio members: Members who hold membership by virtue of an office they hold.

fixed membership: The number of members specifically authorized to compose a board or committee, as distinguished from the current number of members actually serving on the board or committee (when less than the total number authorized).

friendly amendment: An improper form of amendment conditioned on the approval of the maker of the motion to which it is to be applied.

fundamental principle of parliamentary law: A rule of order so basic that it's held to be inviolate and unsuspendable.

general consent: See *unanimous consent.*

general order: An item of business that, in the prior meeting, was pending when the meeting adjourned or otherwise was postponed to the current meeting without being made a special order.

germane: Pertaining to the subject. Amendments are required to be germane to the motion being amended.

honorary officers and members: Persons granted a special title or membership status, but in name only and without any rights of office or membership except as specified in the bylaws.

illegal vote: Refers to a ballot cast for a fictional character or unidentifiable candidate, a ballot with a vote for too many candidates, or a ballot that's otherwise unintelligible. An illegal vote cast by a member entitled to vote, however, still counts as a vote cast when determining the number of votes required to adopt or elect.

immediately pending question: The motion that must be decided before any other pending motions may be considered further. Yields only to a higher-ranking motion.

incidental main motion: A main motion that deals with the business of the assembly or its past or future action.

incidental motion: A motion that deals with questions of procedure.

informal consideration: Occurs when an assembly suspends the rules relating to the number of times a member may speak in debate on a question or on proposed amendments.

item of business: A specific report or motion within a particular class of business. For example, when moving from the report of your Finance Committee to the report of your Membership Committee, the chair will say, "The next item of business is the report of the Membership Committee."

main motion: A motion whose introduction brings substantive business before the assembly.

majority: More than half.

majority of entire membership: More than half of the total membership, including absentees.

majority vote: The vote of more than half of the members present and voting at a properly called meeting at which a quorum is present.

mass meeting: A meeting of an unorganized assembly that is called for a particular purpose. The mass meeting is open to invitees interested in a particular subject who are generally in favor of accomplishing the announced objectives of the meeting.

meeting: An official gathering of the members of a deliberative assembly or committee, for any length of time, to transact official business, with no break in the proceedings for more than a few minutes. Such a break is called a recess, not to be confused with an adjournment.

member: A person with unrestricted rights of participation in meetings of a society, including the right to make motions, debate, and vote.

minutes: A concise and official record of the proceedings of a meeting, containing (generally) what was done in the meeting but not what was said.

motion: A proposal formally offered by a member in a meeting, requesting that the assembly take specific action.

nomination: Lat. "to name." A name offered as a proposal that someone be elected or appointed to an office or other service position. Nominations don't require a second.

officer: An elected or appointed person holding office as may be defined in bylaws and who is assigned specific duties, responsibilities, and term of office.

old business: An improper term sometimes used in place of the term unfinished business. Should be avoided because it implies that it's appropriate to discuss business already disposed of.

order of business: The sequence by which business comes before an assembly as established by rule. An order of business in which times are assigned to the items or classes of business is commonly referred to as a program or an agenda. Also sometimes used to refer to a single class of business, such as new business.

order of precedence of motions: The ranking of motions such that one motion takes precedence over another, which must yield to the higher-ranked motion.

order of the day: A prescheduled item of business.

original main motion: A main motion which, when introduced, brings before the assembly a substantially new question on a new subject that is not related to the internal business of the assembly.

parliamentarian: A consultant who advises on matters of parliamentary procedure.

parliamentary authority: A manual of parliamentary procedure that is adopted by an assembly and is binding unless superseded by the charter, bylaws, or special rules of order of the organization.

parliamentary inquiry: A question about parliamentary procedure raised by a member during a meeting.

parliamentary law: Generally, the body of rules applicable to procedures for the conduct of business in deliberative assemblies.

parliamentary motion: Any motion relating to procedure and to the conduct of business in a deliberative assembly; includes secondary motions (subsidiary, privileged, and incidental motions) and motions which bring a question again before the assembly.

parliamentary procedure: Generally, the rules and procedures under which a deliberative assembly conducts its business and arrives at decisions in the name of the group; the application of common parliamentary law and rules of order.

pending question: A motion currently under consideration, even if it's not the immediately pending question. A motion subject to becoming the immediately pending question whenever a pending motion of higher rank is disposed of.

plurality: Largest number of votes received in situations with more than two choices. A plurality is not decisive unless the assembly has a special rule of order (or a bylaw in the case of elections) that permits it to be the basis for a decision.

preferential voting: A form of voting used when more than one position is to be filled and voters indicate the relative preference of each candidate. Preferential voting yields the election of the most preferable by eliminating the least preferable.

prevailing side: The constituency voting in the affirmative if a motion passes, or in the negative if the motion fails.

previous notice: A notice that a particular motion will be introduced at the next meeting. The motion's exact content is included in the notice. Depending on provisions in bylaws and intervals between meetings, previous notice is given in the call of a meeting or at the prior meeting.

primary amendment: An amendment applied to any main motion or amendable secondary motion, except to another amendment. (When an amendment is applied to a pending primary amendment, it is called a secondary amendment.)

privileged motion: A secondary motion of higher rank than any subsidiary motion; deals with the privileges of the assembly.

pro tem: Lat. Pro tempore meaning "for the time (being)"; temporary.

program: 1) The nonbusiness part of a meeting, such as when a guest speaker makes a presentation. 2) A written schedule of events. See *agenda.*

proviso: A provision related to transition; a condition precedent usually to the enactment of a bylaw. Often deals with an effective date.

proxy: 1) A power of attorney authorizing a person to vote in the stead of another. 2) The person holding a proxy.

putting the question: Putting a motion to a vote.

quarterly time interval: A period beginning on the date of a meeting and extending to the last day of the calendar month three months beyond the calendar month in which the first meeting occurs. For example, if a meeting is held on the first day of January, then a meeting held on April 30 is within a quarterly time interval.

quasi: Lat. "as if"; commonly used as quasi-committee of the whole.

question: The decision to be made. As in, "The question is on the adoption of the motion to send George out for pizza."

quorum: The minimum number of persons legally entitled to vote that must be present at a properly called meeting in order that business may be legally conducted.

ratify: To affirm or uphold a decision made in the name of the assembly but without proper authority at the time the decision was made or carried out.

recess: A short break in the proceedings of a meeting during which members may leave the room. A recess doesn't end the meeting.

reconsider: To vote again on a motion in the same meeting in which the motion was first decided.

refer: To send a motion to a committee.

renew: To offer again a motion that was disposed of without being adopted. Generally, failed main motions are renewable only at a new session. Renewable secondary motions can be in order in the same meeting as long as business has transpired making such a motion, in essence, a new question.

rescind: To repeal or annul action taken by the assembly.

resolution: A written form for a main motion that begins with the word "Resolved," setting forth in specific terms the action to be taken. Often, but not necessarily, a resolution is preceded by a preamble of one or more paragraphs formally stating the rationale for the resolution.

revision of bylaws: A procedure for the amendment of bylaws in which a set of amendments makes such substantive changes throughout the current bylaws that it's offered and considered as a substitution for the current bylaws.

rising vote: A vote in which members stand to express their support or opposition to a proposal. Allows for visual, rather than aural, determination of the prevailing side. Used instead of a voice vote when a two-thirds vote is required

or any time a member calls for a division of the assembly, unless a counted vote or a ballot is ordered.

Robert's Rules: 1) Parliamentary procedure. 2) The parliamentary authority that is *Robert's Rules of Order Newly Revised.* The current title in the series of official revisions and editions of the parliamentary authority originally published as *Robert's Rules of Order* in 1876 by Henry M. Robert.

roll-call vote: Yeas and nays. A vote in which each voting member (or delegation) is called by name and a record is made of his or her vote. This type of voting procedure should only be used in representative or constituent bodies.

rules of order: Any written rules of parliamentary procedure adopted by a deliberative assembly.

scope of notice: The range within which amendments may be applied to motions that require and have been given previous notice. Amendments outside the scope of notice are not in order because the notice protects the rights of absentees.

second: An acknowledgement by a second member that a motion should come before the assembly. A second doesn't imply agreement with the object of the motion; it only indicates that the seconder wishes the motion to be decided. If discussion or debate ensues without a second having been obtained, the fact that there was no second is of no consequence.

secondary amendment: An amendment applied to a primary amendment.

secondary motions: A collective term for subsidiary, privileged, and incidental motions.

secret ballot: Under Robert's Rules, all ballots are secret ballots unless specifically designated otherwise, such as with a signed ballot. See *ballot.*

select committee: See *special committee.*

seriatim: Lat. "step by step." Used in the incidental motion consideration by paragraph or seriatim. A procedure for consideration of a document — such as bylaws — one section or paragraph at a time.

session: A meeting or series of meetings devoted to one continuous order of business.

signed ballot: A ballot that identifies the person who casts it. This voting procedure is a substitute for roll call when a record is required of who voted and how. Advisable when dealing with a large number of voting members.

sine die: Lat. "without day." See *adjourn sine die.*

society: The entity (association or organization) that's governed by a deliberative assembly.

special committee: A committee that is formed for a specific task and that ceases to exist after the task is complete. Also known as a select or ad hoc committee.

special meeting: A meeting other than a regular meeting at which only business specified in the notice for the meeting may be considered. Special meetings usually are reserved for urgent matters that can't wait until the next regular meeting. Must be authorized in bylaws.

special order: An item of business that is set for a particular time in a meeting and that takes precedence over any other business with very few exceptions.

special rules of order: Rules (adopted by an assembly) related to parliamentary procedure that supersede an assembly's written rules of parliamentary procedure (usually contained in the parliamentary authority.)

specification: In disciplinary proceedings, a statement of what the accused has allegedly done to warrant being charged with an offense.

stand at ease: A request by the chair for the assembly to pause briefly in its proceedings (but not recess or adjourn).

This request may be used to accommodate the chair's brief consultation with the parliamentarian or secretary, to permit adjustment of audio-visual equipment, and so on.

standing committee: A permanent committee that performs a continuing function, usually established in the bylaws.

standing rules: Adopted rules that establish policy and usually aren't related to meeting procedures. Require a majority vote without notice to adopt. Standing rules may not be suspended unless their application is in the context of a meeting.

standing rules of a convention: See *convention standing rules.*

straw poll: An informal poll to determine voters' leanings. A straw poll is never in order because it doesn't decide anything.

subcommittee: A committee that's subordinate to another committee.

subsidiary motion: A motion that aids in the disposal of other motions.

substitute: A form of amendment, the purpose of which is to strike out and insert an entire paragraph (or paragraphs).

substitute motion: See *substitute.*

suspend the rules: An incidental motion to enable action that would otherwise be in violation of the rules of order. This motion requires a two-thirds vote and is applicable only to rules of order, not to bylaws.

tellers: Persons appointed to receive and count ballots.

two-thirds vote: A voting threshold of two-thirds of the members present and voting. This threshold is required to adopt certain motions as a means of protecting the interests of a minority greater than one-third.

unanimous ballot: A ballot cast by an officer (usually the secretary) to elect a sole candidate to office. A unanimous ballot is out of order if the bylaws require a ballot vote because the unanimous ballot denies members the right to vote against the candidate by casting write-in votes.

unanimous consent: An expedient procedure for adopting a motion or confirming agreement by the assembly to a course of action without the formality of a vote or, in some cases, even a motion. The chair obtains unanimous consent by requesting it, and if no objection is raised, the chair may proceed as if the assembly had voted formally.

unanimous vote: A vote in which all members present and voting vote the same. This term is often misused; it's never correct to vote to declare a vote unanimous if the outcome of the ballot vote was not unanimous to begin with, unless the motion to make the ballot vote unanimous is itself voted on by ballot.

undebatable motion: A motion on which the question is not subject to discussion.

unfinished business: Questions carried over from the immediately preceding meeting that didn't complete its order of business before adjournment. Unfinished business includes motions pending when the last meeting adjourned and any other business left on the prior meeting's agenda that wasn't reached before it adjourned. Unfinished business is not an applicable order of business in meetings separated by more than a quarterly time interval.

vacancy in office: Occurs when, due to death or resignation, an officer doesn't complete his or her term. Unless a vacancy is to be filled according to the assembly's standard procedure for appointing or electing a person to that office, provisions for filling vacancies should be specified in the bylaws. Under Robert's Rules, when there's a vacancy in the office of president, the vice-president automatically succeeds to the presidency, creating a vacancy in the office of vice-president.

viva voce: Lat. "voice vote."

vote of no confidence: Not a parliamentary term under Robert's Rules. To express disapproval of an officer, adopt a motion of censure.

with power: Describes a committee that's authorized to take binding action in matters referred to it.

withdraw or modify a motion: Up until the chair states a question (bringing it officially before the assembly), the member making the motion has a right to withdraw it or modify it without the permission of the assembly. Once stated by the chair, however, the member must obtain the permission of the assembly in order to withdraw or modify the motion. A withdrawn motion is considered one that has never been made, so it can be offered again during the same session without violating any rules.

without objection: See *unanimous consent.*

write-in: A vote for an individual or choice not nominated or shown on a preprinted ballot.

yeas and nays: See *roll-call vote.*

Appendix B

Sample Agendas, Reports, and Minutes

● ●

*O*ne thing that all organizations probably have in common is a propensity to accrue cardboard storage boxes full of old paperwork. The paperwork wasn't always old, though. At one time or another, the officers, directors, and members were reading it and referring to it for important information. The future of your organization may someday depend on the paperwork you leave behind.

In this appendix, I've assembled some sample agendas, reports of various officers and committees, and meeting minutes. These are all included not only as examples to supplement the text, but also to serve as guides to good form. Hopefully, they'll help you have better meetings and leave an excellent record of your organization's accomplishments.

In addition, at the very end of this appendix is a section containing Web links to bonus information and some very useful forms, designed to help you and your organization have more efficient meetings. I won't say any more about the goodies here — You'll have to go to the end of the appendix to see what they are!

Member's Copy of Meeting Agenda

This sample agenda for a meeting of a small board follows Robert's Rules' standard order of business (see Chapter 5). The items listed under each heading represent the actual agenda items known to be on the calendar for this specific meeting.

Meeting Agenda

June 19, 1999

Call to order: **3:00 p.m.**

Approval of minutes

Reports of Officers

- ✔ Treasurer's Report
- ✔ President's Report
- ✔ Executive Director's Report

Reports of Standing Committees

- ✔ Membership Committee Report
- ✔ Finance Committee Report
- ✔ Convention Committee Report

Reports of Special Committees

- ✔ Special Certification Committee Report
- ✔ Special Chapter Charter Revision Committee Report

New Business

- ✔ AB has motion
- ✔ CD has motion

Announcements

Adjourn

Presiding Officer's Working Agenda

This is a presiding officer's working agenda for the meeting of a small board. This agenda not only contains the items on the calendar for the meeting, but it's annotated in great detail to assist the presiding officer in conducting the meeting. Anticipated motions are even scripted. A good presiding officer prepares for meetings by outlining his agenda in as much detail as possible.

Meeting Agenda

June 19, 1999

Call to order: 3:00 p.m.

Approval or correction of minutes
Adopt May 2 meeting as corrected or as distributed — use general consent.

Reports of Officers
Treasurer's Report

- ✔ Treasurer will be absent

- ✔ President will report

- ✔ 281 dues paid members, $21,272 total cash accounts. Members have in their packets some financial reports for period 1/1–5/31

    - Say, *"You have an itemized income and expense report covering our year to date in your materials. Mr. J has an expense detail available; if you have any questions, we'll be glad to try and answer them."*

- ✔ No action is taken on the treasurer's report.

President's Report

- ✔ Report Committee Chairmen and membership appointments so far

Executive Director's Report

- ✔ This report contains recommendations for action

- ✔ President assumes the motion on each of the recommendations by saying *"There are a number of recommendations here and we'll take them up one at a time. . . ."*

- 1: *"On the establishment of a special committee to develop a question bank for use in competency examinations, will the secretary read the recommendation. . . ."* [Ask Secretary to read the recommendation. Someone then should move the adoption of the recommendation just read.] State the motion as, *"It is moved to adopt the recommendation just read. Is there discussion?"* Handle discussion; put the question when ready by saying, *"All those in favor say 'Aye' [pause] Opposed say 'No'. . . ."* Then, *"The motion passes (fails) and the recommendation is (not) adopted."*

[Note: If passes, advise board that chairman will need to schedule the meetings for the work day for July 17 in Greenville or Riverton.]

- 2: *"On the recommendation that the board authorize the production of a General Practice Workshop . . . will the secretary read the recommendation. . . ."* [Ask Secretary to read the recommendation. Someone then should move the adoption of the recommendation just read.] State the motion as, *"It is moved to adopt the recommendation just read. Is there discussion?"* Handle discussion; put the question when ready by saying, *"All those in favor. . . ."* Then, *"The motion passes (fails) and the recommendation is (not) adopted."*

[If passes, advise board that committee will be appointed and directed to meet as soon as possible.]

- 3: *"On the recommendation that the board authorize the production of an Advanced Practice Workshop . . . will the secretary read the recommendation. . . ."* [Ask Secretary to read the recommendation. Someone then should move the adoption of the recommendation just read.] State the motion as, *"It is moved to adopt the recommendation just read. Is there discussion?"* Handle discussion; put the question when ready by saying, *"All those in favor. . . ."* Then, *"The motion passes (fails) and the recommendation is (not) adopted."*

[If passed, advise board that committee will be appointed and directed to meet as soon as possible.]

[Inform board and the executive director of intent to coordinate volunteer efforts to handle some of the accumulated work that the association is not currently staffed to handle.]

Reports of Standing Committees
Membership Committee Chairman's Report

✔ Motions arising from this report: (handle as necessary)

Finance Committee Chairman's Report

✔ President is current Finance Chairman.

✔ No recommendations. No action required.

Convention Committee Report

✔ Announce that complete information from the 1999 Convention has not been finalized, and the Convention Committee will report at the next meeting.

✔ Announce that the Y2K Committee should plan to report site selection by the next meeting.

Reports of Special Committees
Special Certification Committee Report

✔ Motions arising from this report: (handle as necessary)

Special Chapter Charter Revision Committee Report

✔ The committee reports the recommendation on the adoption of resolutions.

✔ President is chairman of this committee. Read the report/ resolutions and then state, *"The question is on the adoption of the resolutions just read. Is there discussion?"* Handle discussion and so on, and adopt the resolutions. Then, *"The motion passes and the resolutions are adopted."*

New Business
AB has motion

CD has motion

[Ask if there is any other business to come before the meeting.]

Announcements
Establish date for next meeting. Adopt by general consent.

Adjourn

Audited Treasurer's Report

This report is an example of a summary-style cash basis treasurer's report covering a full year's finances for a small local society. During the year, periodic reports are given in the same form, but without the auditors' certifications contained on this report.

**Audited Report of the Treasurer of the
Upwardly Mobile Elevator Operator's Society
April 1, 2003–March 31, 2004**

Balance on hand April 1, 2003 $2,513.70

Receipts
        Members' Dues $600.00
                Total Receipts $ 600.00

Total (opening balance plus total receipts) $3,113.70

Disbursements
        Postage $317.16
        Printing & Binding $233.24
                Total Disbursements $ 550.40

Balance on hand March 30, 2005 [(opening balance plus total receipts) less total disbursements] $2,563.30

_____

S/Otis Levelstopper
Treasurer

Audited on April 15, 2004 and found correct

_____

_____

Audit Committee

Finance Committee Reporting Budget

This form contains important components in addition to a budget. It includes a *resolution adopting the budget* with an *authorization for the treasurer to disburse the budgeted amounts.* The final part of the form includes a form for the secretary to certify to the adoption of the budget and the resolution, providing the treasurer with an official copy for his files.

Elm Acres Civic Association
Proposed General Fund Operating Budget 3/16/96–3/15/97

The following budget is prepared from records available covering the last two years and represents the reasonable and customary expenses anticipated in the routine operation of Elm Acres Civic Association, Inc. The adoption by the board of the resolution following this budget will authorize the treasurer to disburse funds as allocated and available without further board action.

General Fund

Undedicated Cash on Hand 3/16/96	$812	
Anticipated 1996 Dues	400	
Due from Patrol Fund	343	
Total Available Funds	**$1,555**	
Donations	**$50**	T
FCA Dues 1996 & 97	$50	T
Holiday Decorations	50	B
Lawn/Mowing	300	B
Lawn/Water	88	B
Lawn/Plants	150	B
PO Box	40	T
Print/Copy	150	P/W

Prizes	60	T
Postage/Mailing	250	P
Additional Administrative Expenses	150	P
Total Projected Expenses	$1,288	

Treasurer

Beautification Committee Chairman

President

Welcome Committee Chairman

Budget Adoption Resolution w/ disbursement authorization:

Resolved, that the proposed budget be adopted and that the treasurer be authorized to disburse funds as may be available in amounts not to exceed the budgeted totals when presented with proper invoices that have been approved for payment by the appropriate committee chairmen or other officer or designee of the board as noted; further that the treasurer be authorized to disburse funds in excess of the budgeted amounts with the approval of the president, subject to the ratification and approval of the board.

Certificate of Secretary

I certify that the foregoing budget and resolution were adopted at a Regular Meeting of the Board of Directors held on April 10, 1996.

_____

Secretary

Audit Committee Report

In connection with an audited financial report, an Audit Committee may have comments and recommendations. This committee report is a report rendered in connection with an audited treasurer's report similar to the one used in the section by the same name above.

Elm Acres Civic Association
Report of the Audit Committee to the Board of Directors
September 10, 1996

The Audit Committee's audit of the books of account of Elm Acres Civic Association was undertaken at the direction of the president pursuant to the requirement in the bylaws of the association. The audit is not an outside audit, rather it is an authorized verification of disbursement authorizations and the accuracy and completeness of the books of account made by appointed members of the association.

The audit encompasses the period beginning August 15, 1994, and reflects all moneys held, received, and disbursed by the association to and including May 13, 1996. The figures reflect the cash basis accounting method. Because we use a system wherein dues are posted when paid but credited for a particular period, the actual books of account are maintained using accrual method accounting. Adjustments to provide a cash-basis report are incorporated into this report.

Included in this report are all receipts and disbursements for the patrol fund as well as the general fund. The treasurer of the association maintained the records of both funds. The Patrol Committee's authorization was required to disburse funds, and committee members approved all invoices and maintained the bookkeeping records. However, the treasurer and the president of the association signed all checks and reviewed all invoices for proper approval prior to issuing the checks.

The records for the audit period are, with few exceptions, very complete for receipts and disbursements under both funds.

No breakdown of income sources and items are included in the reports, but permanent detailed records of the source of dues have been inspected and no discrepancies were found. There were, however, no records available to substantiate the neighborhood social ticket sales. This activity generates a large number of cash payments to the association. While the treasurer should not be expected to record each payment transaction in the books, a list of payor names should be compiled by any person collecting these funds and it should be submitted with the funds to the treasurer. The treasurer should log total amounts received from each person remitting such payments. We recommend this procedure be followed in the future.

In the disbursement records of the general fund, there is a deficiency in that some reimbursements were made without proper itemization and without required written certification by the recipient that the expenses were authorized and incurred for the benefit of the association. Further, some disbursements were made for items of which there is no record of authorization by the Board of Directors.

It is recommended that the treasurer shall require an appropriate reimbursement request, bearing an appropriate "approved for payment" certification by an authorized person when issuing payment to a director or other individual to reimburse for expenses. It is further recommended that any invoices being paid be properly noted as "approved for payment" by an authorized person.

A few of the minutes filed in the minute book were found to be without signature, and none of the minutes were noted as "approved . . ." on the minutes themselves. For auditors to rely on the authenticity of minutes, they should be signed by the recording secretary who took the minutes and further noted thereon when they are approved. Any corrections or additions to minutes should be noted on the affected minutes and not merely referred to in subsequent minutes.

It is recommended that the unsigned minutes for the period of this audit which are filed in the minute book shall be signed by the appropriate recorder, and that each set of approved minutes be so noted as to the date approved, and that corrections be reflected directly on the minutes so corrected.

The Audit Committee recommends the audited financial reports be accepted as correct, and that this report and the recommendations contained in this report be adopted and incorporated as standard operating procedures of the corporation.

S/_____

Chairman

Convention Committee on Standing Rules Report

A convention of delegates adopts its own convention standing rules for a single session. The organization's Committee on Standing Rules is charged with recommending the rules for adoption at the opening meeting of the convention.

Sample Report of Convention Committee on Standing Rules

The Committee on Standing Rules reports the following proposed standing rules for the 2000 Convention and recommends their adoption:

Proposed Convention Standing Rules

1. Attendees shall register with the Credentials Committee before receiving an identifying badge.

2. No one will be admitted to the convention meetings without an identifying badge and a specific admission pass for each event or designated area.

3. The presiding officer may make minor changes to the adopted agenda as may be made necessary during the meetings.

4. The Initiation Ritual shall be made the special order of business for 11:05 a.m. on Tuesday, November 14, 2000.

5. All main motions and resolutions shall be in writing and unless originating from an established committee, board, or agency of the organization, will be automatically referred to the Resolutions Committee. The Resolutions Committee shall admit the member proposing the motion or resolution to speak to his proposal before the committee.

6. All announcements offered from the chapters shall be type-written or hand printed, signed by an authorized delegate of the chapter, and submitted to the convention recording secretary.

7. Nominating speeches for officers may not exceed one nominating speech and one seconding speech per nominee per office, and each shall be limited to three minutes.

8. Persons addressing the president and seeking the floor shall state their name and their chapter represented.

9. Debate on main motions shall be limited to two speakers for and two speakers against, with no speech in debate exceeding three minutes.

10. A timekeeper shall signal when allotted time has expired.

11. There will be no smoking indoors in any area where convention activities are taking place.

Sample Minutes

Everything you need to know to prepare minutes in good form is in Chapter 17. But the rules may make more sense to you after you see them applied to the actual minutes of an actual meeting. If you're a secretary, especially, you'll encounter all sorts of parliamentary situations that need to be included in minutes.

The two detailed sample minutes in this section provide some examples of style for documenting things like motions laid on the table (or taken from the table), points of order, appeals, referrals to committee, and recesses, to name a few. The minutes are based on real-life examples that I think you can benefit from, because they were prepared in general conformity with the principles in Robert's Rules.

Monthly Board Meeting

These minutes are representative of the form you use to create minutes of a regular monthly board meeting of a large local or state professional association:

Greater Luxopolis Electrical Engineers Professional Society Regular Monthly Board Meeting Minutes June 19, 1999

The regular monthly meeting of the board of the GLEEPS was called to order by the president, Stumpy Luckless, at 3:05 p.m. on Saturday, June 19, 1999, at the association's office. Frank Cleemadeer, secretary, was present.

The minutes of the May 2, 1999, meeting were approved as corrected.

President Luckless reported for the treasurer. The society has $11,600 in cash and 281 dues-paid members. Written reports were placed on file.

President Luckless reported that he has appointed Nick McGlick as Membership Committee chairman and JanieMae Joltz as Y2K Expo Committee chairman, but he had not yet been able to appoint a chairman for the Finance Committee. He reported that until he could find a capable member who would accept appointment, he would serve as chairman pro tem.

Mr. J. Alphonse Calabash, vice-president and executive director, furnished a written report and made several recommendations. From those recommendations arose the following motions:

Hoss Grumplotta moved that there be established a special committee chaired by Grover Koerners to develop a question bank for use in competency examinations. Grumplotta moved to request the committee meet in July and report back to us at the August meeting. The motion passed.

Gomer Dabblehoofer moved that "there be established a special committee appointed by the president to work closely with the Executive Director to develop, schedule, and provide for the presentation of a General Practice Workshop, to cover generally the material included in the Practice Manual and to authorize such funds to be advanced as may be necessary and prudent to promote and present such a workshop at such time and location as the committee deems practicable." The motion was postponed to the July meeting and on a two-thirds vote was made a special order for that meeting.

Dilly Dooleman moved that the association order for the research library one copy each of *Nuclear-Powered Sparkplug Design Techniques* and *Effective Marketing and Networking Using Pocket Protector Art,* at a total cost not to exceed $225.00. During the discussion of the motion, Nick McGlick moved to lay the motion on the table in order to take up his committee report and recommendations because he needed to leave early. The motion was laid on the table in order to hear Mr. McGlick's report.

Mr. McGlick reported the Membership Committee's recommendation that the association print and mail 2,500 brochures to newly licensed professionals identified by the committee in the last two months. The motion was referred to the Communications Committee to develop a proposed brochure and to report back next month.

Dilly Dooleman's motion for the book purchases was taken from the table, and the motion carried.

Pasqualetta Puffglopper reported for the 1999 Expo Committee that the financials for the 1999 Expo were not yet finalized, but the committee would make its final report next month. She moved that the secretary go ahead and send the thank-you letters to the exhibitors on a list she provided. The motion passed.

The Special Certification Committee chairman, Bennie Blather, reported that his committee's progress on the Professional Certification Exam Preparation workshop was developing. On behalf of the committee, he moved that the president appoint a special committee to obtain locations for the seminar to be presented and to report back next month. The motion passed, and the president appointed the secretary and the Hospitality Committee chairman to serve on the special committee.

Mr. Blather then moved on behalf of his committee that an additional $2,000 be allocated for graphics art and design for the course materials. After amendment to strike out $2,000 and insert $1,500, the motion was postponed to the next meeting.

JanieMae Joltz moved that a scholarship be given to a deserving student each year. The motion was ruled out of order because it was outside the scope of the purpose of the organization as stated in the bylaws.

Joltz appealed from the decision of the chair. The decision of the chair was sustained.

J. Alphonse Calabash moved to lease out a section of the office building for $300 per month. Frank Cleemadeer moved to strike out $300 and insert $400. After considerable discussion, JanieMae Joltz noted the lateness of the hour and moved the previous question. Secretary Cleemadeer moved to adjourn. Motion to adjourn carried.

President Luckless announced the next meeting would be July 22, 1999, at 3:00 p.m., and declared the meeting adjourned at 6:30 p.m.

s/ Frank Cleemadeer
Secretary   Date approved: 07/22/99

Annual Membership Meeting

These minutes are representative of form for minutes of the annual membership meeting of a state professional association:

Pembleton Kickboxers Association
Annual Meeting of the Membership
May 5-7, 2000

The annual meeting of the membership of the Pembleton Kickboxers Association kicked off at 12:05 p.m. on May 5, 2000, at the Five Corners City Convention Center in Starsville by President Manny Bumpus. Luther Lockhold, secretary, was present.

President Bumpus announced the following appointments:

- ✔ Meeting Parliamentarian: J. Littleton Biltrock, PRP

- ✔ Hospitality Committee: Goldie Betterbatter, Jacob Strainstretcher, Clint Clockclabber, Mervin Stillstammer

- ✔ Resolutions Committee: Casey Brownbear, Dodley Rodley, Beanpole Stackstepper, Terry C. Guessergin, and Chastain. B. Danbold

- ✔ Tellers Committee: Nonmembers appointed with the consent of the membership: Hans von Donneman, Perry Derryberry, Harsapple Strangebird

- ✔ Timekeeper: Clark Washer

- ✔ Committee to approve minutes of this meeting: Will Reed, Mae Reed, Lark Tatum

The annual meeting special rules (as published on page 7 of the Book of Reports) were read and adopted by general consent.

Winnie Marplemoney presented the auditors' report (published on page 19 of the Book of Reports) and moved to adopt the audited treasurer's report and commend the treasurer for a job well done. The motion passed.

Scuffy Stamus, the chairman of the Nominating Committee, reported nine nominees for the board of directors (as published on page 25 of the Book of Reports). The president called for further nominations. Nominated were: Sly Calcaneous and Ben Hatter.

The election of directors was then conducted, after which a 30-minute recess was taken while the tellers counted the ballots.

The Tellers Committee reported the following election results:

Number of ballots cast: 188; Illegal ballots: 3

Nominee	Total Votes
Hornsby Barnum	126
Tank Bricksome	158
Marley Dittletrip	155
Helga Dittletrip	159
Dilbert Rodwinky	156
Clyde Schmalzapple	162
Lillie Locknuckle	162
Scuffy Slamus	160
Jackie Normus	167
Sly Calcaneous	160
Ben Hatter	31
Hubert Pugwhistle	13
Thumper Wheezer	12
Norbert Bumpmaple	3
Will Reed	3
Pablo Loman	1

The president thanked the Tellers Committee and announced the newly elected directors for year 2000–2001 as follows:

> Tank Bricksome
>
> Sly Calcaneous
>
> Marley Dittletrip
>
> Helga Dittletrip
>
> Lillie Locknuckle
>
> Jackie Normus
>
> Dilbert Rodwinky
>
> Clyde Schmalzapple
>
> Scuffy Slamus

The following proposed bylaw amendment, properly noticed and submitted by Tank Bricksome and Thumper Wheezer, was then taken up:

Proposed, To amend the bylaws by inserting a new article after Article IX: Committees, with such article to read as follows:

Position Statements

A. The membership of this association may adopt position statements or resolutions declaring a position of the association only by mail ballot.

B. The adoption of any such position statement shall require a majority vote in the affirmative.

C. For the purposes of this article, mail ballots are subject to all rules of the parliamentary authority adopted by the association, and may be ordered as follows:

- By the membership at a regular or special meeting

- By the board of directors

- Upon written request signed by 10 percent of the association's members eligible to vote

The motion to amend the bylaws was amended to include a proviso that the amendment, if adopted, would not take effect until the close of the annual meeting. The proposed bylaw amendment did not receive a vote of two-thirds in the affirmative and accordingly was not adopted.

Goldie Betterbatter then moved the adoption of a resolution, which, after amendment, was adopted as follows:

Resolved, That the publications committee be encouraged to include a 'Letters to the Editor' column in each issue of *Just for Kicks,* the association newsletter.

At that time, Annabel Rumple moved to recess for an hour so that the newly elected board could meet and elect officers. The motion to recess was adopted by general consent.

After the recess, President Bumpus called the meeting back to order and announced that the following were elected by the new board to serve in their respective offices for the year 2000–2001:

President: Clyde Schmalzapple

Vice-president: Helga Dittletrip

Secretary: Sly Calcaneous

Treasurer: Lillie Locknuckle

He then conducted the installation of officers, administering an oath of office to each and charging them with their duties for the coming year.

The meeting adjourned at 4:00 p.m.

s/ Luther Lockhold

    Approved:

s/ Will Reed	09/12/2000
s/ Mae Reed	07/14/2000
s/ Lark Tatum	07/21/2000

On the Web: Bonus Chapters and Forms You Can Use

If you thought the text in this book is the only help I planned to give you in navigating the nuances of parliamentary procedure, I hope the information in this section is a pleasant surprise! Robert's Rules For Dummies has a companion Web site that contains more useful information for you AND some sample forms your association can use to help run your meetings. To gain access to this marvelous bonus material, go here:

www.dummies.com/go/robertsrulesfd

What? You say you don't have an association yet? Then the following bonus chapter, included on the Web site, will help you start one.

Starting a New Association: The Steps to Success

If you have a cause that needs the collective effort of a group of people with the same or similar objectives, there are steps you can take to ensure your group's effectiveness in meeting your goals. Starting a new organization isn't terribly difficult, but like anything else in Robert's Rules, it's all about procedure. This bonus chapter helps you navigate through the technicalities of establishing your association so that it's not only effective but operates as a well-oiled machine. Topics covered in the chapter include:

- Understanding how new organizations are formed
- Managing productive organizational meetings

> ✔ Staffing a committee to draft bylaws
>
> ✔ Enrolling charter members

Yessir, once your new association is up and running (thanks to the information in this chapter), then you can have fun participating in all sorts of parliamentary goings-on, like meetings, voting, and conventions.

What? You're curious to know about the workings of your organization's big annual convention? Well then, take a look at the next bonus chapter on the Web site.

The Convention of Delegates: A Special Kind of Assembly

Some people think conventions are just big excuses to get a bunch of people together to party. Well, I'd be dishonest if I didn't say that some conventions really are like that, but for the most part, conventions are serious business. Work needs to be done to establish your organization's direction for the next year (or two, or four). This bonus chapter shows you how to conduct business in a convention, and shows you the special rules designed to make a convention an efficient and proper operation. Topics covered include:

> ✔ Understanding the special nature of a convention of delegates
>
> ✔ Organizing a convention of delegates
>
> ✔ Using specialized convention committees

Ten Custom Rules to Consider

It's a sad fact that Robert's Rules in no way tries to be one-size-fits-all when it comes to individualizing your own rules. This bonus chapter lists some of the ideas frequently recommended by professional parliamentarians regarding special rules and bylaws. Adopting some of these rules may reduce your chances of having to hire a professional parliamentarian to help straighten out a mess!

Downloadable Forms for Your Meetings

Whether you're having full-blown conventions or small board meetings, someone in your group (yes, probably you) is going to have to do some paperwork. Many people are rather talented in coming up with computerized forms that simplify their meeting paperwork problems, but let's face it, designing forms still isn't much of a picnic.

If I could, I'd load a whole bunch of blank meeting forms onto the Web site so that you and your association would never have to design or tweak a form again. Unfortunately, that's not practical, since every association is different and has different needs. Even so, I have included four Microsoft Word form templates on the Web site that you can download for your own use. I hope they'll be as useful to you as they have been for me.

Teller's Election Worksheet

In any election, it's important to track the nominees and the ballot totals and tallies. This teller's worksheet is designed as a nice, simple way to accumulate all the information you need to prepare a perfect Teller's Report. Of course, once you download the form, you can adapt it according to your own needs, but I personally find its current, simplified layout more than helpful.

Tellers' Reports for Motions and Elections

When your organization votes by ballot reporting the details is important for the record (and for preventing the occasional fist fight). Two forms on the Web site are designed to help you in that process. One form is for reporting the ballot counts in a vote on an election. The other form is for reporting the ballot counts in a vote on a motion. Both forms include the critical components for proper reporting of the following:

- ✔ The number of votes cast
- ✔ The number of votes required to elect (or adopt, as in the case of a motion)
- ✔ The total votes cast for each candidate (or choice, as in the case of a motion)
- ✔ The total number of illegal votes and a short description of each such vote

Notice of Proposed Amendment to Bylaws

Here's the granddaddy of all the forms included on the Web site. Amending the bylaws is serious business, and this form is designed to show you how to prepare and give notice for proposed bylaw amendments, how to show the differences between current and proposed bylaws, when to go out for coffee (no, I'm kidding), and more. This is the prettiest form in the bunch, and you're sure to find that it comes in very handy.

Index

BUSINESS, CAREERS & PERSONAL FINANCE

0-7645-5307-0   0-7645-5331-3 *†

Also available:

Accounting For Dummies †
0-7645-5314-3
Business Plans Kit For Dummies †
0-7645-5365-8
Cover Letters For Dummies
0-7645-5224-4
Frugal Living For Dummies
0-7645-5403-4
Leadership For Dummies
0-7645-5176-0
Managing For Dummies
0-7645-1771-6

Marketing For Dummies
0-7645-5600-2
Personal Finance For Dummies *
0-7645-2590-5
Project Management
For Dummies
0-7645-5283-X
Resumes For Dummies †
0-7645-5471-9
Selling For Dummies
0-7645-5363-1
Small Business Kit For Dummies *†
0-7645-5093-4

HOME & BUSINESS COMPUTER BASICS

0-7645-4074-2   0-7645-3758-X

Also available:

ACT! 6 For Dummies
0-7645-2645-6
iLife '04 All-in-One Desk Reference
For Dummies
0-7645-7347-0
iPAQ For Dummies
0-7645-6769-1
Mac OS X Panther Timesaving
Techniques For Dummies
0-7645-5812-9
Macs For Dummies
0-7645-5656-8
Microsoft Money 2004 For Dummies
0-7645-4195-1

Office 2003 All-in-One Desk
Reference For Dummies
0-7645-3883-7
Outlook 2003 For Dummies
0-7645-3759-8
PCs For Dummies
0-7645-4074-2
TiVo For Dummies
0-7645-6923-6
Upgrading and Fixing PCs
For Dummies
0-7645-1665-5
Windows XP Timesaving
Techniques For Dummies
0-7645-3748-2

FOOD, HOME, GARDEN, HOBBIES, MUSIC & PETS

0-7645-5295-3   0-7645-5232-5

Also available:

Bass Guitar For Dummies
0-7645-2487-9
Diabetes Cookbook For Dummies
0-7645-5230-9
Gardening For Dummies *
0-7645-5130-2
Guitar For Dummies
0-7645-5106-X
Holiday Decorating For Dummies
0-7645-2570-0
Home Improvement All-in-One
For Dummies
0-7645-5680-0

Knitting For Dummies
0-7645-5395-X
Piano For Dummies
0-7645-5105-1
Puppies For Dummies
0-7645-5255-4
Scrapbooking For Dummies
0-7645-7208-3
Senior Dogs For Dummies
0-7645-5818-8
Singing For Dummies
0-7645-2475-5
30-Minute Meals For Dummies
0-7645-2589-1

INTERNET & DIGITAL MEDIA

0-7645-1664-7   0-7645-6924-4

Also available:

2005 Online Shopping Directory
For Dummies
0-7645-7495-7
CD & DVD Recording For Dummies
0-7645-5956-7
eBay For Dummies
0-7645-5654-1
Fighting Spam For Dummies
0-7645-5965-6
Genealogy Online For Dummies
0-7645-5964-8
Google For Dummies
0-7645-4420-9

Home Recording For Musicians
For Dummies
0-7645-1634-5
The Internet For Dummies
0-7645-4173-0
iPod & iTunes For Dummies
0-7645-7772-7
Preventing Identity Theft
For Dummies
0-7645-7336-5
Pro Tools All-in-One Desk
Reference For Dummies
0-7645-5714-9
Roxio Easy Media Creator
For Dummies
0-7645-7131-1

* Separate Canadian edition also available
† Separate U.K. edition also available

Available wherever books are sold. For more information or to order direct: U.S. customers
visit www.dummies.com or call 1-877-762-2974.
U.K. customers visit www.wileyeurope.com or call 0800 243407. Canadian customers visit
www.wiley.ca or call 1-800-567-4797.

SPORTS, FITNESS, PARENTING, RELIGION & SPIRITUALITY

0-7645-5146-9   0-7645-5418-2

Also available:
- Adoption For Dummies
  0-7645-5488-3
- Basketball For Dummies
  0-7645-5248-1
- The Bible For Dummies
  0-7645-5296-1
- Buddhism For Dummies
  0-7645-5359-3
- Catholicism For Dummies
  0-7645-5391-7
- Hockey For Dummies
  0-7645-5228-7

- Judaism For Dummies
  0-7645-5299-6
- Martial Arts For Dummies
  0-7645-5358-5
- Pilates For Dummies
  0-7645-5397-6
- Religion For Dummies
  0-7645-5264-3
- Teaching Kids to Read
  For Dummies
  0-7645-4043-2
- Weight Training For Dummies
  0-7645-5168-X
- Yoga For Dummies
  0-7645-5117-5

TRAVEL

0-7645-5438-7   0-7645-5453-0

Also available:
- Alaska For Dummies
  0-7645-1761-9
- Arizona For Dummies
  0-7645-6938-4
- Cancún and the Yucatán
  For Dummies
  0-7645-2437-2
- Cruise Vacations For Dummies
  0-7645-6941-4
- Europe For Dummies
  0-7645-5456-5
- Ireland For Dummies
  0-7645-5455-7

- Las Vegas For Dummies
  0-7645-5448-4
- London For Dummies
  0-7645-4277-X
- New York City For Dummies
  0-7645-6945-7
- Paris For Dummies
  0-7645-5494-8
- RV Vacations For Dummies
  0-7645-5443-3
- Walt Disney World & Orlando
  For Dummies
  0-7645-6943-0

GRAPHICS, DESIGN & WEB DEVELOPMENT

0-7645-4345-8   0-7645-5589-8

Also available:
- Adobe Acrobat 6 PDF
  For Dummies
  0-7645-3760-1
- Building a Web Site For Dummies
  0-7645-7144-3
- Dreamweaver MX 2004
  For Dummies
  0-7645-4342-3
- FrontPage 2003 For Dummies
  0-7645-3882-9
- HTML 4 For Dummies
  0-7645-1995-6
- Illustrator CS For Dummies
  0-7645-4084-X

- Macromedia Flash MX 2004
  For Dummies
  0-7645-4358-X
- Photoshop 7 All-in-One Desk
  Reference For Dummies
  0-7645-1667-1
- Photoshop CS Timesaving
  Techniques For Dummies
  0-7645-6782-9
- PHP 5 For Dummies
  0-7645-4166-8
- PowerPoint 2003 For Dummies
  0-7645-3908-6
- QuarkXPress 6 For Dummies
  0-7645-2593-X

NETWORKING, SECURITY, PROGRAMMING & DATABASES

0-7645-6852-3   0-7645-5784-X

Also available:
- A+ Certification For Dummies
  0-7645-4187-0
- Access 2003 All-in-One Desk
  Reference For Dummies
  0-7645-3988-4
- Beginning Programming
  For Dummies
  0-7645-4997-9
- C For Dummies
  0-7645-7068-4
- Firewalls For Dummies
  0-7645-4048-3
- Home Networking For Dummies
  0-7645-42796

- Network Security For Dummies
  0-7645-1679-5
- Networking For Dummies
  0-7645-1677-9
- TCP/IP For Dummies
  0-7645-1760-0
- VBA For Dummies
  0-7645-3989-2
- Wireless All In-One Desk Reference
  For Dummies
  0-7645-7496-5
- Wireless Home Networking
  For Dummies
  0-7645-3910-8